INUYASHA

VOL. 38
Shonen Sunday Edition

Story and Art by
RUMIKO TAKAHASHI

English Adaptation by Gerard Jones

Translation/Mari Morimoto
Touch-up Art & Lettering/Bill Schuch
Cover and Interior Graphic Design/Yuki Ameda
Editors/Ian Robertson & Shaenon K. Garrity

VP, Production/Alvin Lu
VP, Publishing Licensing/Rika Inouye
VP, Sales & Product Marketing/Gonzalo Ferreyra
VP, Creative/Linda Espinosa
Publisher/Hyoe Narita

INUYASHA 38 by Rumiko TAKAHASHI
© 2005 Rumiko TAKAHASHI
All rights reserved. Original Japanese edition
published in 2005 by Shogakukan Inc., Tokyo.

The stories, characters and incidents mentioned
in this publication are entirely fictional.

Printed in the U.S.A.

Published by VIZ Media, LLC
P.O. Box 77010
San Francisco, CA 94107

10 9 8 7 6 5 4 3 2 1
First printing, July 2009

www.viz.com   WWW.SHONENSUNDAY.COM

INUYASHA

VOL. 38

Shonen Sunday Edition

STORY AND ART BY
RUMIKO TAKAHASHI

CONTENTS

THE STORY THUS FAR

Long ago, in the "Warring States" era of Japan's Muromachi period (Sengoku-jidai, approximately 1467-1568 CE), a legendary dog-like half-demon called "Inuyasha" attempted to steal the Shikon Jewel—or "Jewel of Four Souls"—from a village, but was stopped by the enchanted arrow of the village priestess, Kikyo. Inuyasha fell into a deep sleep, pinned to a tree by Kikyo's arrow, while the mortally wounded Kikyo took the Shikon Jewel with her into the fires of her funeral pyre. Years passed.

Fast-forward to the present day. Kagome, a Japanese high school girl, is pulled into a well one day by a mysterious centipede monster and finds herself transported into the past—only to come face to face with the trapped Inuyasha. She frees him, and Inuyasha easily defeats the centipede monster.

The residents of the village, now 50 years older, readily accept Kagome as the reincarnation of their deceased priestess Kikyo, a claim supported by the fact that the Shikon Jewel emerges from a cut on Kagome's body. Unfortunately, the jewel's rediscovery means that the village is soon under attack by a variety of demons in search of this treasure. Then, the jewel is accidentally shattered into many shards, each of which may have the fearsome power of the entire jewel.

Although Inuyasha says he hates Kagome because of her resemblance to Kikyo, the woman who "killed" him, he is forced to team up with her when Kaede, the village leader, binds him to Kagome with a powerful spell. Now the two grudging companions must fight to reclaim and reassemble the shattered shards of the Shikon Jewel before they fall into the wrong hands...

THIS VOLUME Inuyasha and the crew are locked deep in combat with the scheming Hakudoshi. The plot thickens as Kagura's plans as well as Hakudoshi's plans come to light. In a rare moment, Inuyasha fights on the side of Kagura. It seems that Hakudoshi will stop at nothing to achieve his goals! But will he succeed?!

CHARACTERS

INUYASHA
Half-demon hybrid, son of a human mother and demon father. His necklace is enchanted, allowing Kagome to control him with a word.

KAGOME
Modern-day Japanese schoolgirl who can travel back and forth between the past and present through an enchanted well.

NARAKU
Enigmatic demon-mastermind behind the miseries of nearly everyone in the story.

MIROKU
Lecherous Buddhist priest cursed with a mystical "hellhole" in his hand that's slowly killing him.

KOGA
Leader of the Wolf Clan, Koga is himself a Wolf Demon and, because of several Shikon shards in his legs, possesses super speed. Enamored of Kagome, he quarrels with Inuyasha frequently.

SANGO
"Demon Exterminator" or slayer from the village where the Shikon Jewel was first born.

SCROLL 1

HAKUDOSHI'S SCHEME

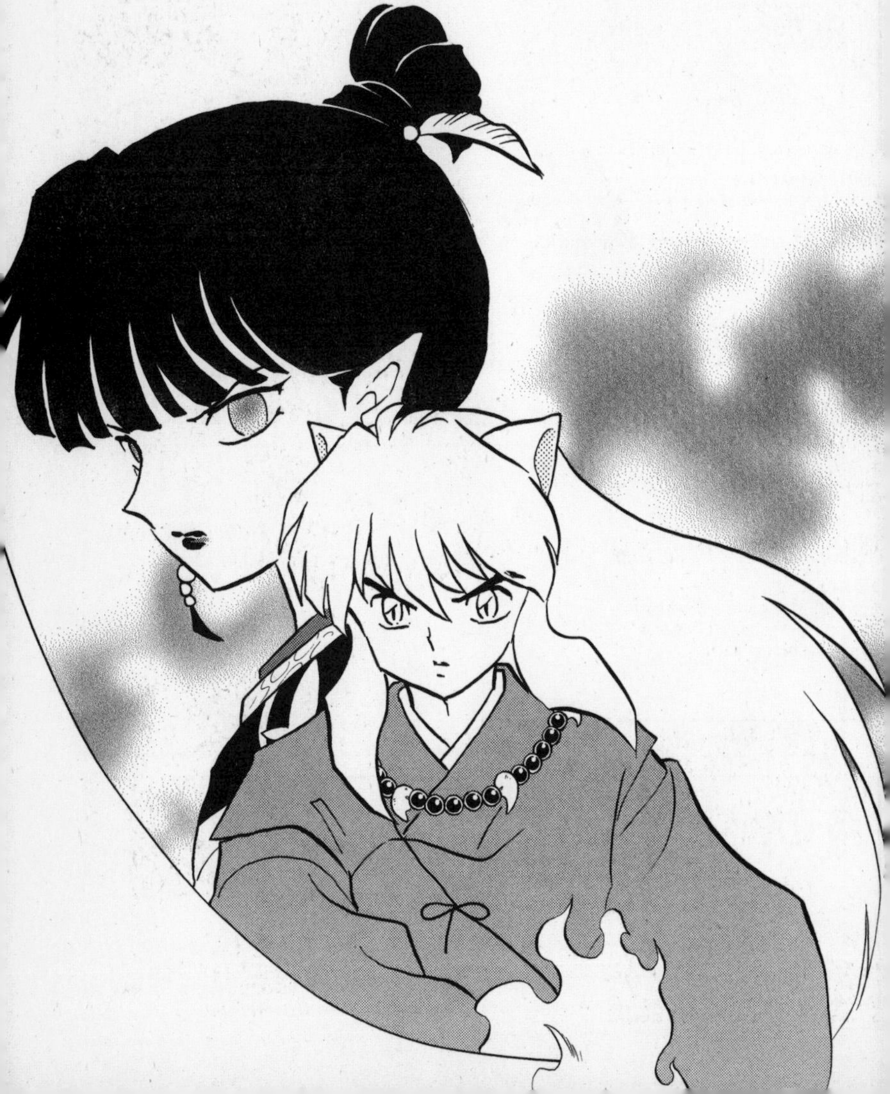

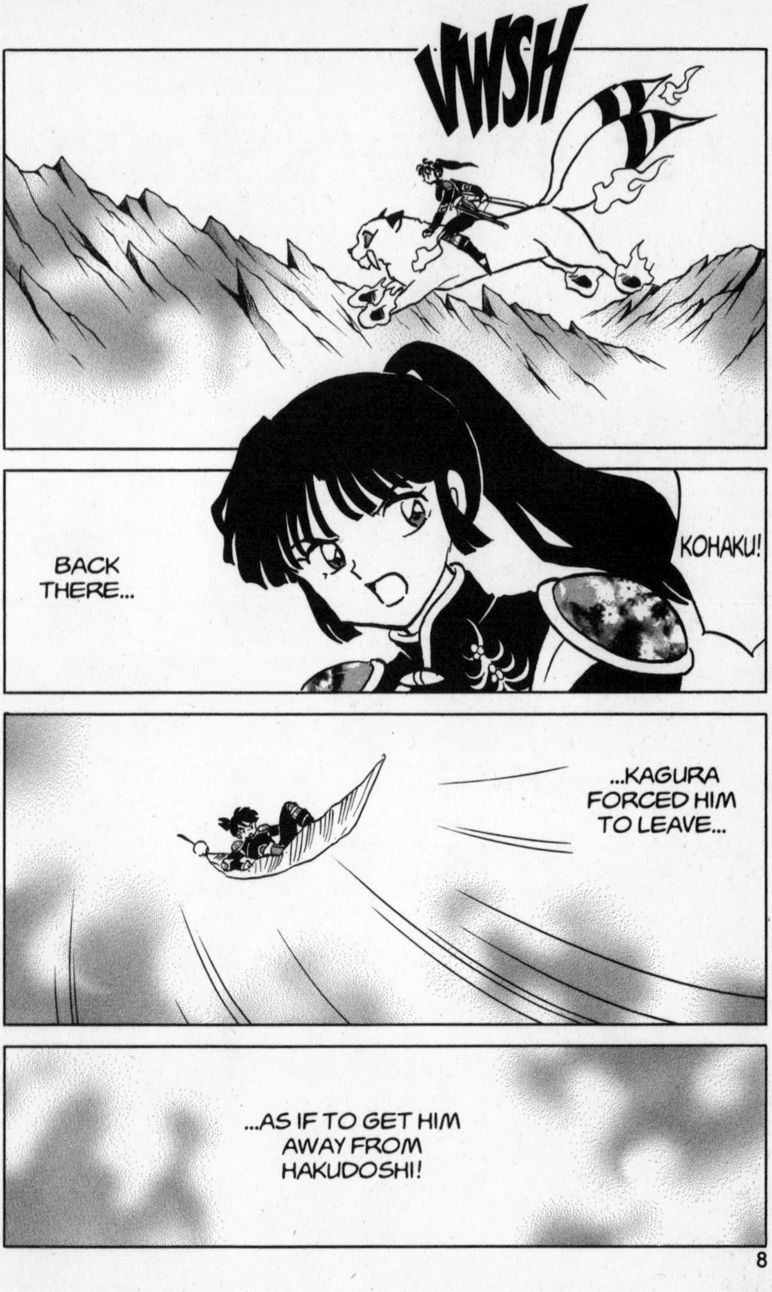
VWSH
KOHAKU!
BACK THERE...
...KAGURA FORCED HIM TO LEAVE...
...AS IF TO GET HIM AWAY FROM HAKUDOSHI!

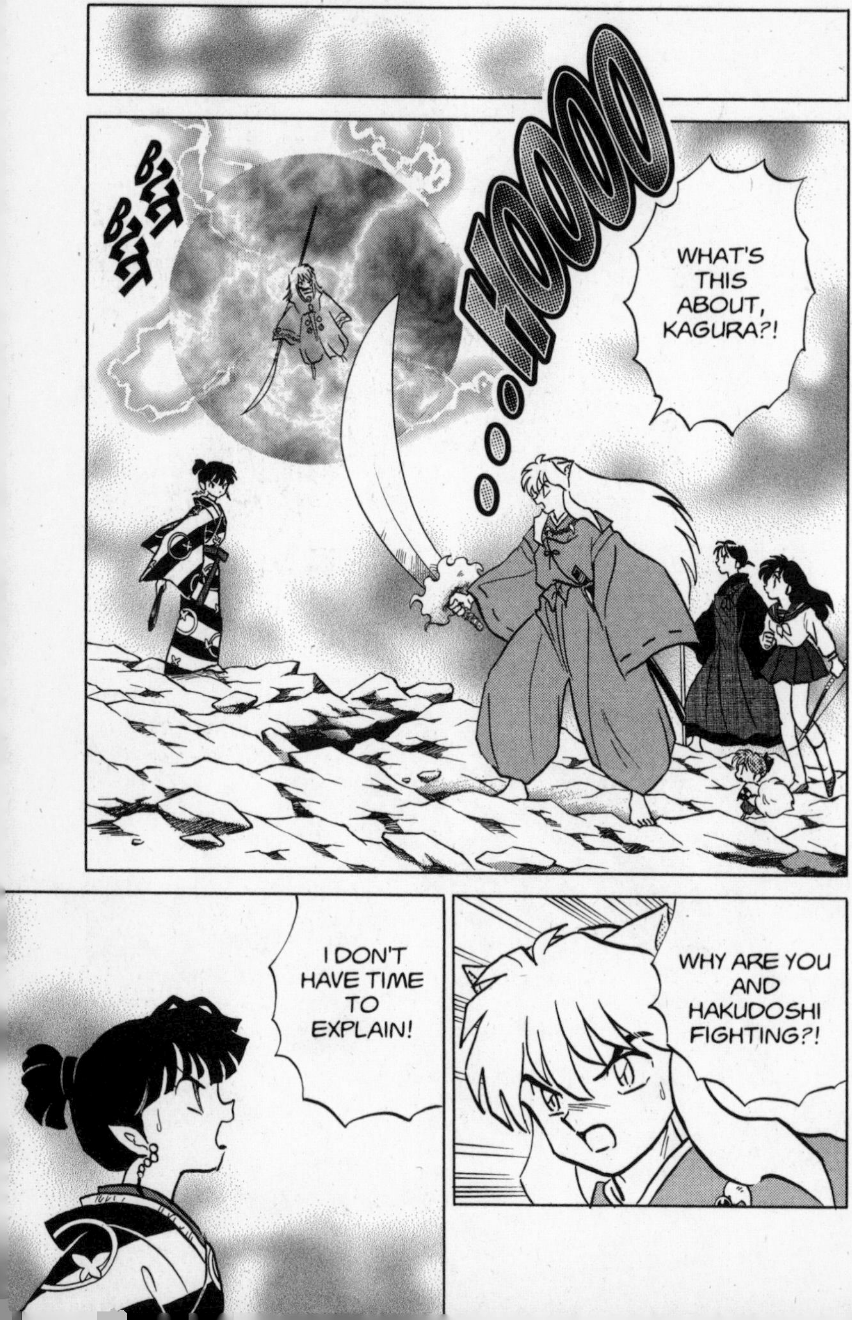
WHAT'S THIS ABOUT, KAGURA?!
HOOOOO...
BZZT BZZT
WHY ARE YOU AND HAKUDOSHI FIGHTING?!
I DON'T HAVE TIME TO EXPLAIN!

BZZT
BZZT
BZZT

HEH...

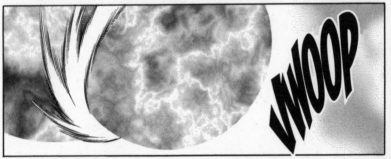

VWOOP

HE'S SHOOTING BACK YOUR WIND SCAR!

FEH!

OH!

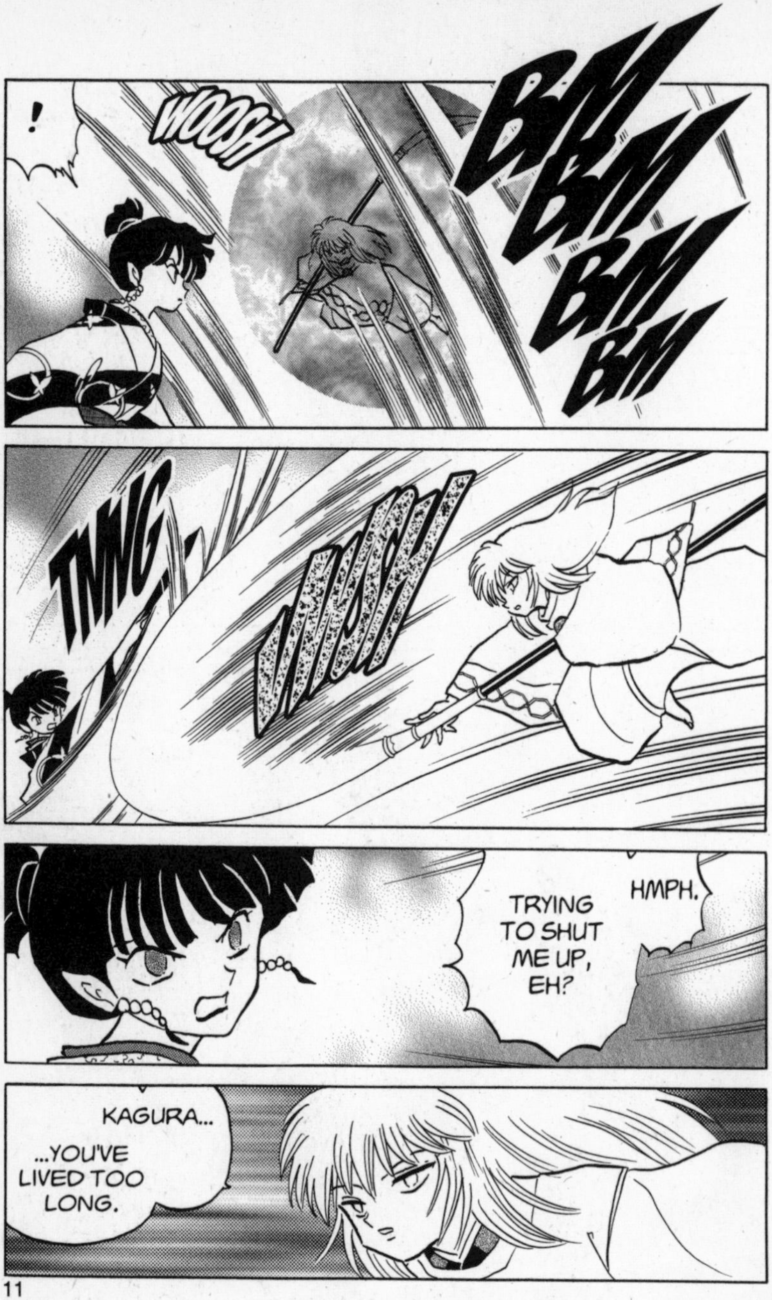
BAM
BAM
BAM
BAM
BAM
WOOSH
!
VWOSH
TWING...
HMPH.
TRYING TO SHUT ME UP, EH?
KAGURA...
...YOU'VE LIVED TOO LONG.

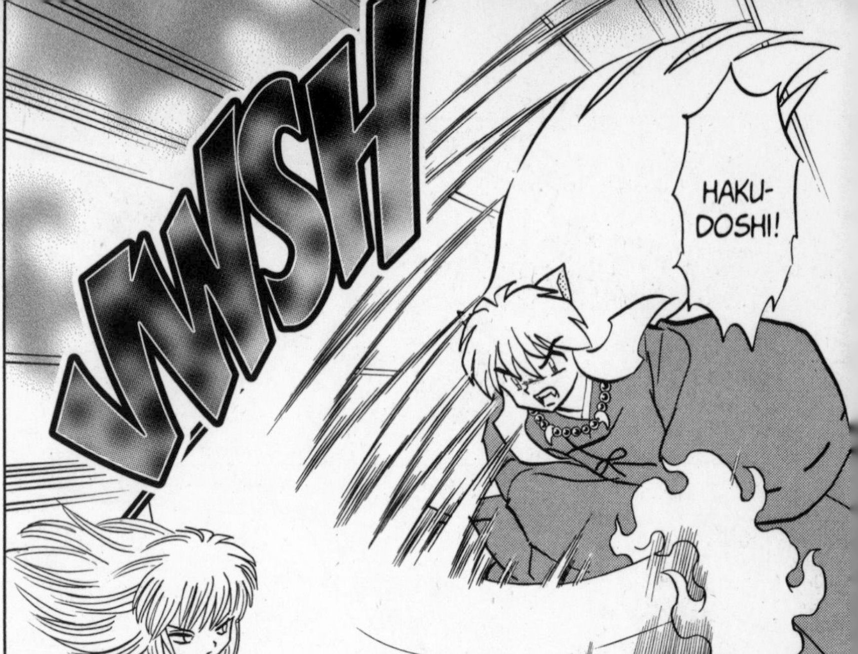
HAKU-
DOSHI!
WHSH

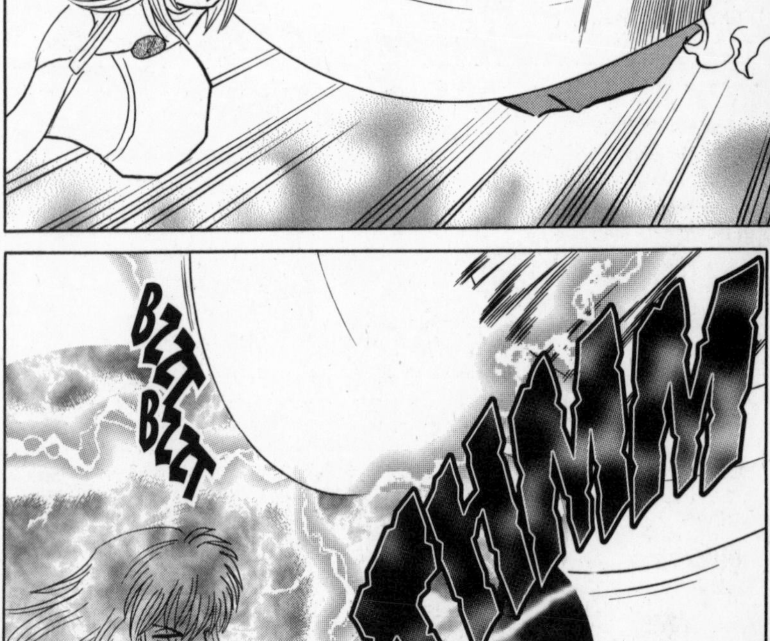
THMM
BZZT
BZZT

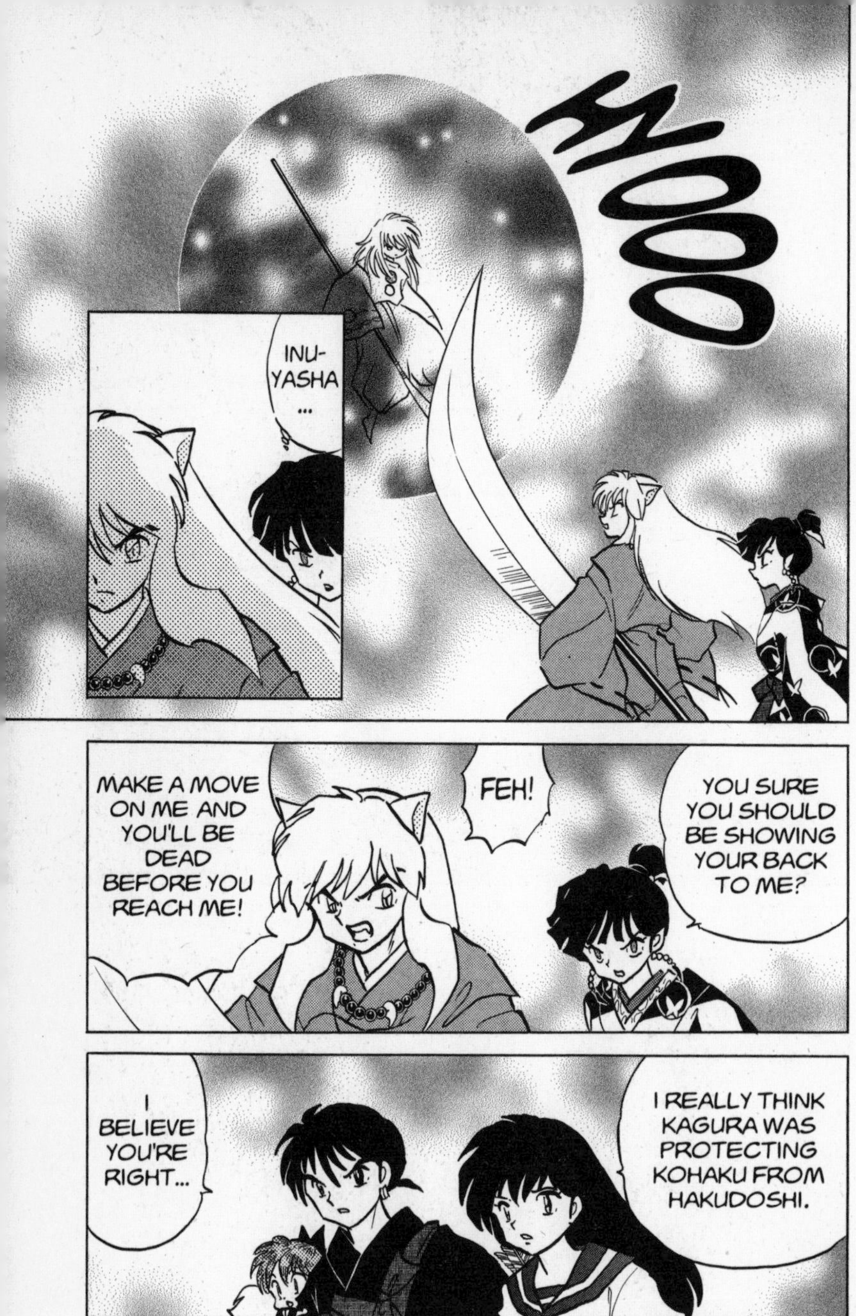
HYOOO
INU-YASHA ...
YOU SURE YOU SHOULD BE SHOWING YOUR BACK TO ME?
FEH!
MAKE A MOVE ON ME AND YOU'LL BE DEAD BEFORE YOU REACH ME!
I REALLY THINK KAGURA WAS PROTECTING KOHAKU FROM HAKUDOSHI.
I BELIEVE YOU'RE RIGHT...

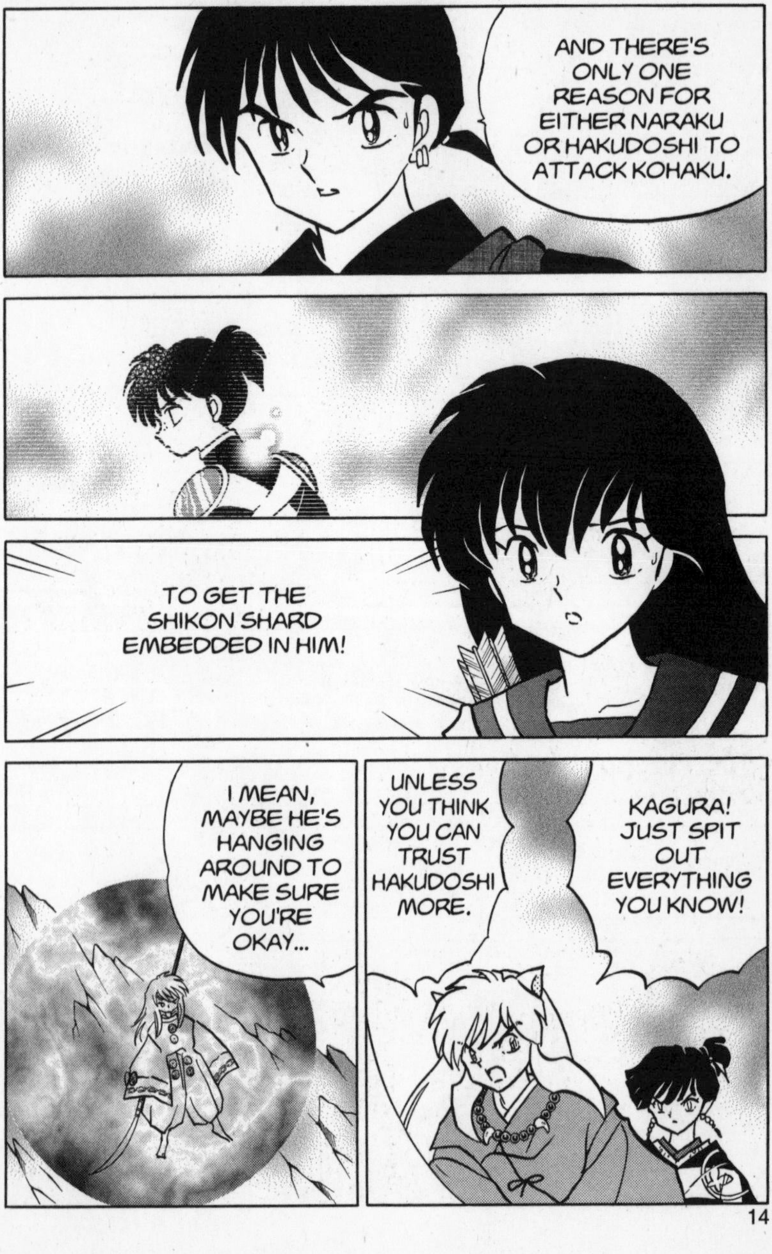
AND THERE'S ONLY ONE REASON FOR EITHER NARAKU OR HAKUDOSHI TO ATTACK KOHAKU.
TO GET THE SHIKON SHARD EMBEDDED IN HIM!
KAGURA! JUST SPIT OUT EVERYTHING YOU KNOW!
UNLESS YOU THINK YOU CAN TRUST HAKUDOSHI MORE.
I MEAN, MAYBE HE'S HANGING AROUND TO MAKE SURE YOU'RE OKAY...

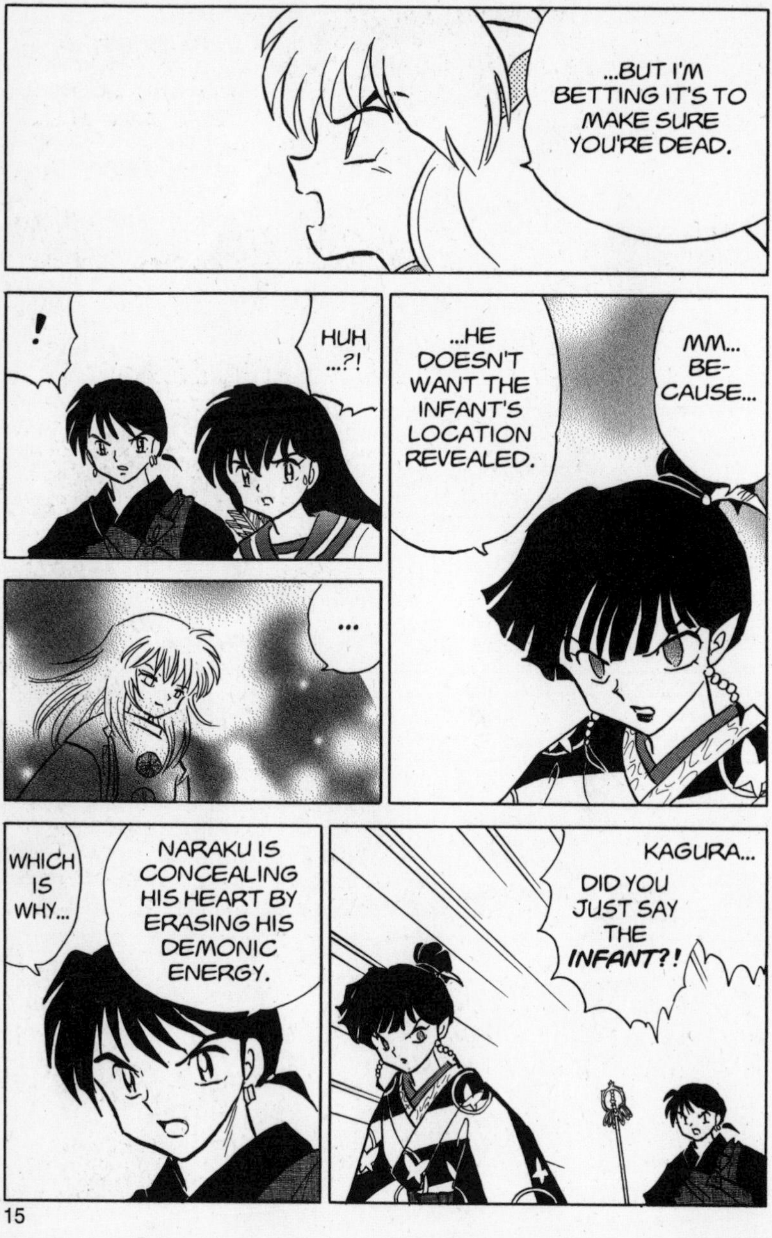
...BUT I'M BETTING IT'S TO MAKE SURE YOU'RE DEAD.
MM... BE-CAUSE...
...HE DOESN'T WANT THE INFANT'S LOCATION REVEALED.
HUH ...?!
!
...
KAGURA...
DID YOU JUST SAY THE *INFANT*?!
NARAKU IS CONCEALING HIS HEART BY ERASING HIS DEMONIC ENERGY.
WHICH IS WHY...

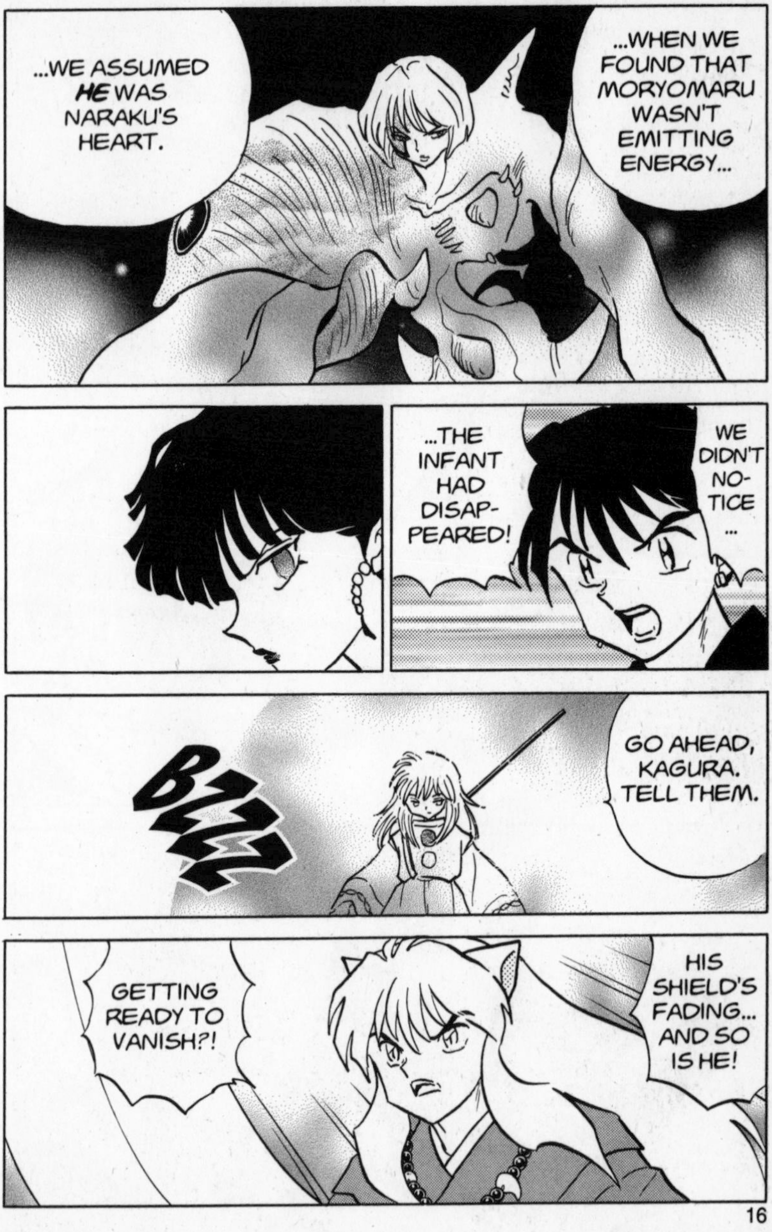
...WHEN WE FOUND THAT MORYOMARU WASN'T EMITTING ENERGY...
...WE ASSUMED *HE* WAS NARAKU'S HEART.
WE DIDN'T NO-TICE ...
...THE INFANT HAD DISAP-PEARED!
GO AHEAD, KAGURA. TELL THEM.
BZZZ
HIS SHIELD'S FADING... AND SO IS HE!
GETTING READY TO VANISH?!

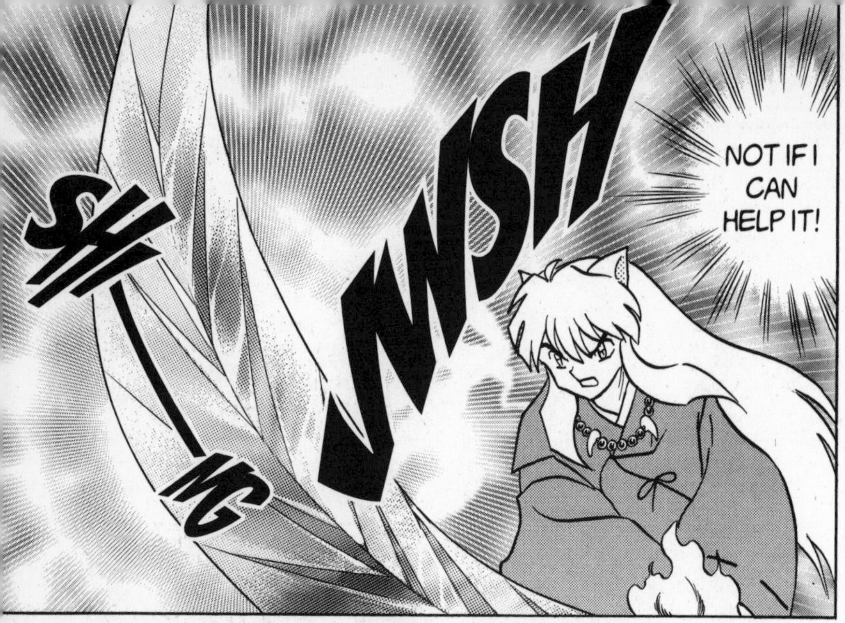
NOT IF I CAN HELP IT!
SWISH
SHI—NG

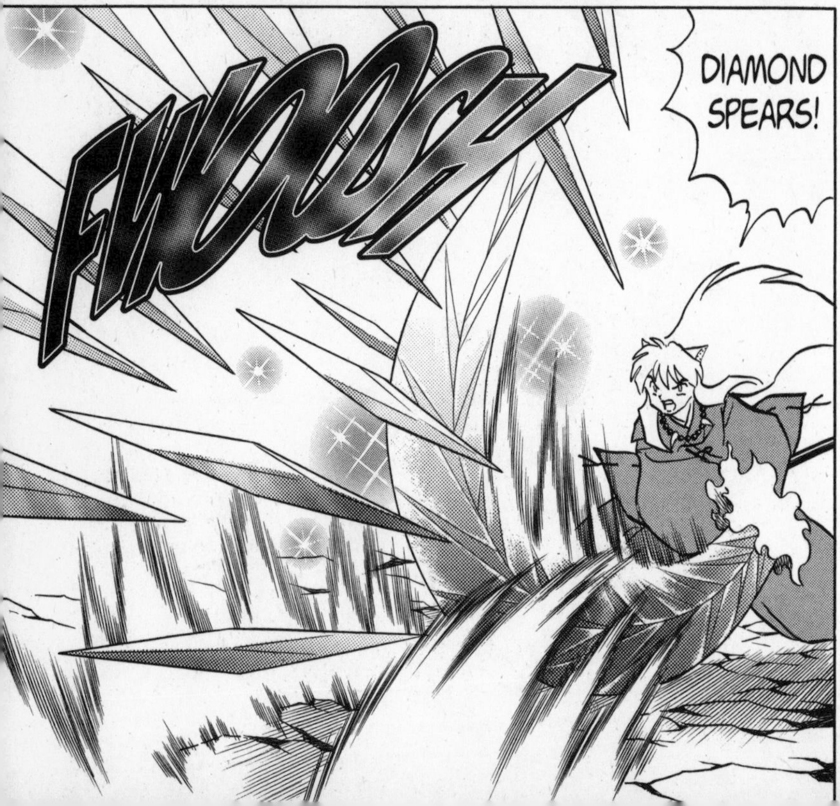
DIAMOND SPEARS!
FWOOSH

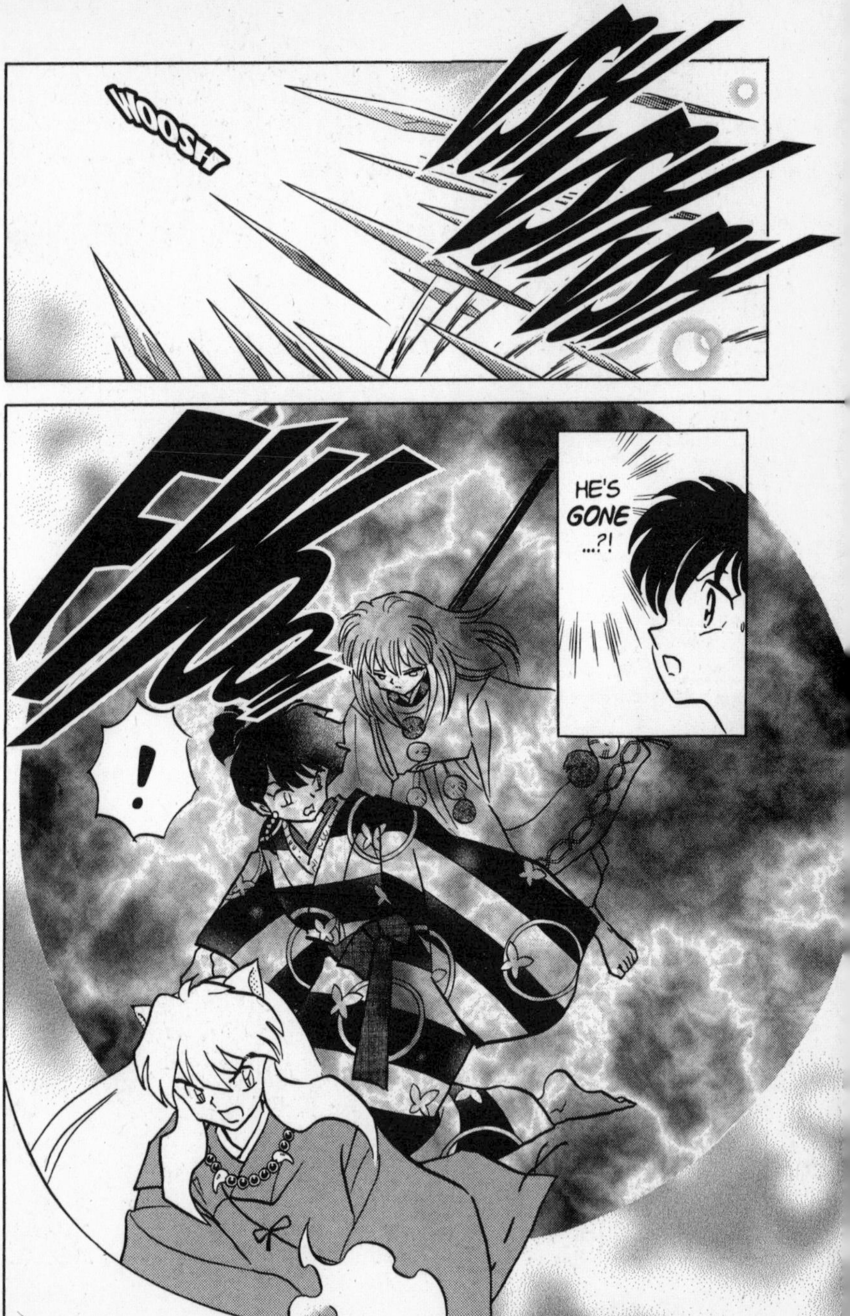
WOOSH
HE'S GONE ...?!
!

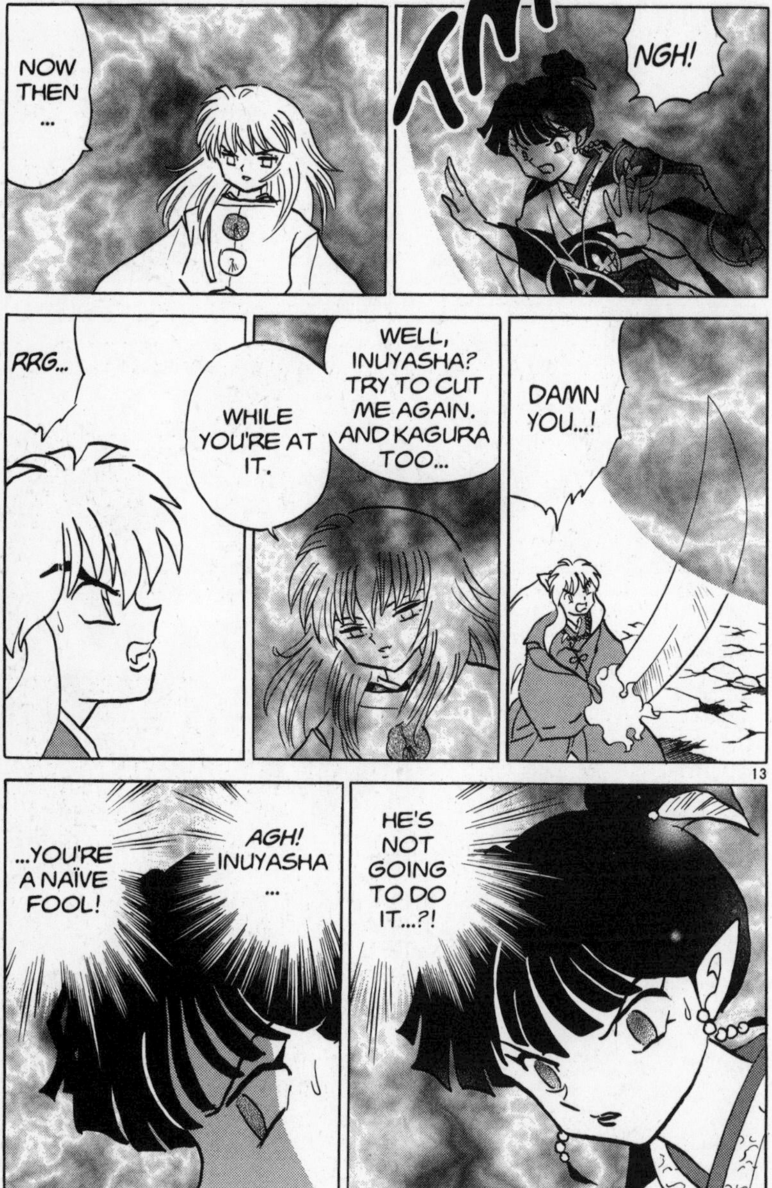
TM
NGH!
NOW THEN ...
DAMN YOU...!
WELL, INUYASHA? TRY TO CUT ME AGAIN. AND KAGURA TOO...
WHILE YOU'RE AT IT.
RRG...
HE'S NOT GOING TO DO IT...?!
AGH! INUYASHA ...
...YOU'RE A NAÏVE FOOL!

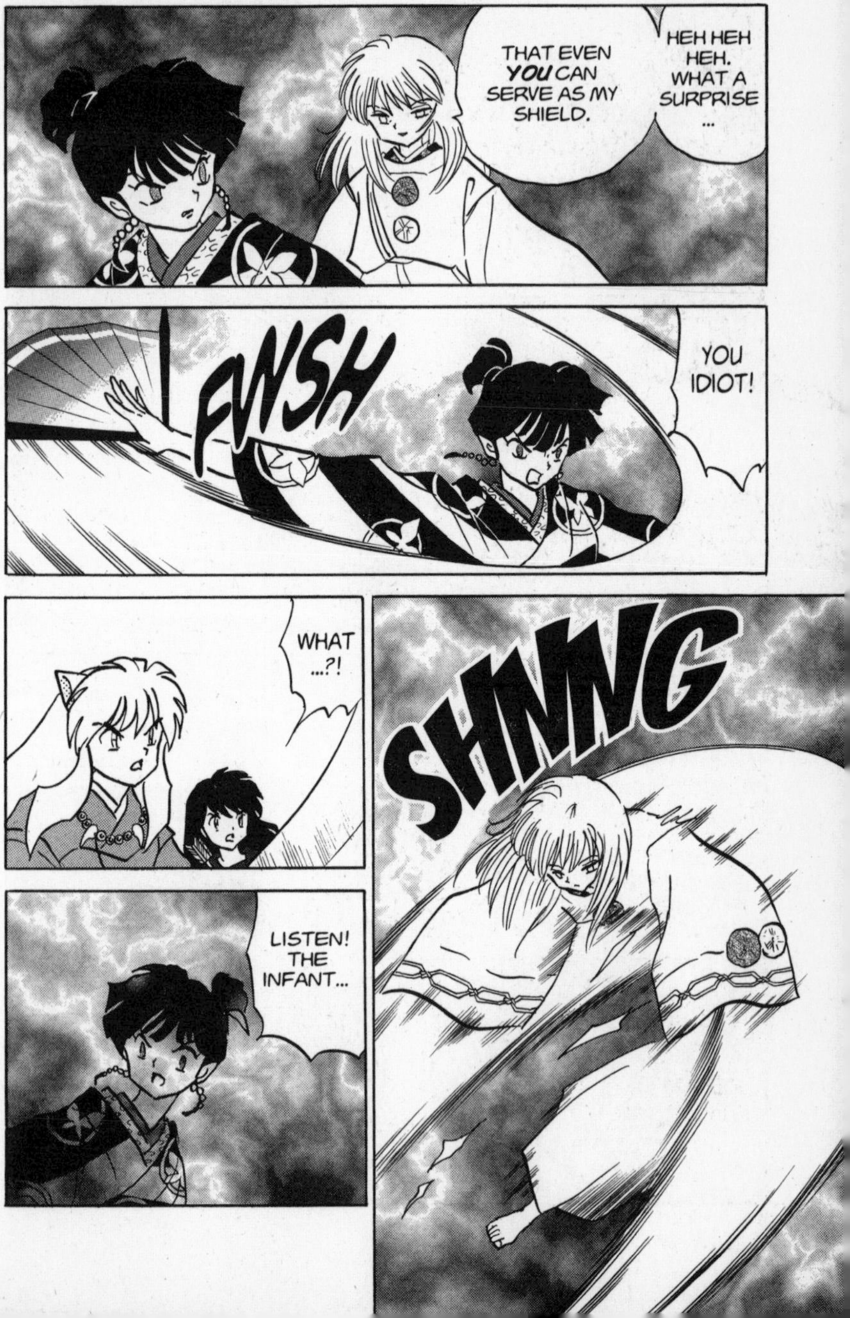
HEH HEH HEH. WHAT A SURPRISE ...
THAT EVEN *YOU* CAN SERVE AS MY SHIELD.
YOU IDIOT!
FWSH
SHNNG
WHAT ...?!
LISTEN! THE INFANT...

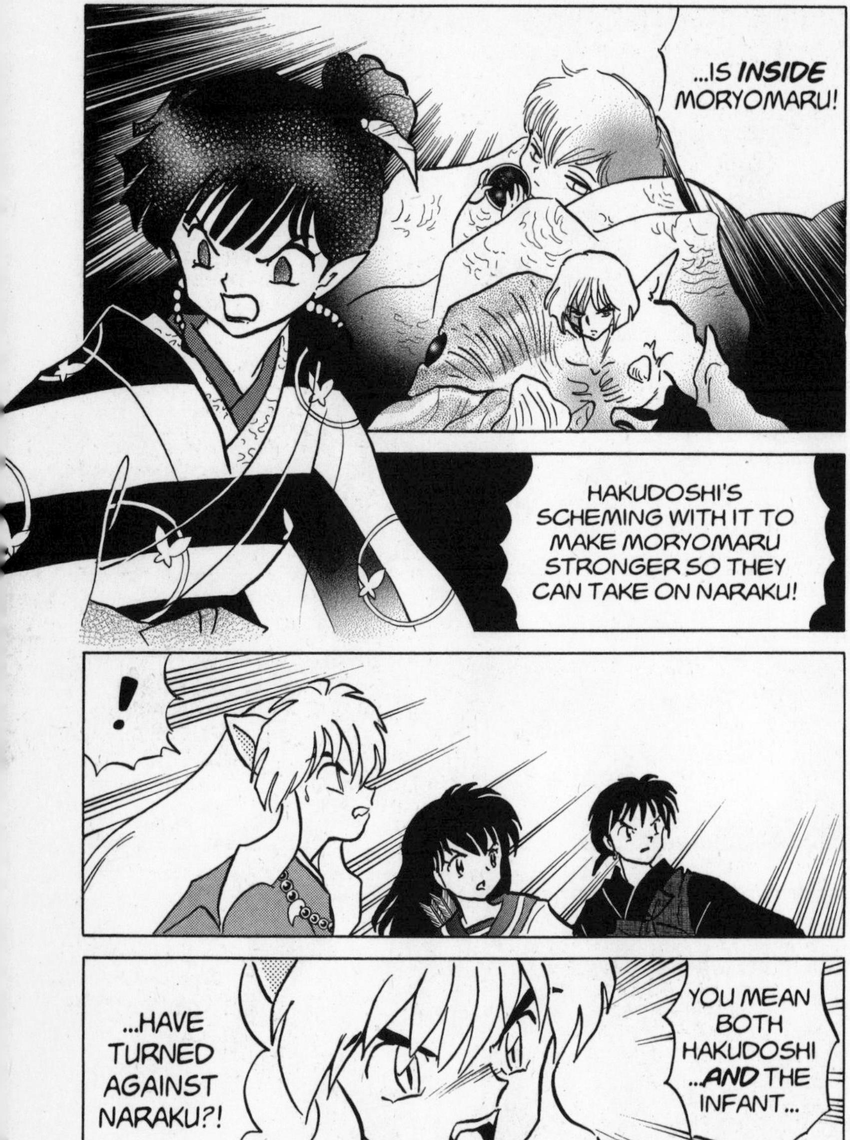
...IS INSIDE MORYOMARU!
HAKUDOSHI'S SCHEMING WITH IT TO MAKE MORYOMARU STRONGER SO THEY CAN TAKE ON NARAKU!
!
YOU MEAN BOTH HAKUDOSHI ...AND THE INFANT...
...HAVE TURNED AGAINST NARAKU?!

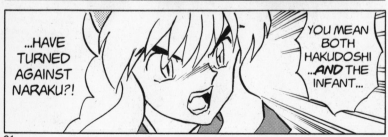

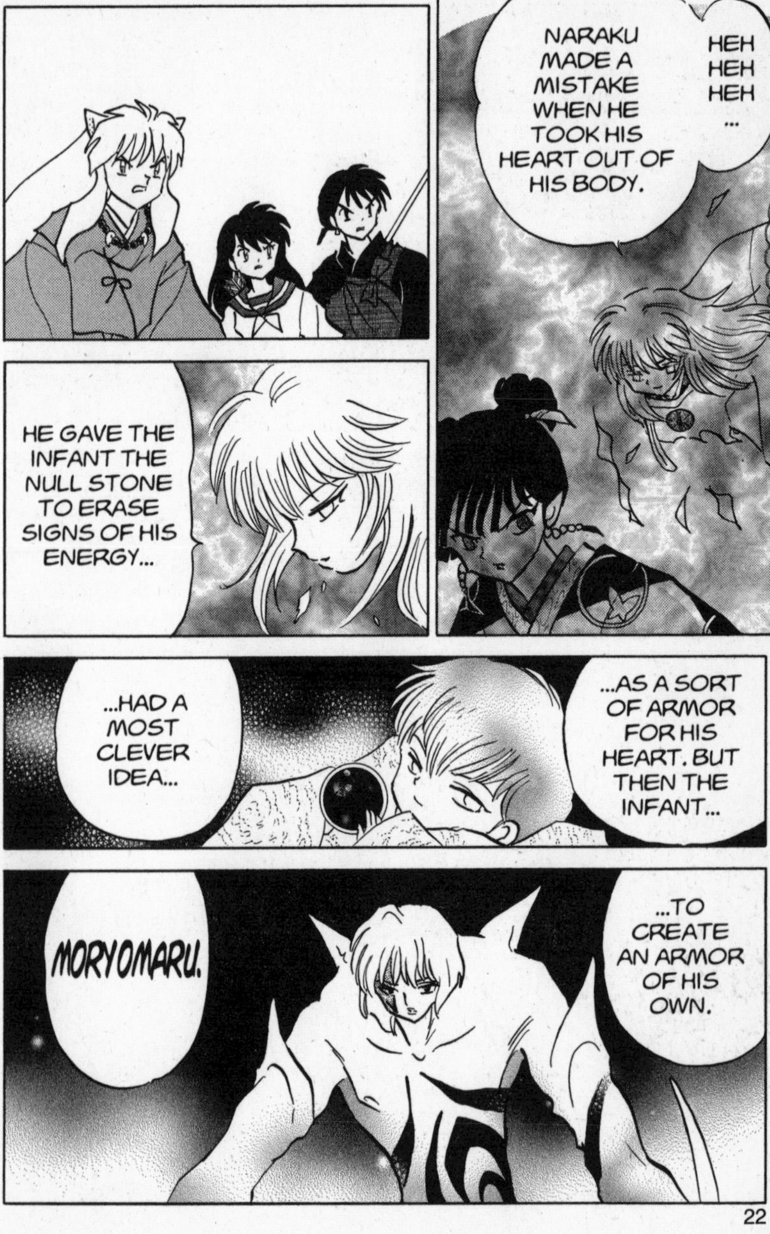
HEH HEH HEH ...
NARAKU MADE A MISTAKE WHEN HE TOOK HIS HEART OUT OF HIS BODY.
HE GAVE THE INFANT THE NULL STONE TO ERASE SIGNS OF HIS ENERGY...
...AS A SORT OF ARMOR FOR HIS HEART. BUT THEN THE INFANT...
...HAD A MOST CLEVER IDEA...
...TO CREATE AN ARMOR OF HIS OWN.
MORYOMARU.

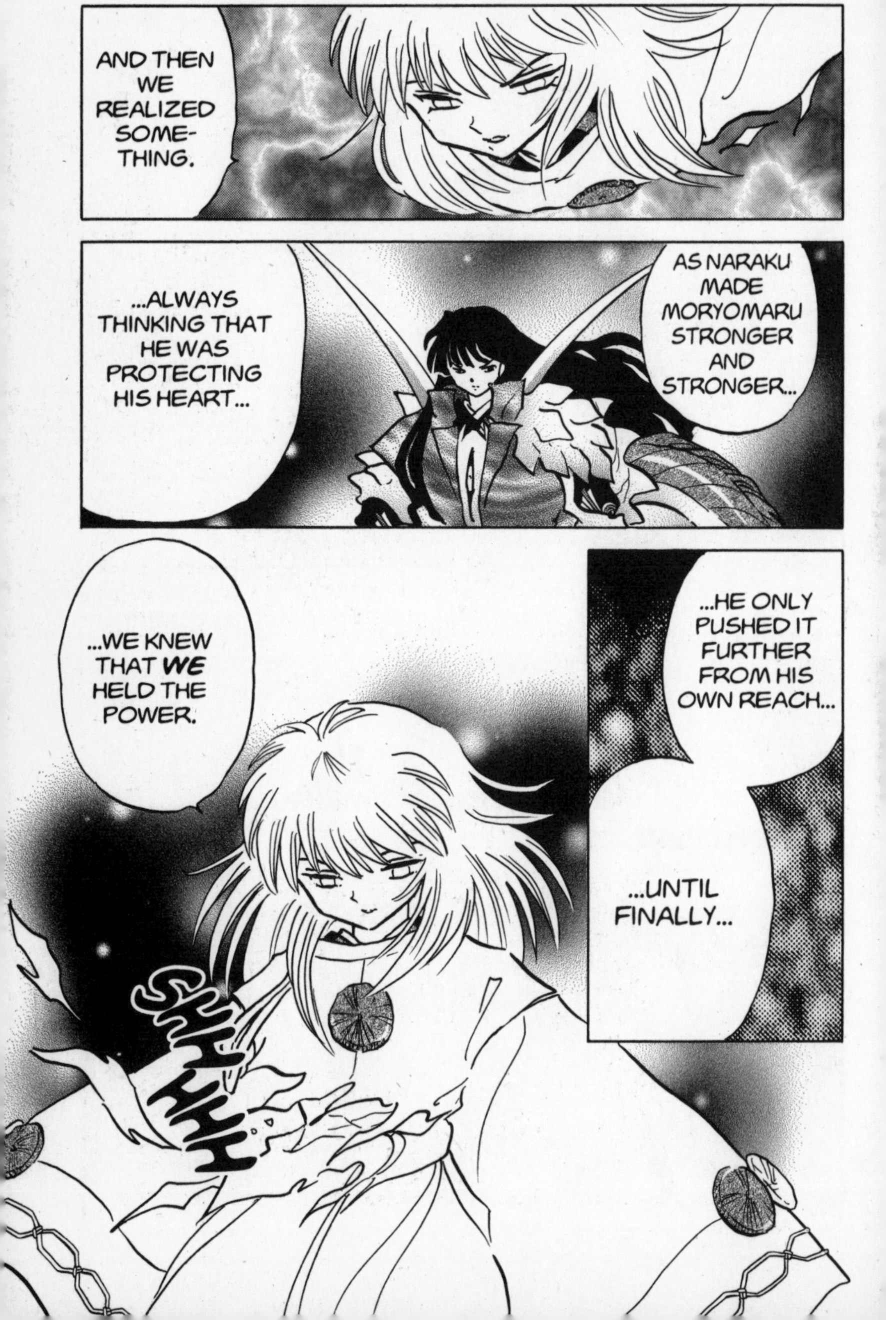
AND THEN WE REALIZED SOME-THING.
AS NARAKU MADE MORYOMARU STRONGER AND STRONGER...
...ALWAYS THINKING THAT HE WAS PROTECTING HIS HEART...
...HE ONLY PUSHED IT FURTHER FROM HIS OWN REACH...
...UNTIL FINALLY...
...WE KNEW THAT **WE** HELD THE POWER.
SHHHH

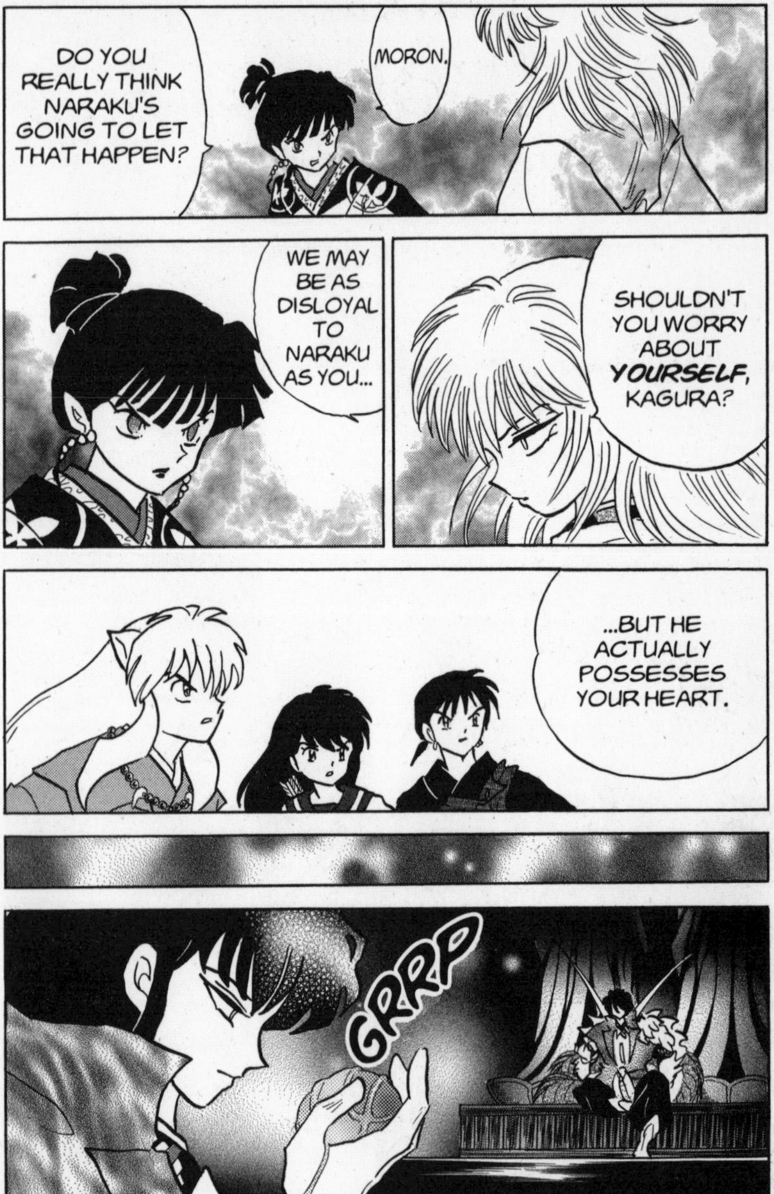
MORON.
DO YOU REALLY THINK NARAKU'S GOING TO LET THAT HAPPEN?
SHOULDN'T YOU WORRY ABOUT YOURSELF, KAGURA?
WE MAY BE AS DISLOYAL TO NARAKU AS YOU...
...BUT HE ACTUALLY POSSESSES YOUR HEART.
GRRP

SCROLL 2
HAKUDOSHI'S END

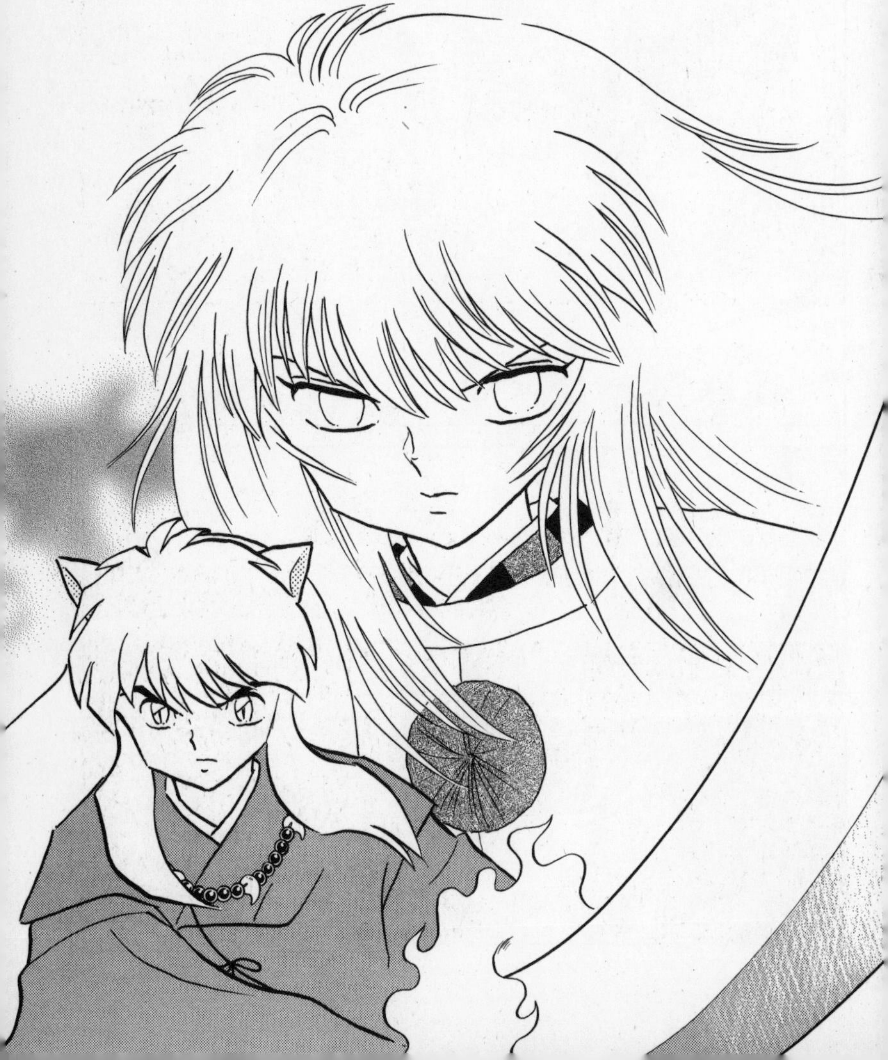

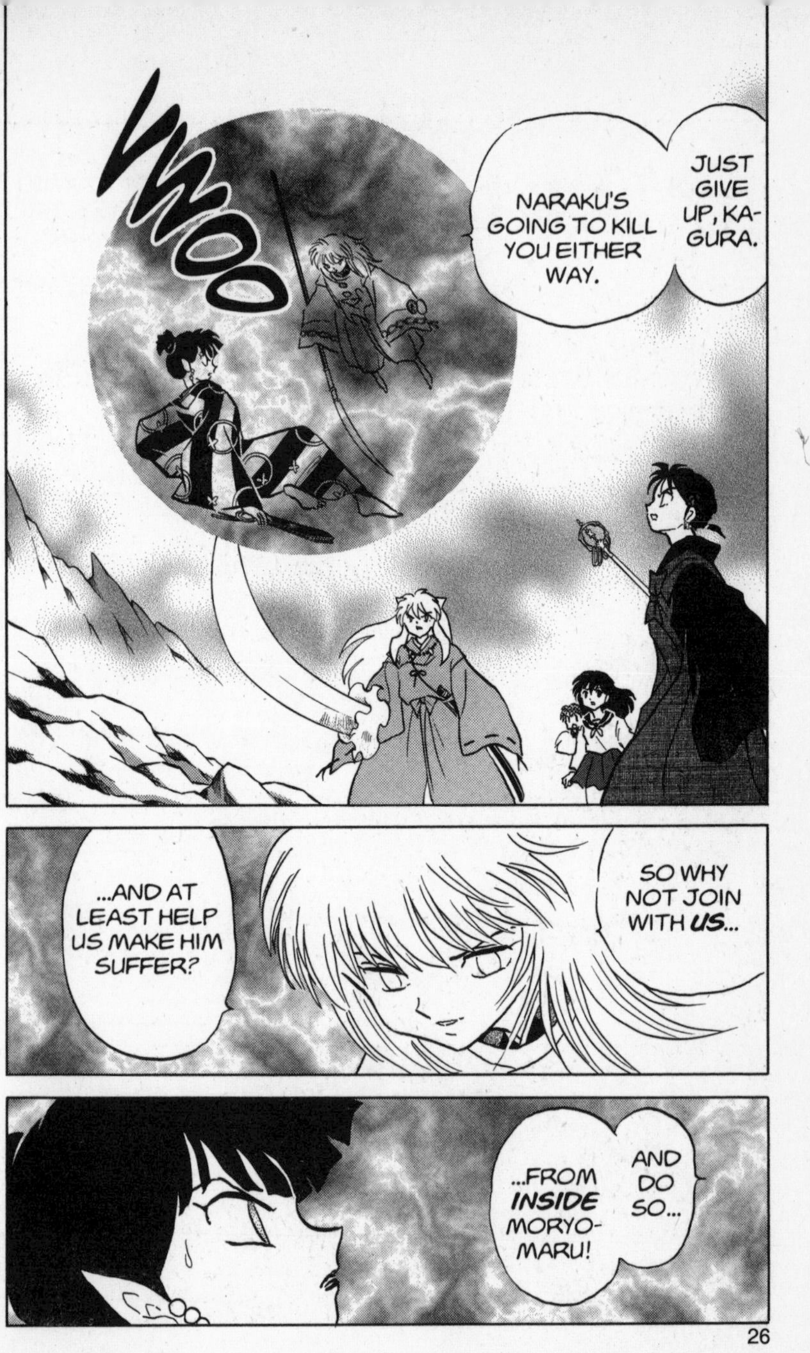
JUST GIVE UP, KA-GURA.
NARAKU'S GOING TO KILL YOU EITHER WAY.
VWOO
SO WHY NOT JOIN WITH US...
...AND AT LEAST HELP US MAKE HIM SUFFER?
AND DO SO...
...FROM INSIDE MORYO-MARU!

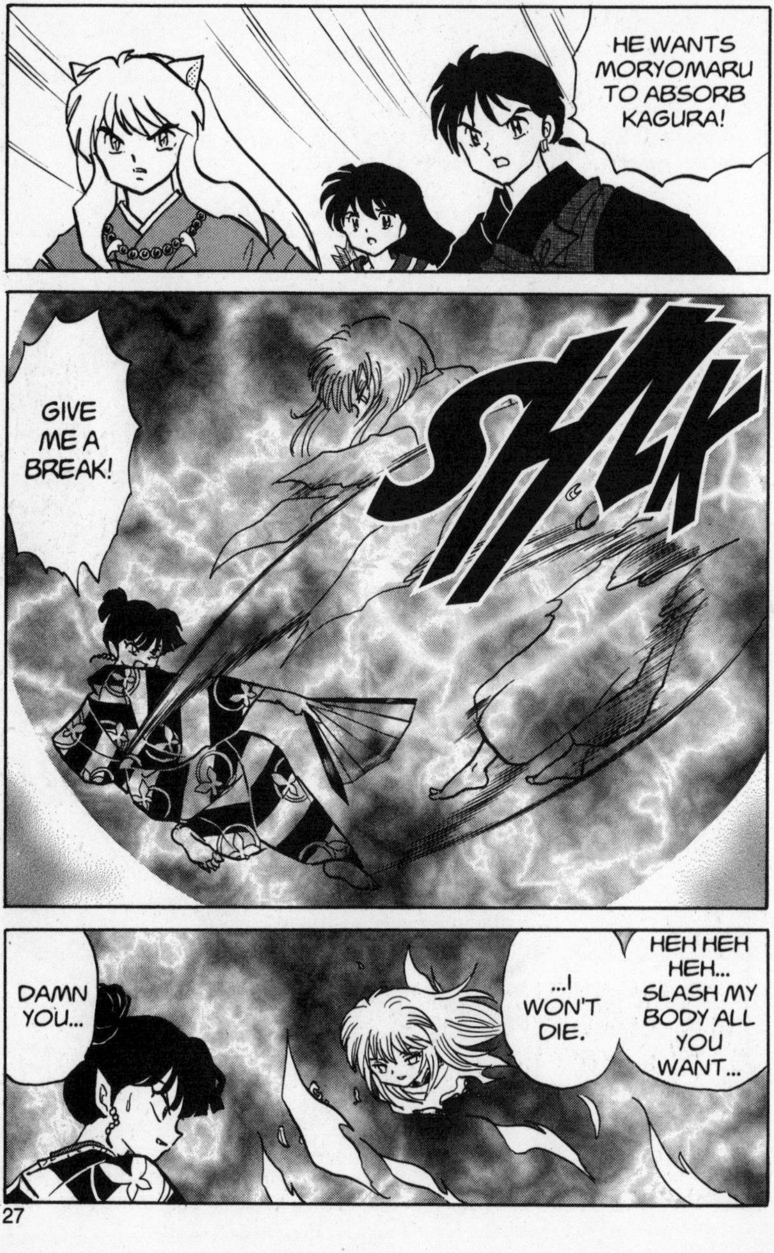
HE WANTS MORYOMARU TO ABSORB KAGURA!
SHAK
GIVE ME A BREAK!
HEH HEH HEH... SLASH MY BODY ALL YOU WANT...
...I WON'T DIE.
DAMN YOU...

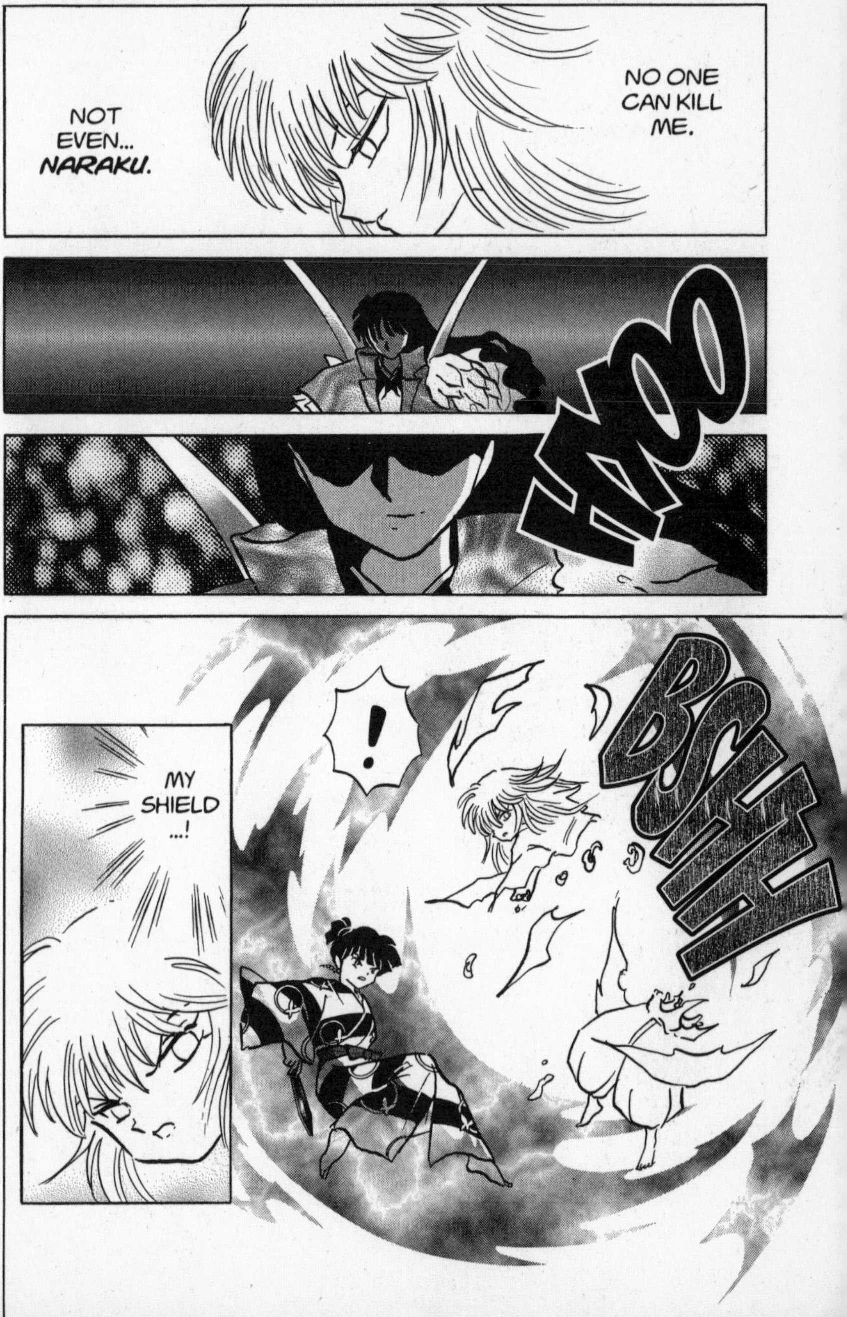
NO ONE CAN KILL ME.
NOT EVEN... NARAKU.
WHOO
BSHH!
!
MY SHIELD ...!

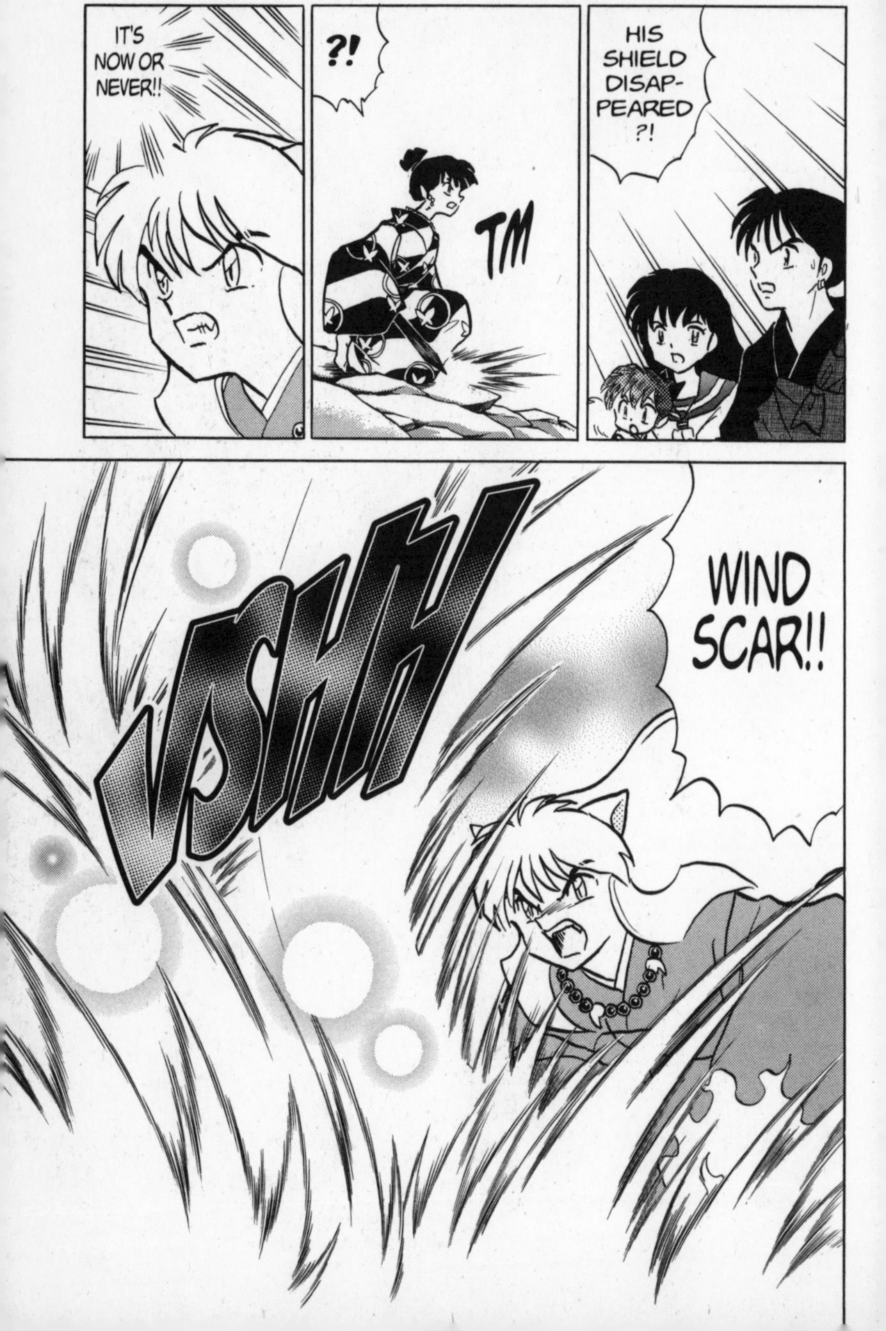
HIS SHIELD DISAPPEARED?!
?!
TM
IT'S NOW OR NEVER!!
WIND SCAR!!
VSHH

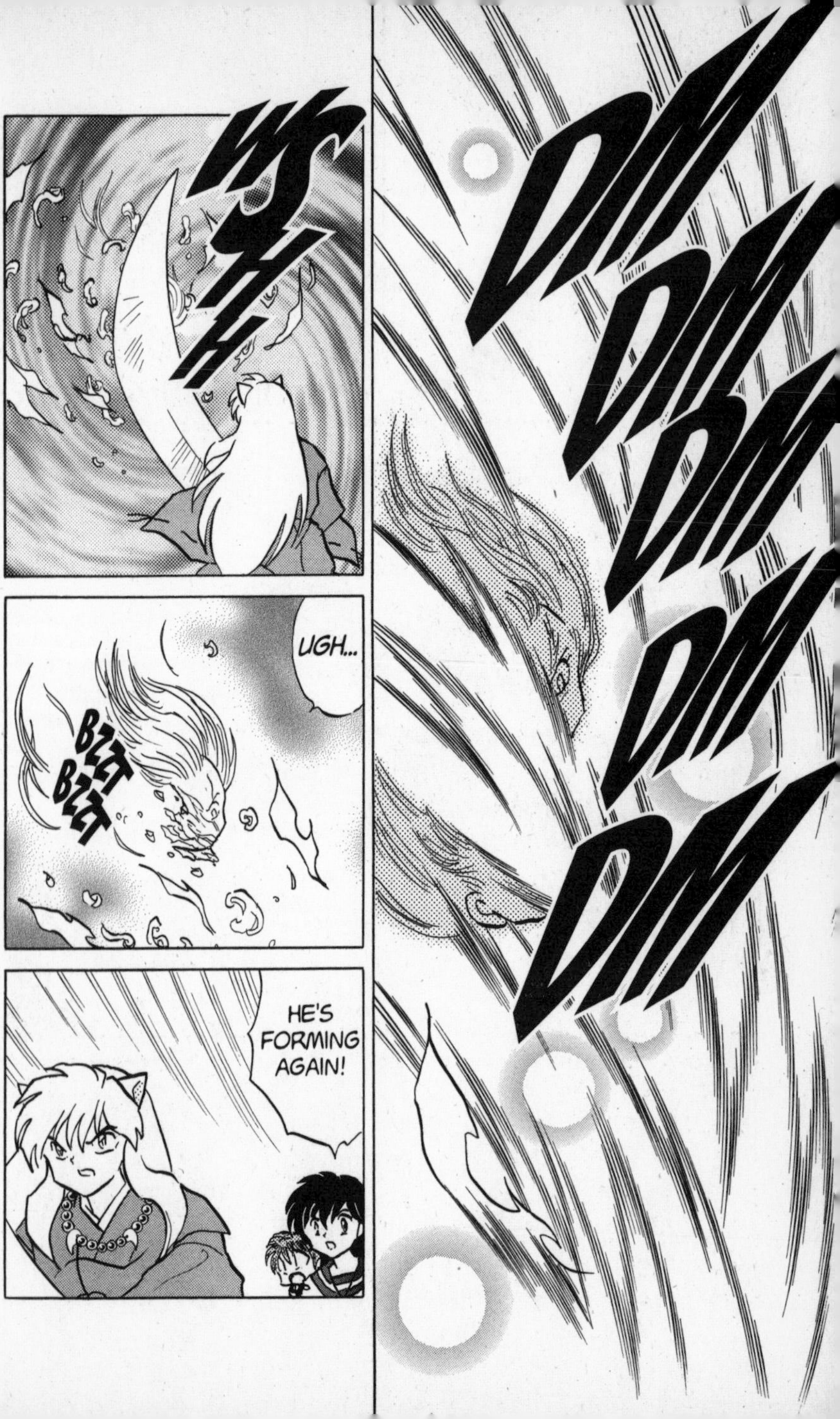
DM DM DM DM DM DM
WSHH
UGH...
BZZT BZZT
HE'S FORMING AGAIN!

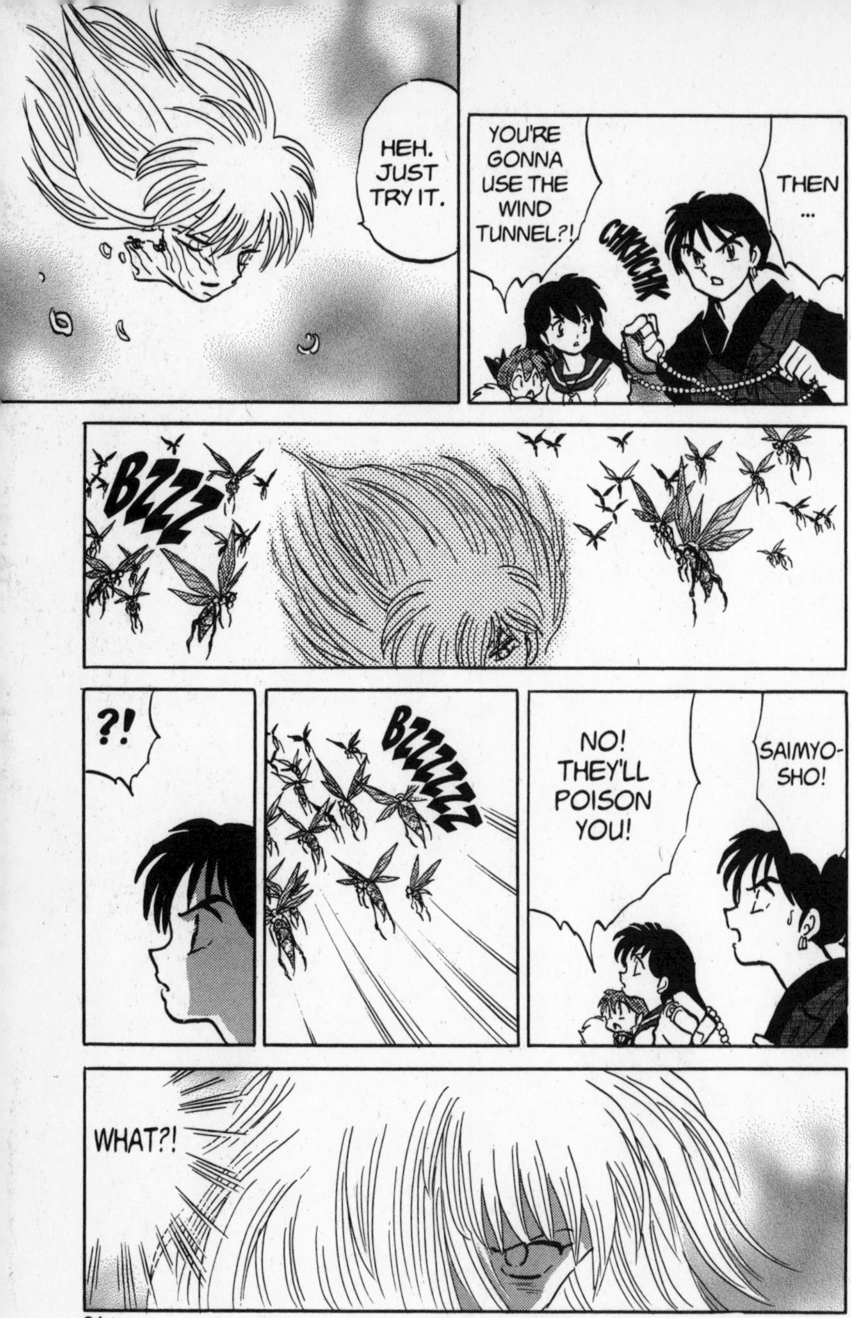
THEN ...
YOU'RE GONNA USE THE WIND TUNNEL?!
CHKCHCHK
HEH. JUST TRY IT.
BZZZ
SAIMYO-SHO!
NO! THEY'LL POISON YOU!
BZZZZZZZ
?!
WHAT?!

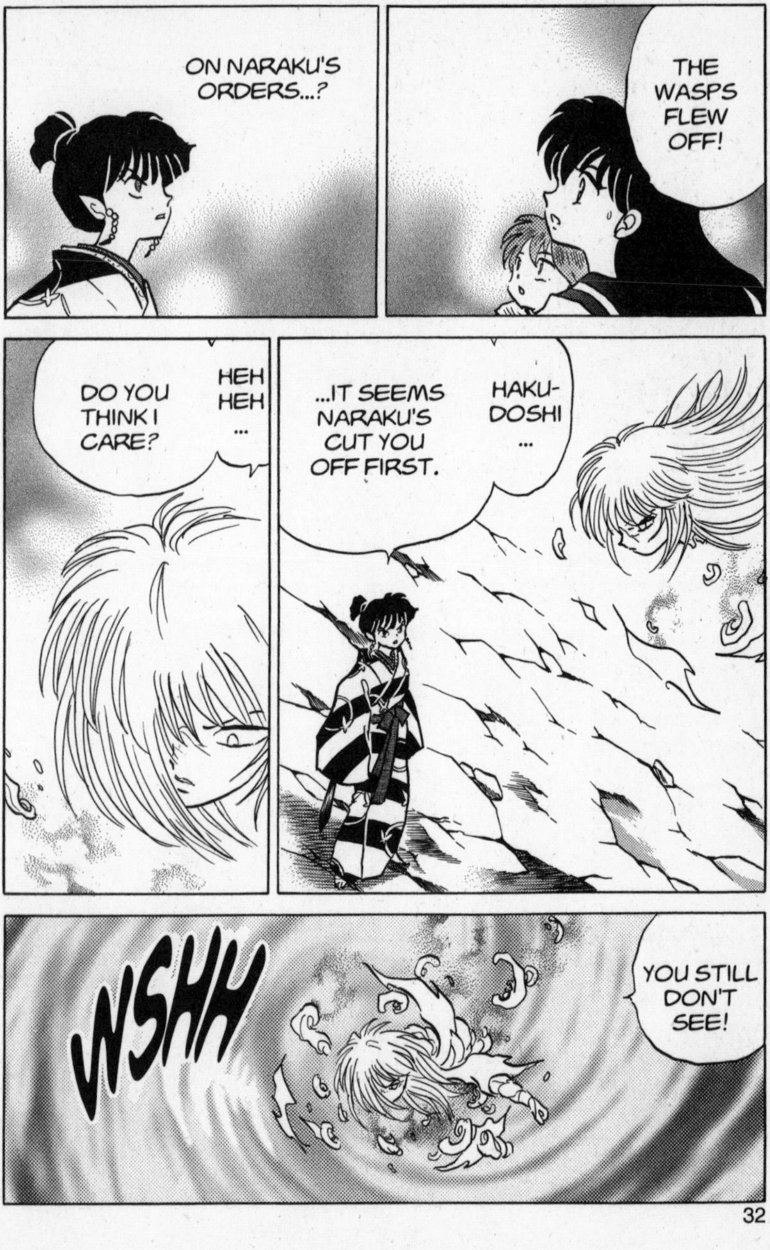
THE WASPS FLEW OFF!
ON NARAKU'S ORDERS...?
HAKU-DOSHI ...
...IT SEEMS NARAKU'S CUT YOU OFF FIRST.
HEH HEH ...
DO YOU THINK I CARE?
YOU STILL DON'T SEE!
WSHH

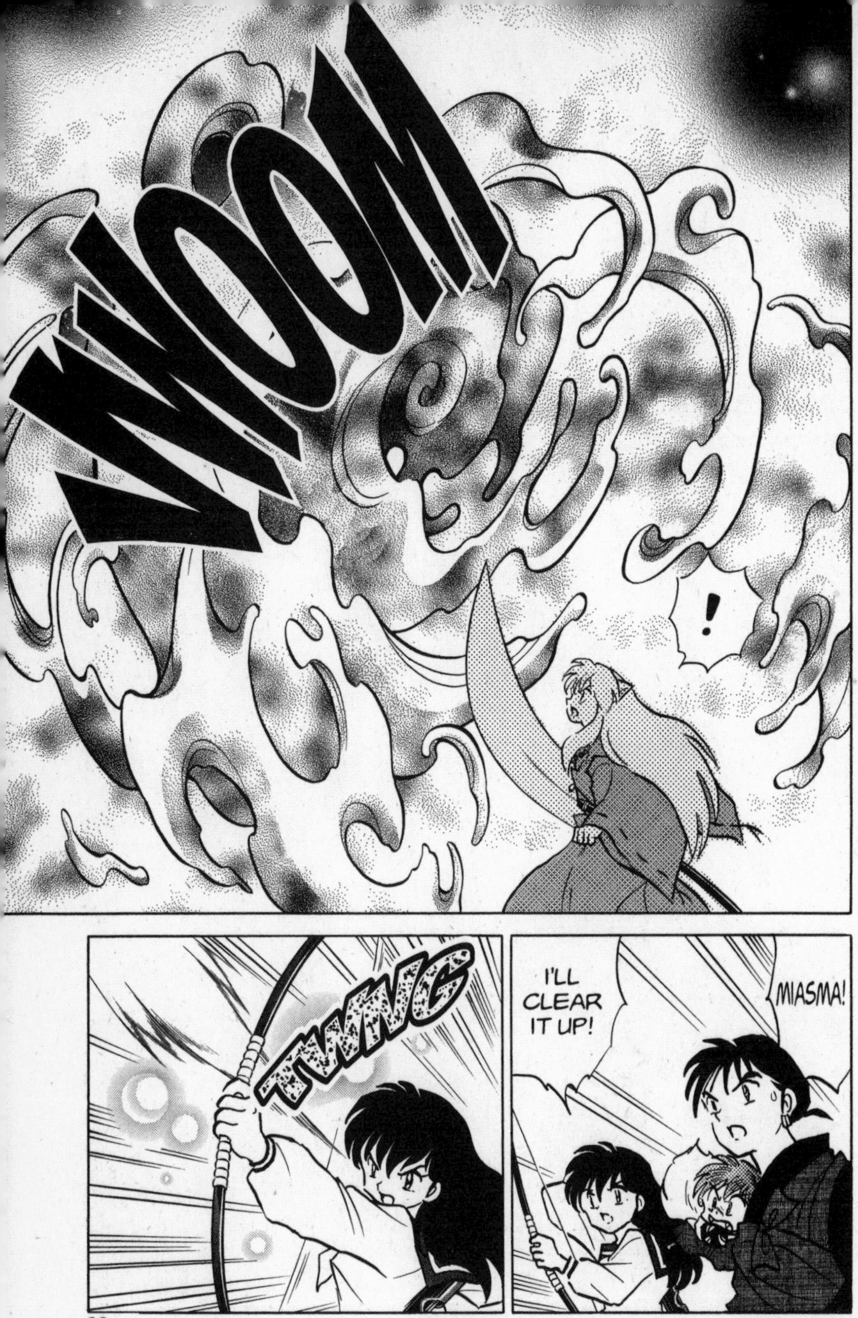
VWOOM
!
MIASMA!
I'LL CLEAR IT UP!
TWNG

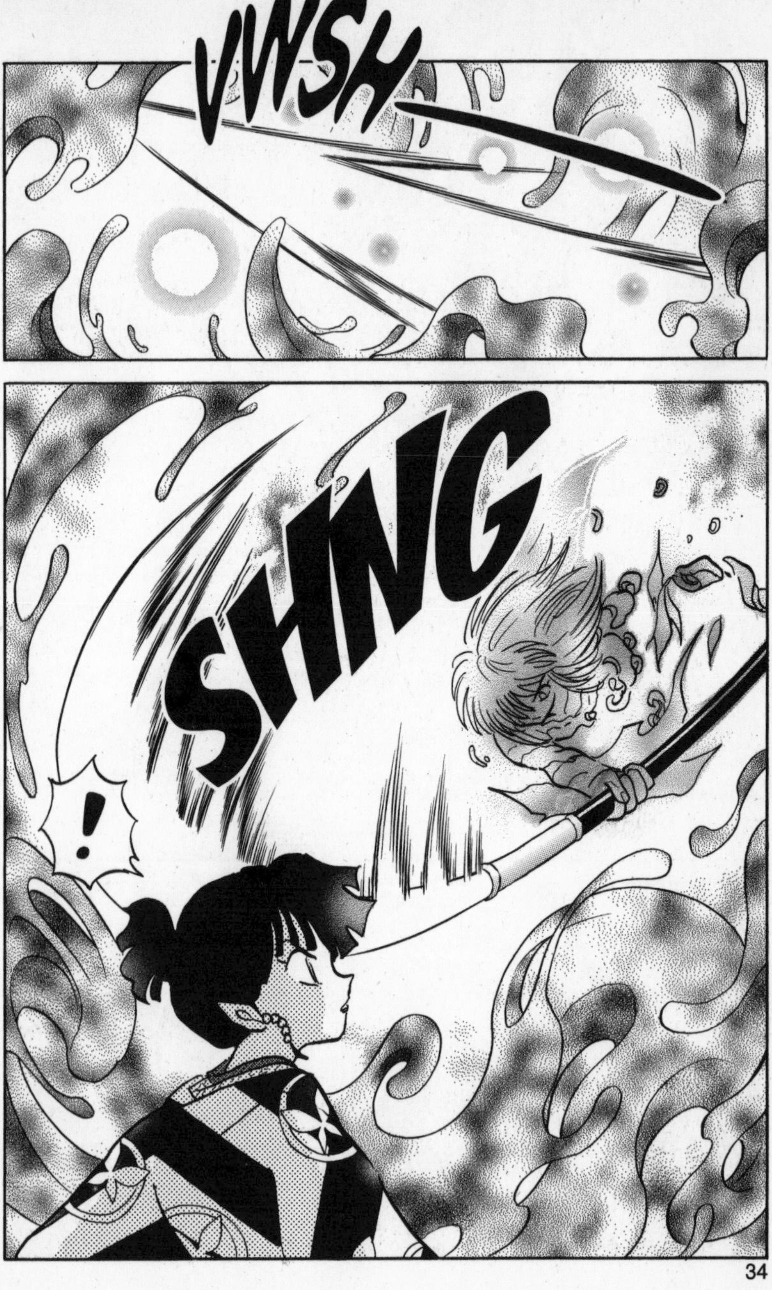
VWSH
SHING
!

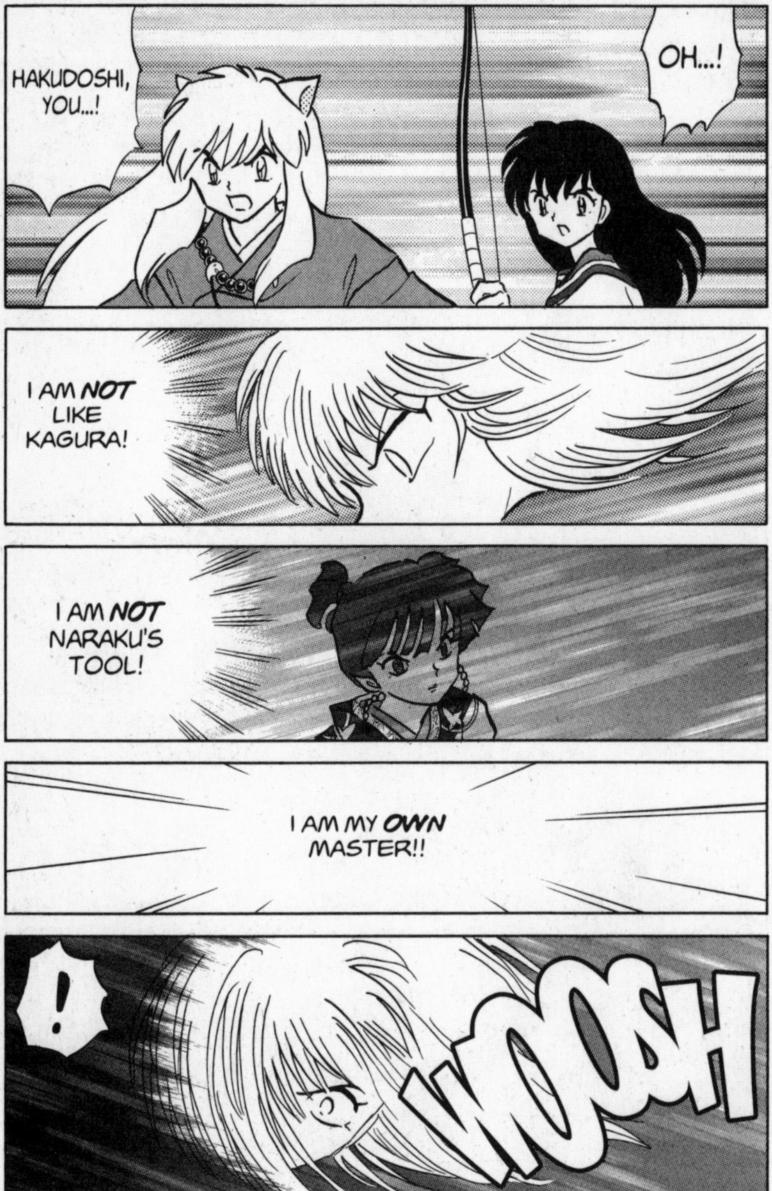
OH...!
HAKUDOSHI, YOU...!
I AM NOT LIKE KAGURA!
I AM NOT NARAKU'S TOOL!
I AM MY OWN MASTER!!
WOOSH
!

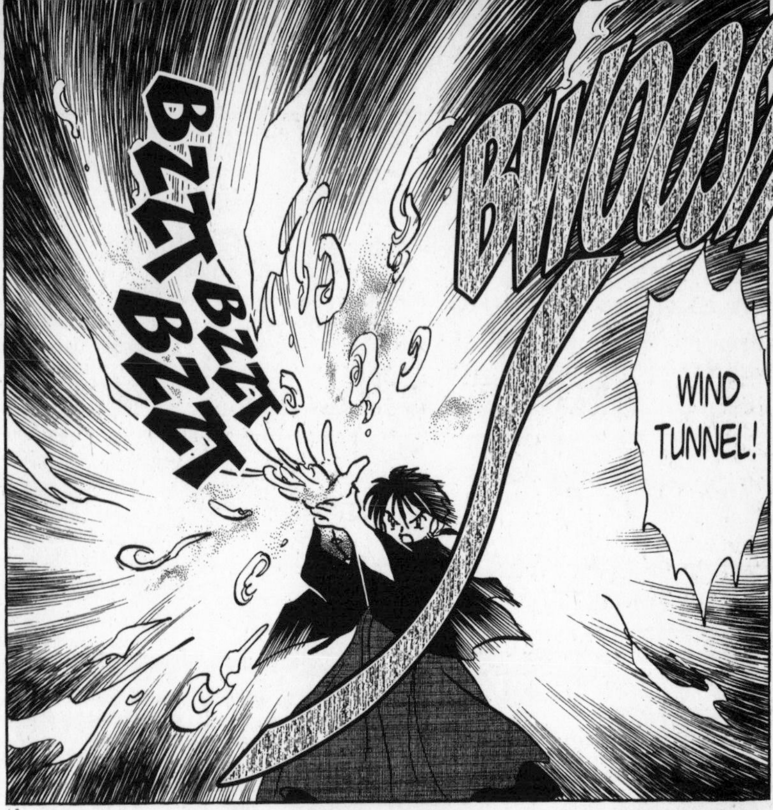
BWOOSH
WIND TUNNEL!
BZZT BZZT BZZT

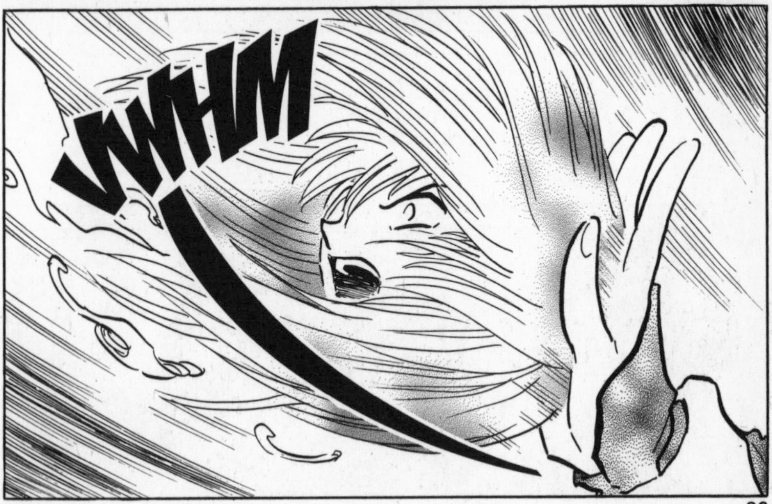
VWHM

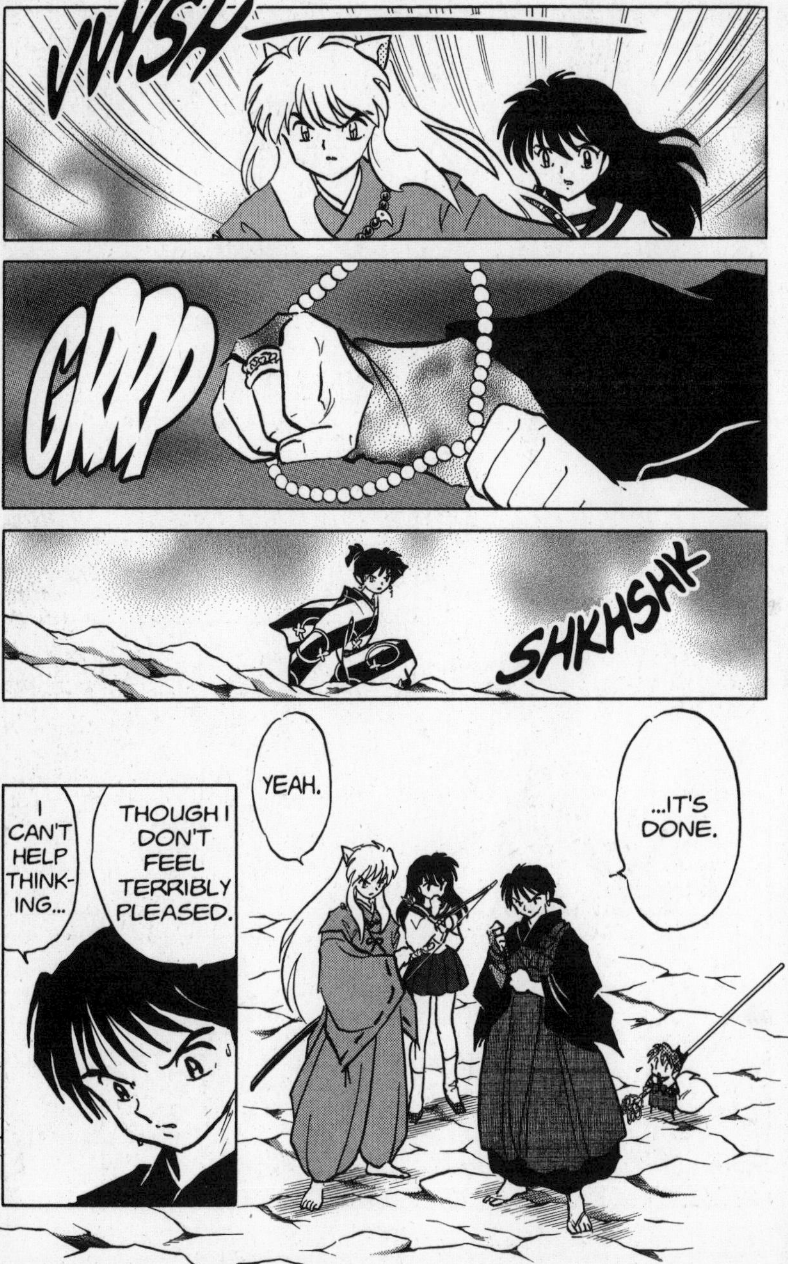
VWSH
GRRP
SHKSHK
...IT'S DONE.
YEAH.
THOUGH I DON'T FEEL TERRIBLY PLEASED.
I CAN'T HELP THINKING...

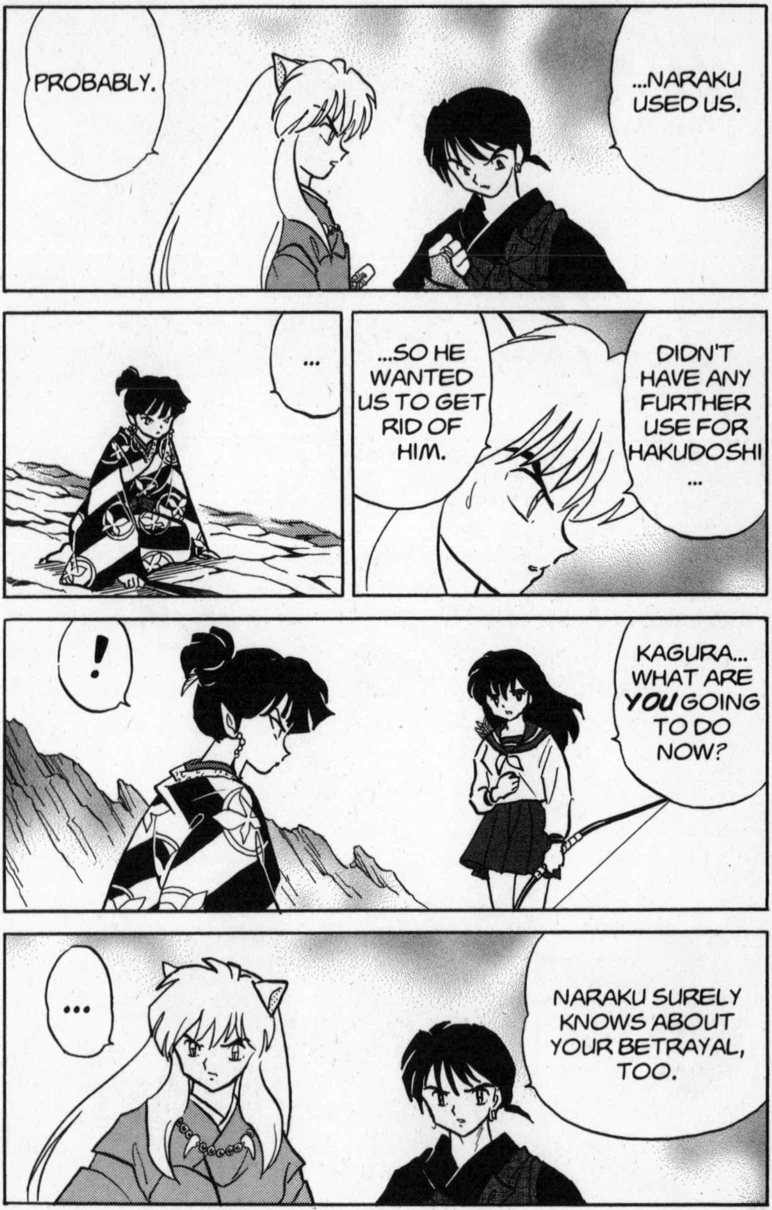
...NARAKU USED US.
PROBABLY.
DIDN'T HAVE ANY FURTHER USE FOR HAKUDOSHI ...
...SO HE WANTED US TO GET RID OF HIM.
...
KAGURA... WHAT ARE YOU GOING TO DO NOW?
!
NARAKU SURELY KNOWS ABOUT YOUR BETRAYAL, TOO.
...

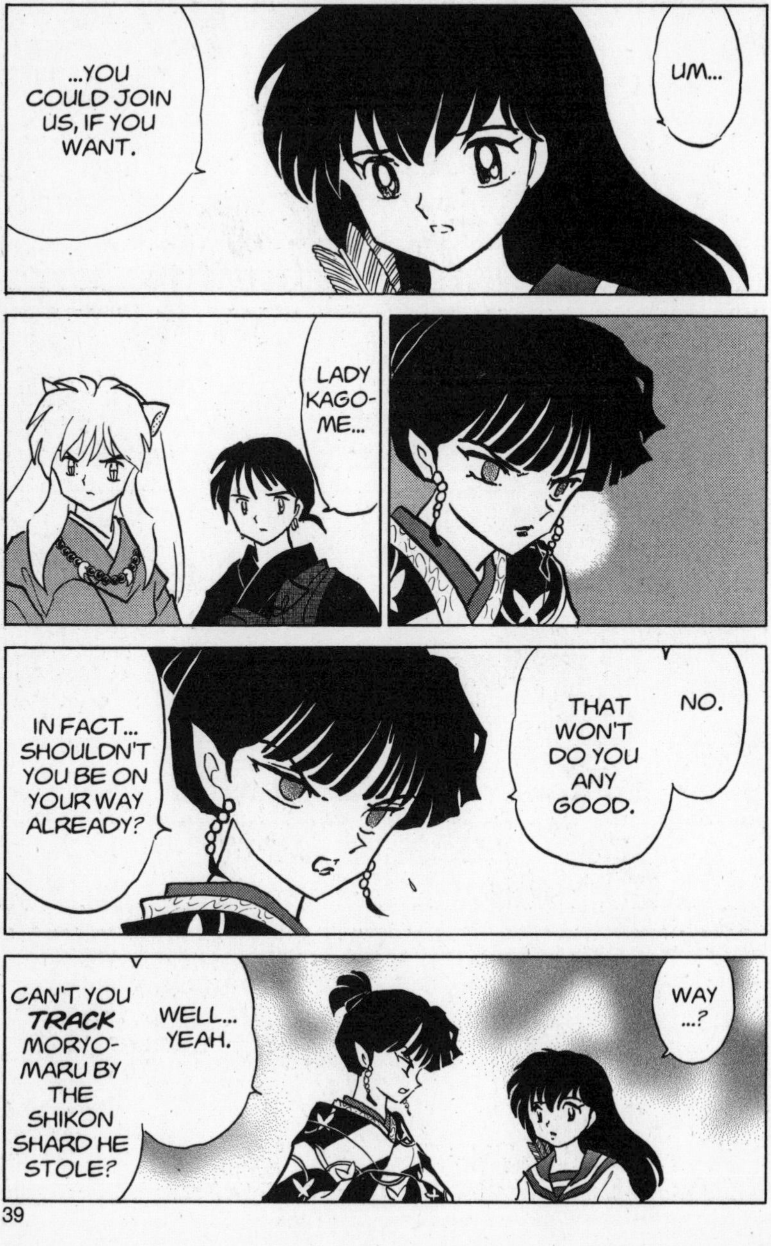
UM...
...YOU COULD JOIN US, IF YOU WANT.
LADY KAGO-ME...
NO.
THAT WON'T DO YOU ANY GOOD.
IN FACT... SHOULDN'T YOU BE ON YOUR WAY ALREADY?
WAY ...?
WELL... YEAH.
CAN'T YOU TRACK MORYO-MARU BY THE SHIKON SHARD HE STOLE?

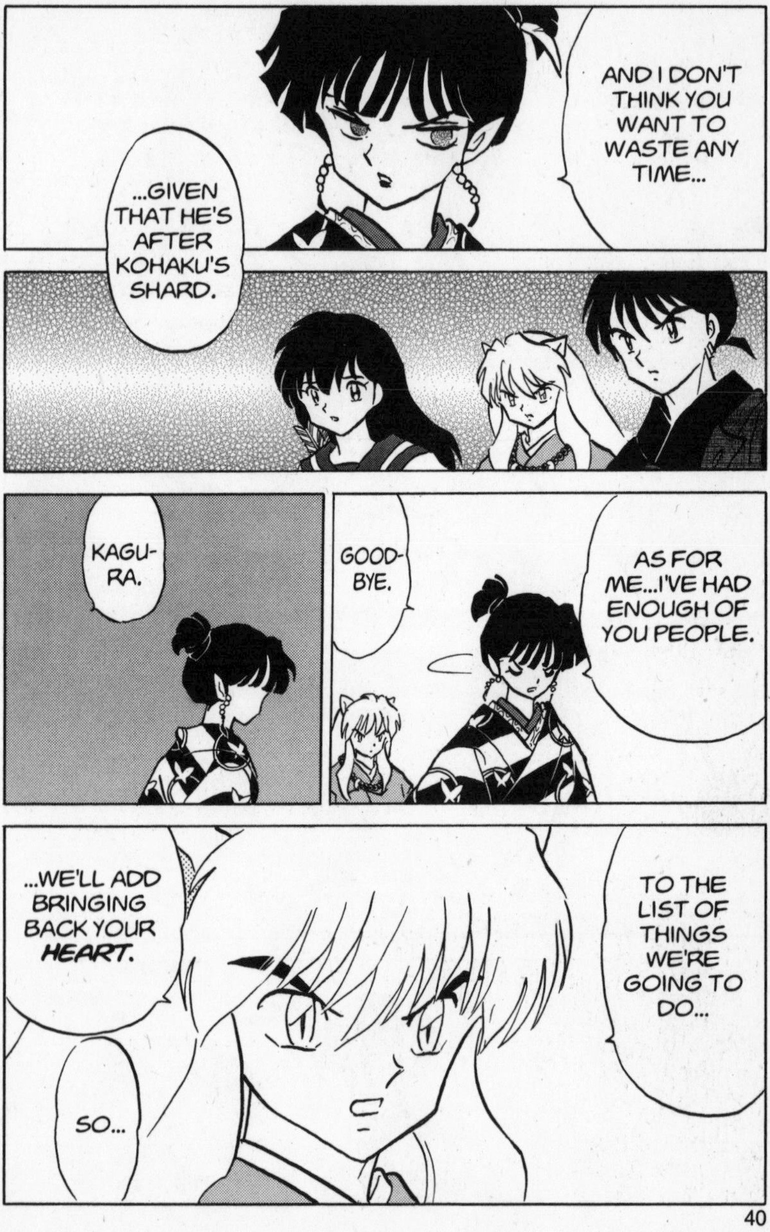
AND I DON'T THINK YOU WANT TO WASTE ANY TIME...
...GIVEN THAT HE'S AFTER KOHAKU'S SHARD.
AS FOR ME...I'VE HAD ENOUGH OF YOU PEOPLE.
GOOD-BYE.
KAGU-RA.
TO THE LIST OF THINGS WE'RE GOING TO DO...
...WE'LL ADD BRINGING BACK YOUR ***HEART***.
SO...

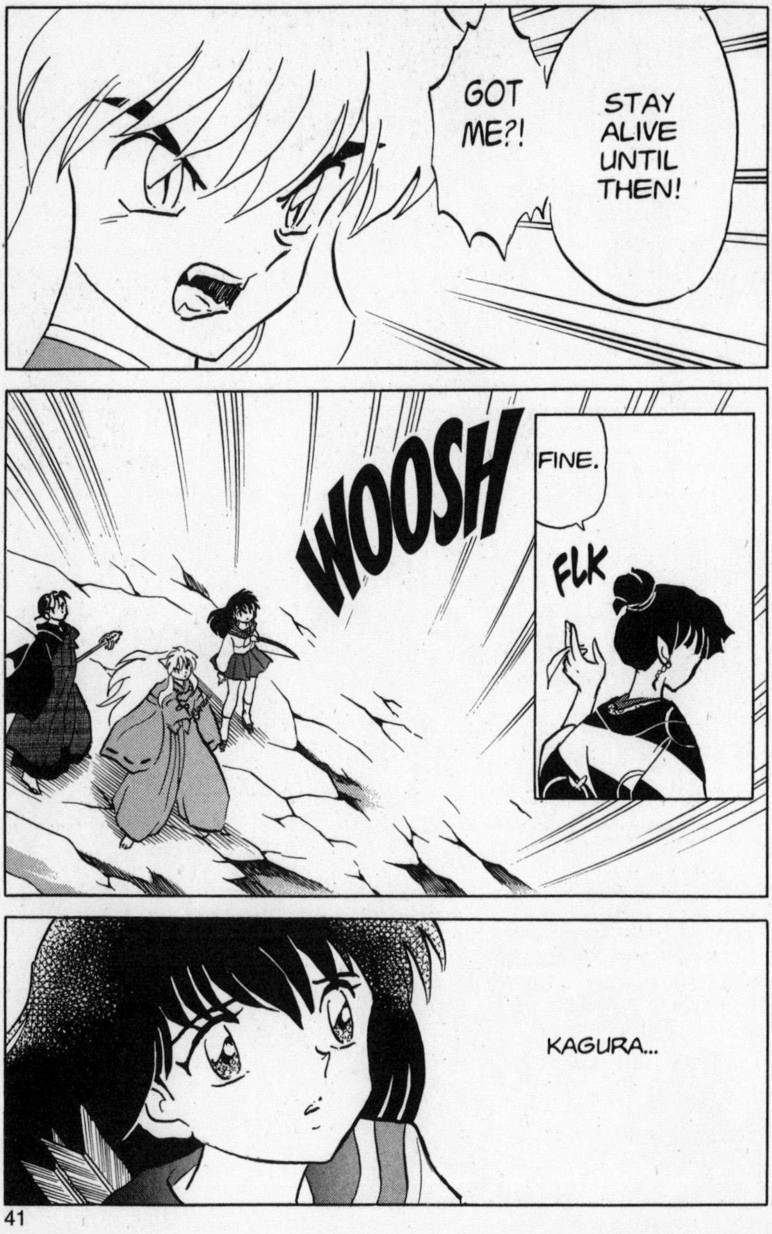
STAY ALIVE UNTIL THEN!
GOT ME?!
FINE.
FLK
WOOSH
KAGURA...

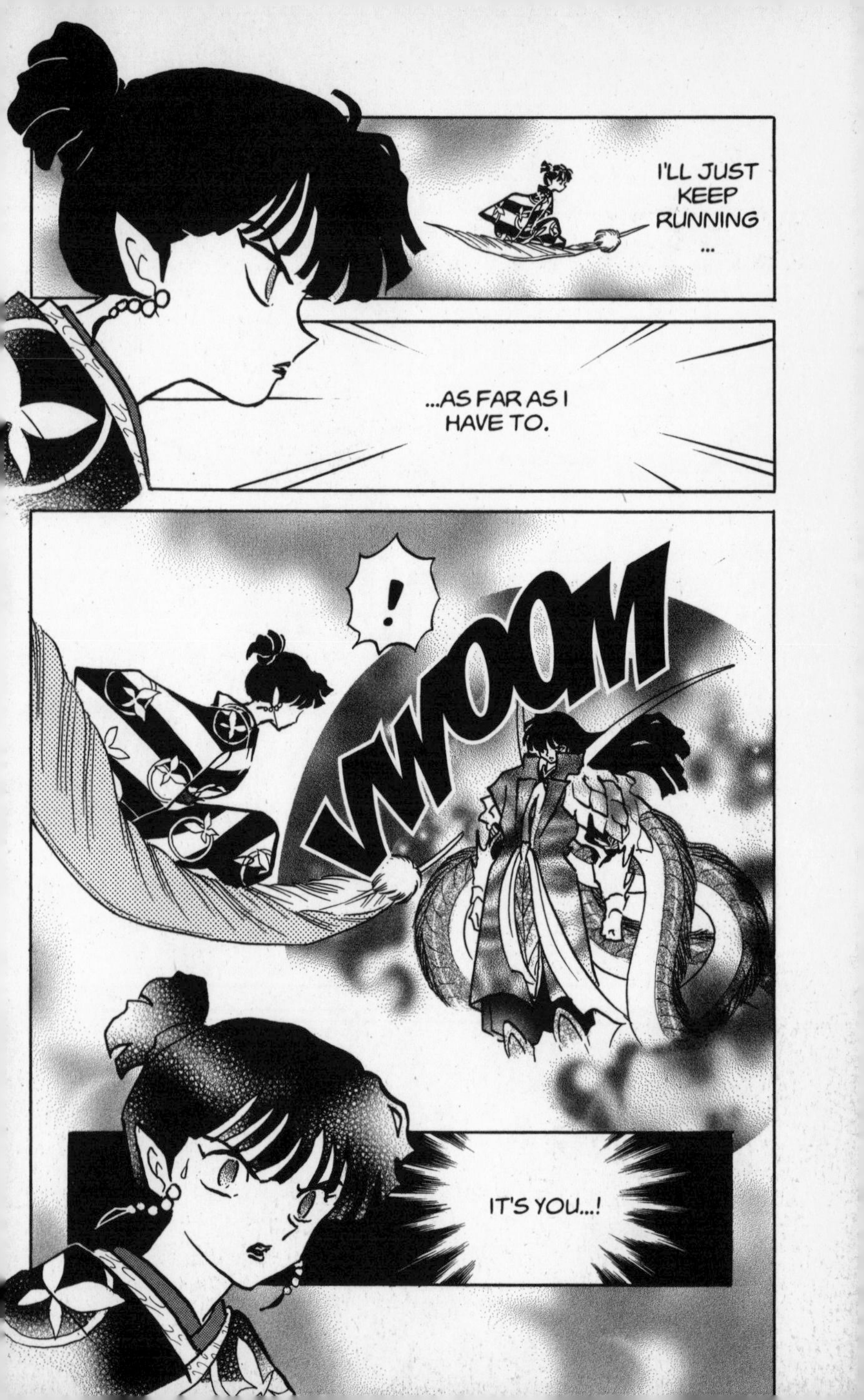
I'LL JUST KEEP RUNNING ...
...AS FAR AS I HAVE TO.
!
VWOOM
IT'S YOU...!

SCROLL 3
KAGURA'S HEART

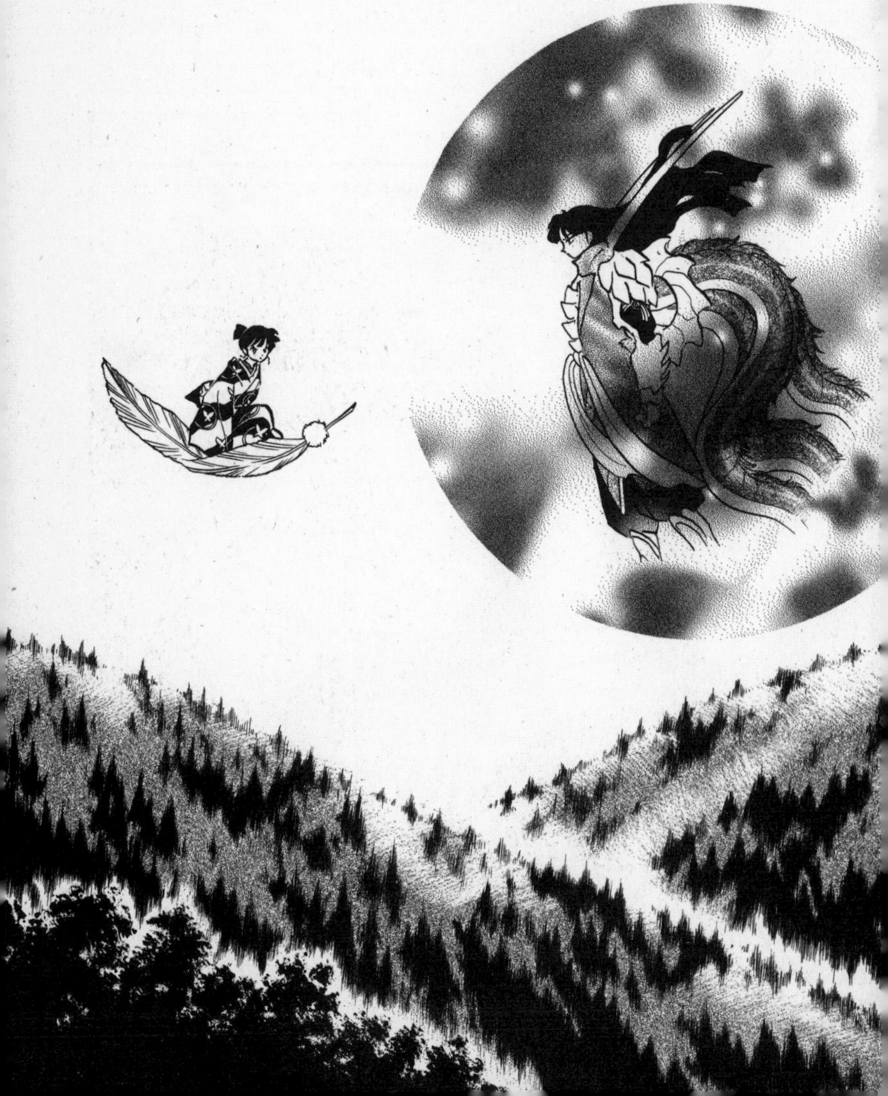

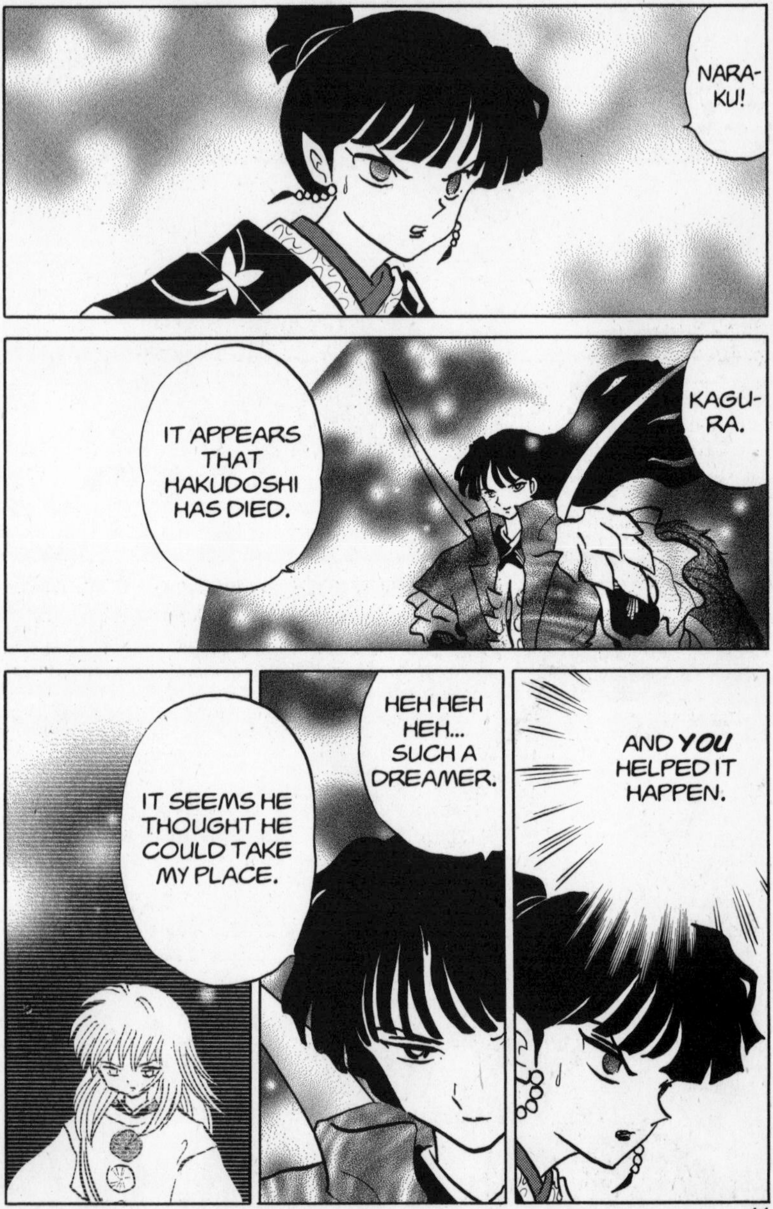
NARAKU!
KAGURA.
IT APPEARS THAT HAKUDOSHI HAS DIED.
AND ***YOU*** HELPED IT HAPPEN.
HEH HEH HEH... SUCH A DREAMER.
IT SEEMS HE THOUGHT HE COULD TAKE MY PLACE.

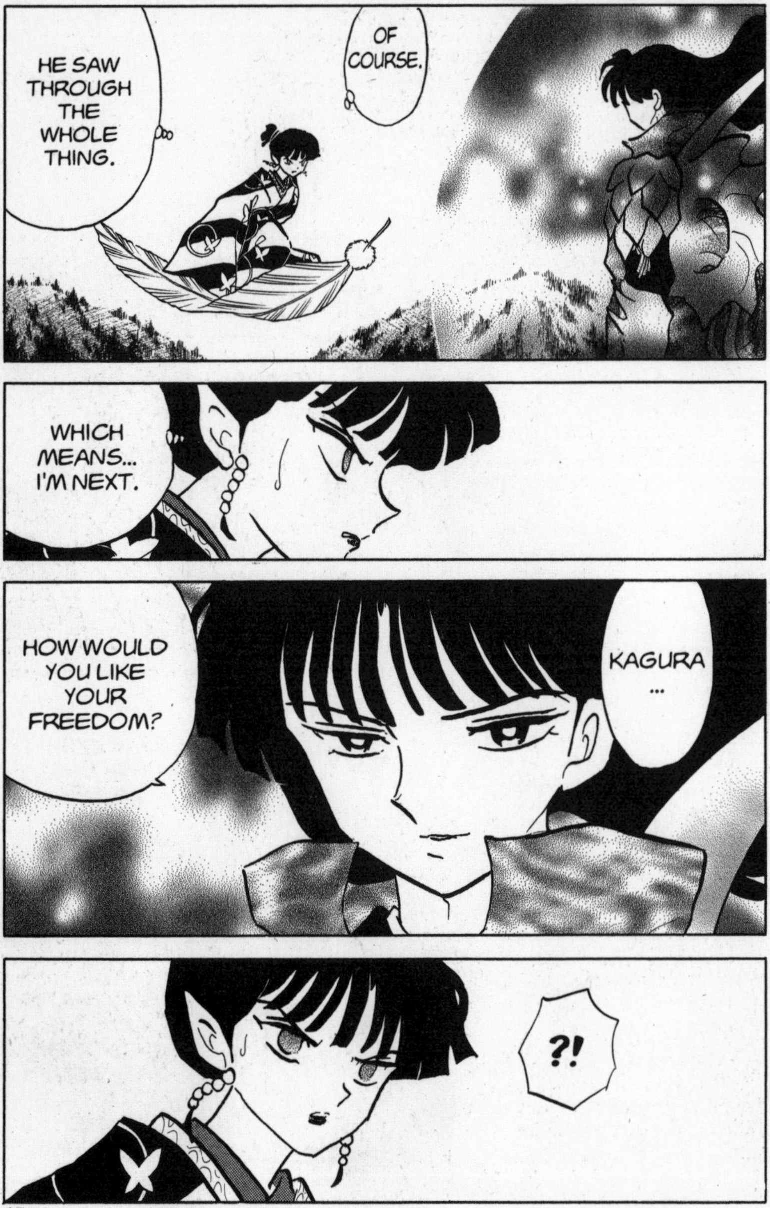
OF COURSE.
HE SAW THROUGH THE WHOLE THING.
WHICH MEANS... I'M NEXT.
KAGURA ...
HOW WOULD YOU LIKE YOUR FREEDOM?
?!

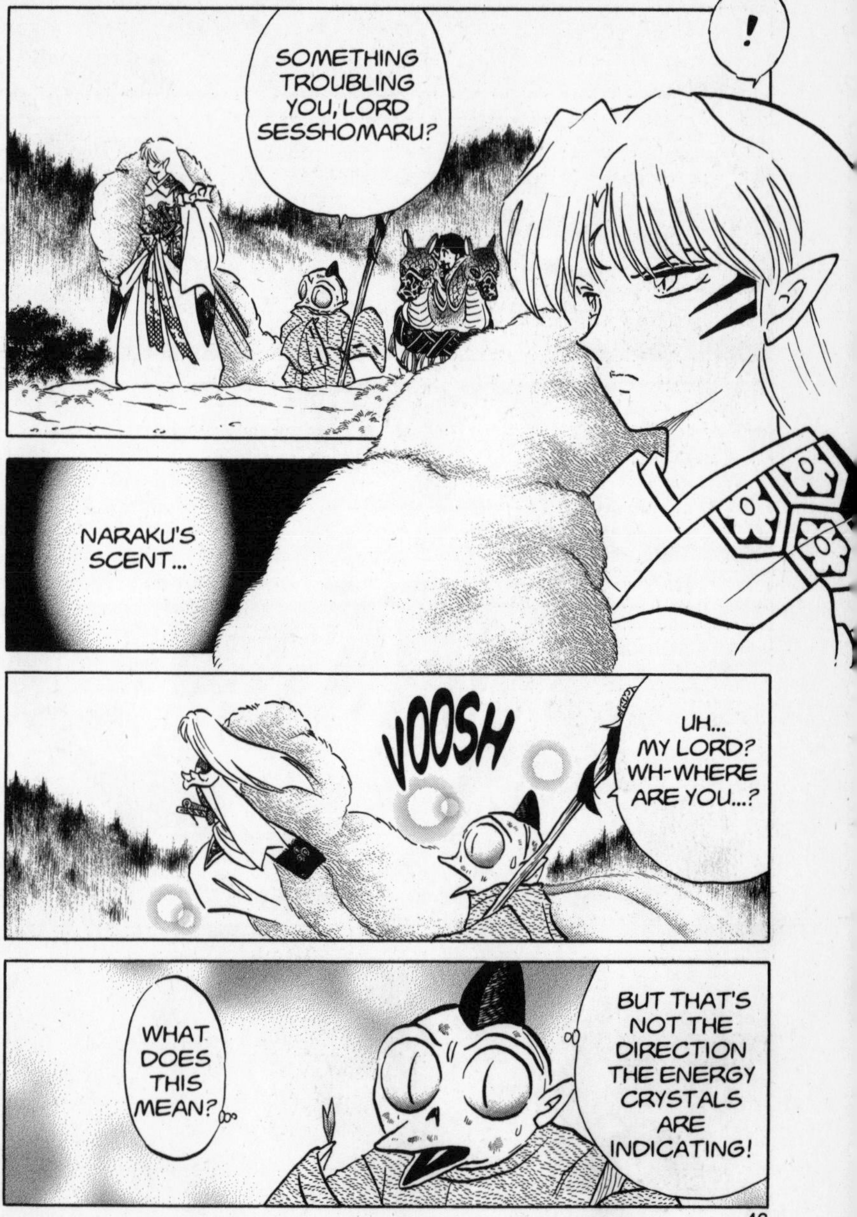
!
SOMETHING TROUBLING YOU, LORD SESSHOMARU?
NARAKU'S SCENT...
UH... MY LORD? WH-WHERE ARE YOU...?
VOOSH
BUT THAT'S NOT THE DIRECTION THE ENERGY CRYSTALS ARE INDICATING!
WHAT DOES THIS MEAN?

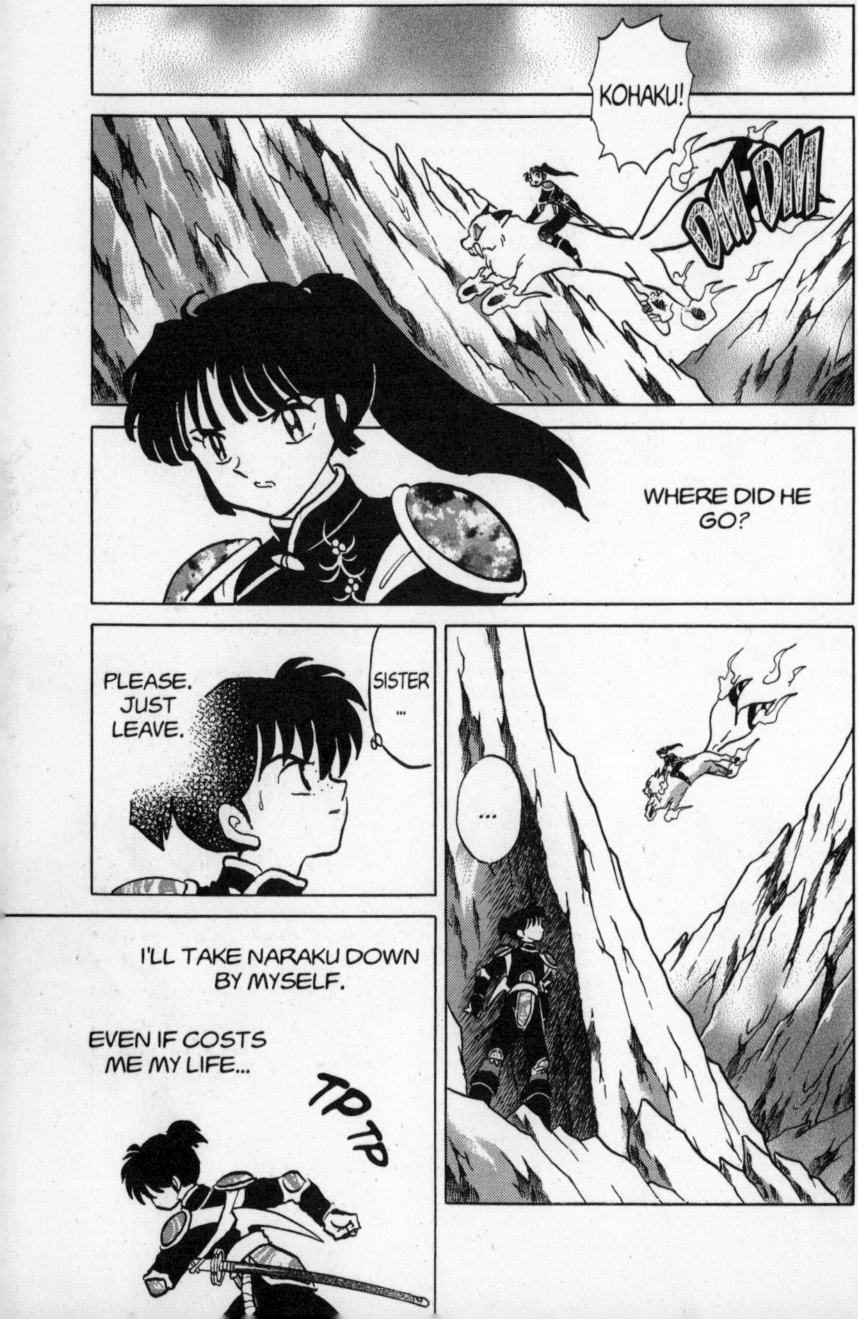
KOHAKU!
DM DM
WHERE DID HE GO?
...
SISTER ...
PLEASE. JUST LEAVE.
I'LL TAKE NARAKU DOWN BY MYSELF.
EVEN IF COSTS ME MY LIFE...
TP TP

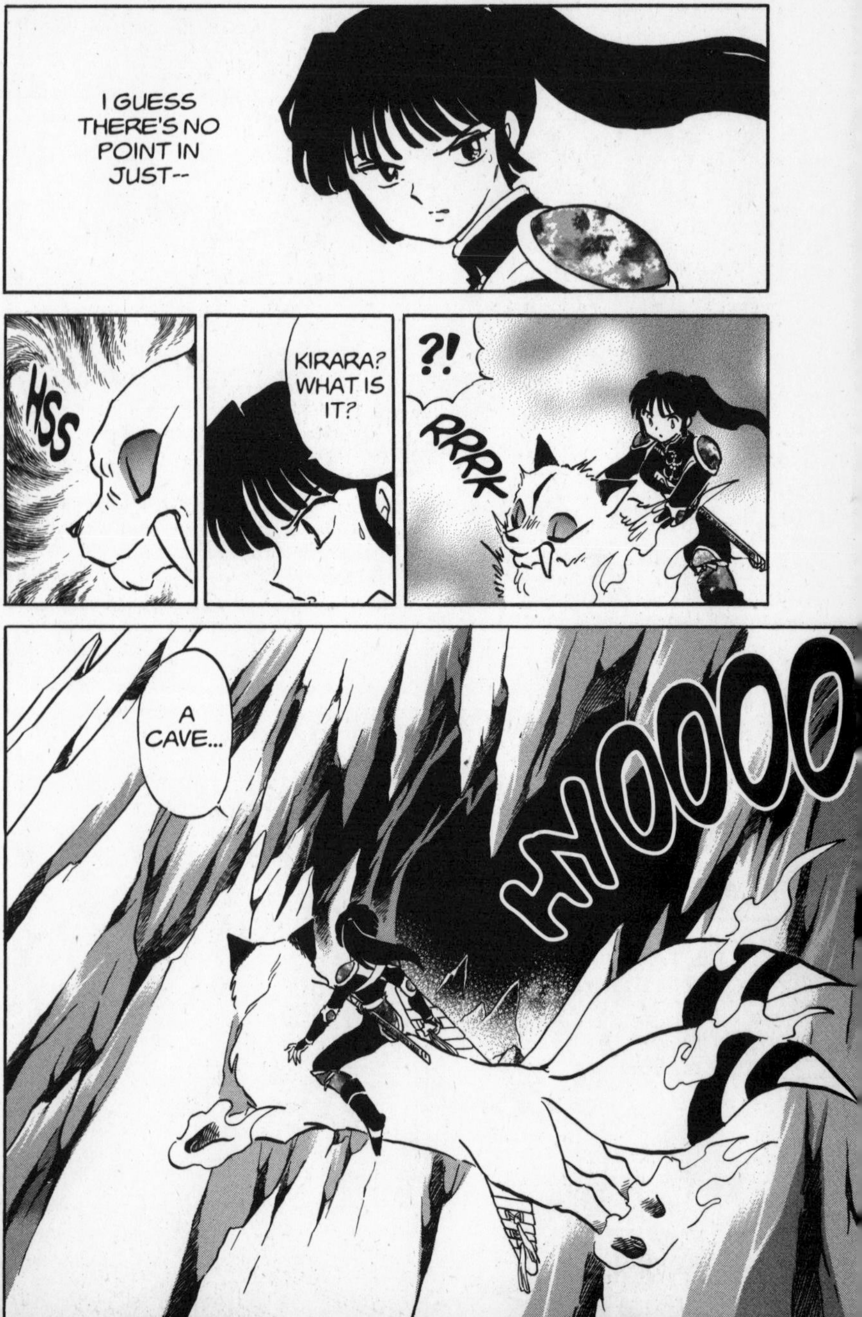

I GUESS THERE'S NO POINT IN JUST--
?!
RRRK
KIRARA? WHAT IS IT?
HSS
HYOOOO
A CAVE...

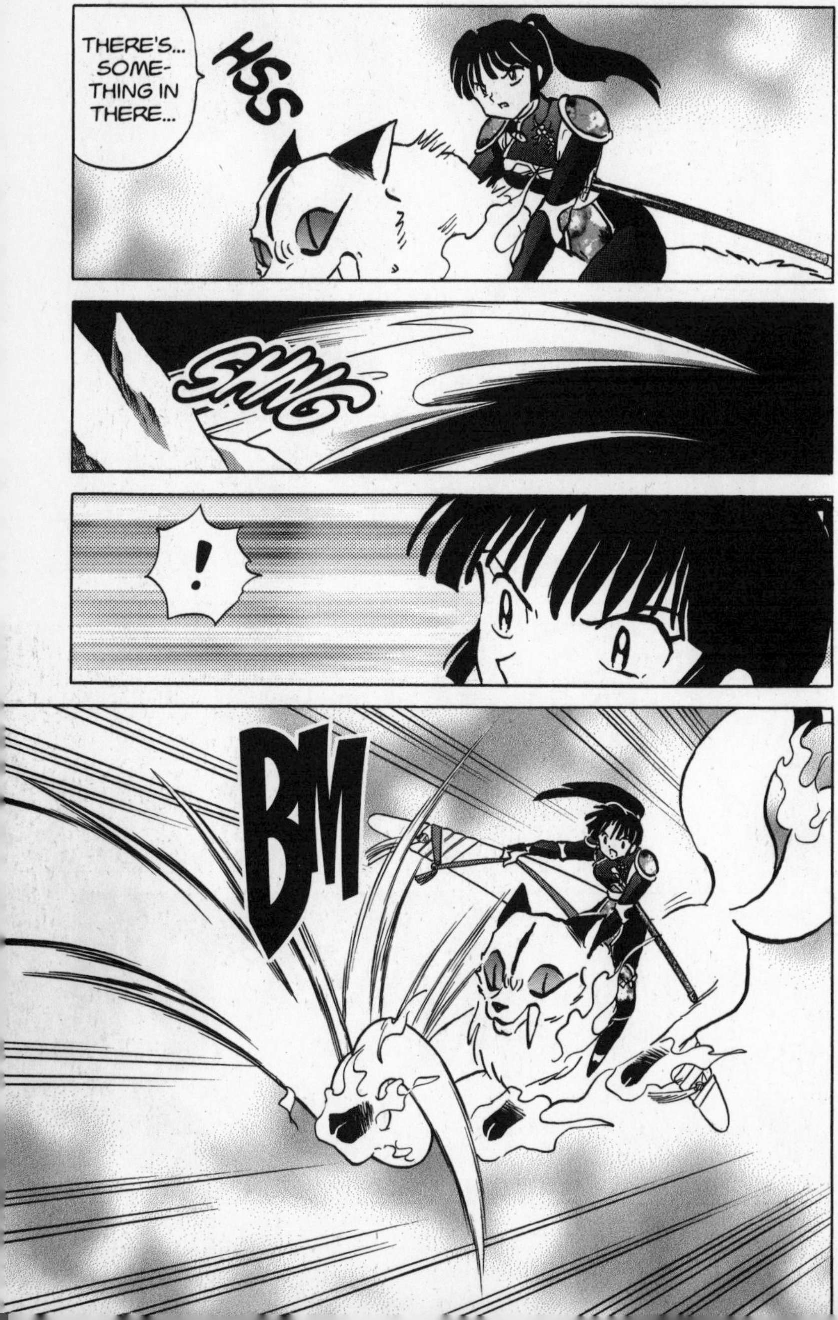
THERE'S... SOMETHING IN THERE...
HSS
SHING
!
BM

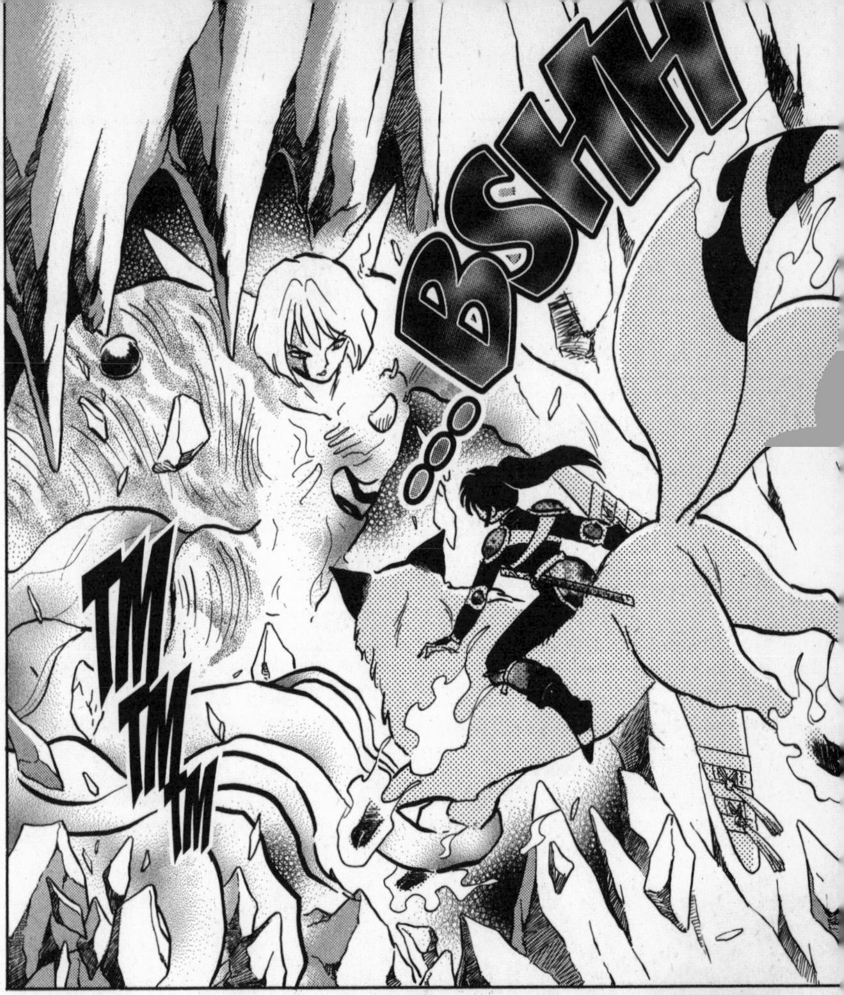
BSHH...
TM TM TM
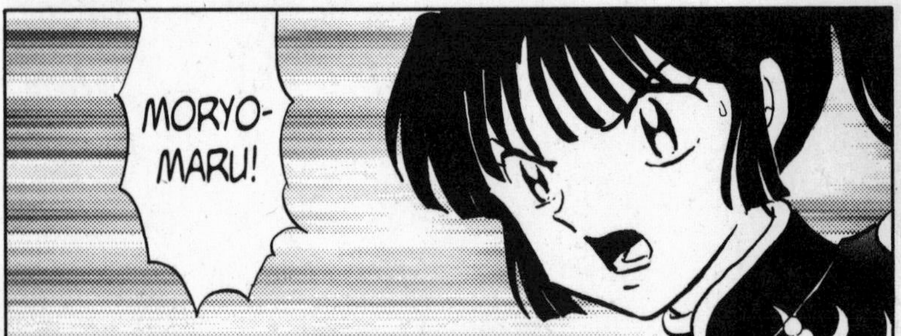
MORYO-MARU!

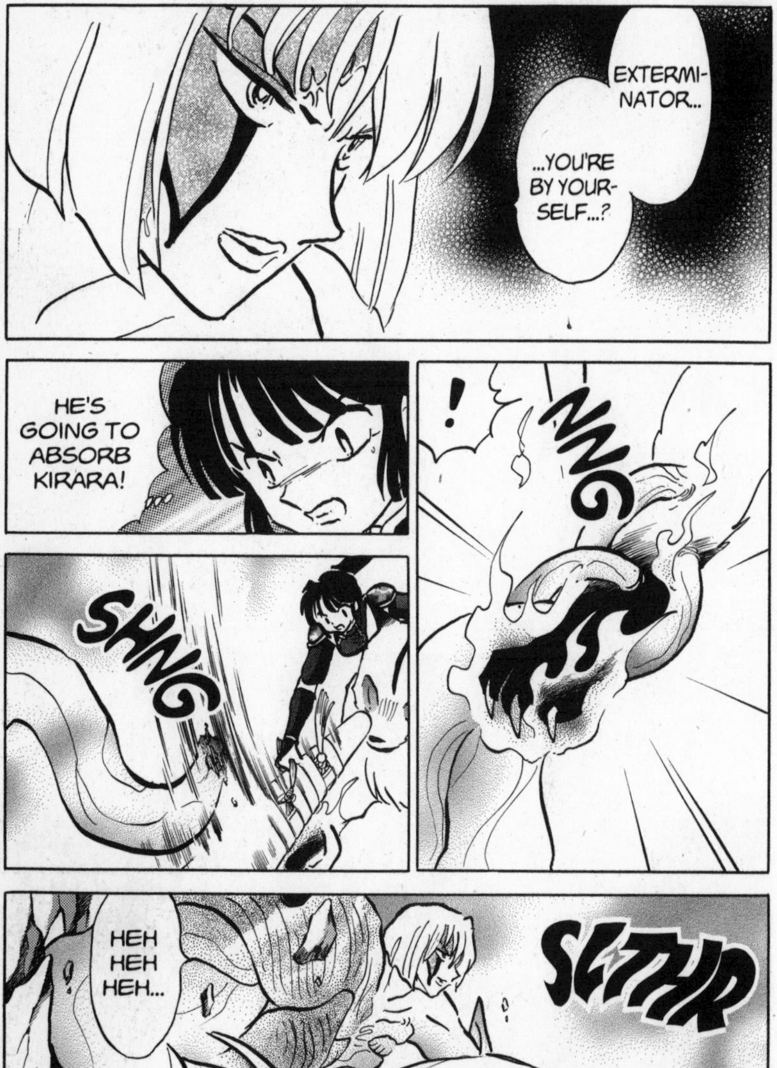
EXTERMINATOR...
...YOU'RE BY YOURSELF...?
!
NNG
HE'S GOING TO ABSORB KIRARA!
SHNG
SLTHR
HEH HEH HEH...

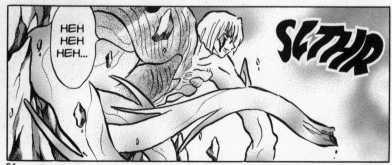

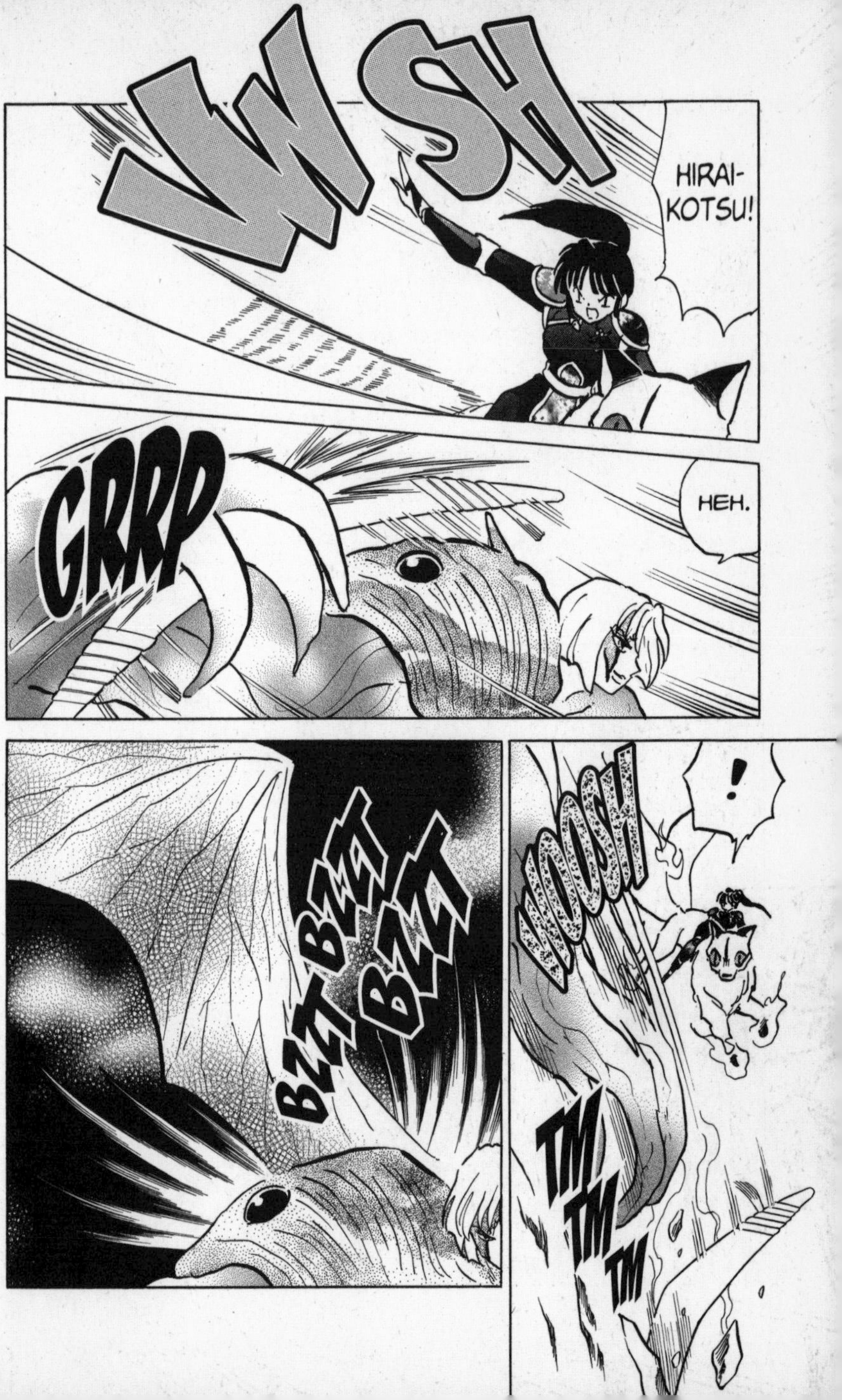
VWSH
HIRAI-KOTSU!
GRRP
HEH.
!
WOOSH
TM TM TM
BZZT BZZT BZZT

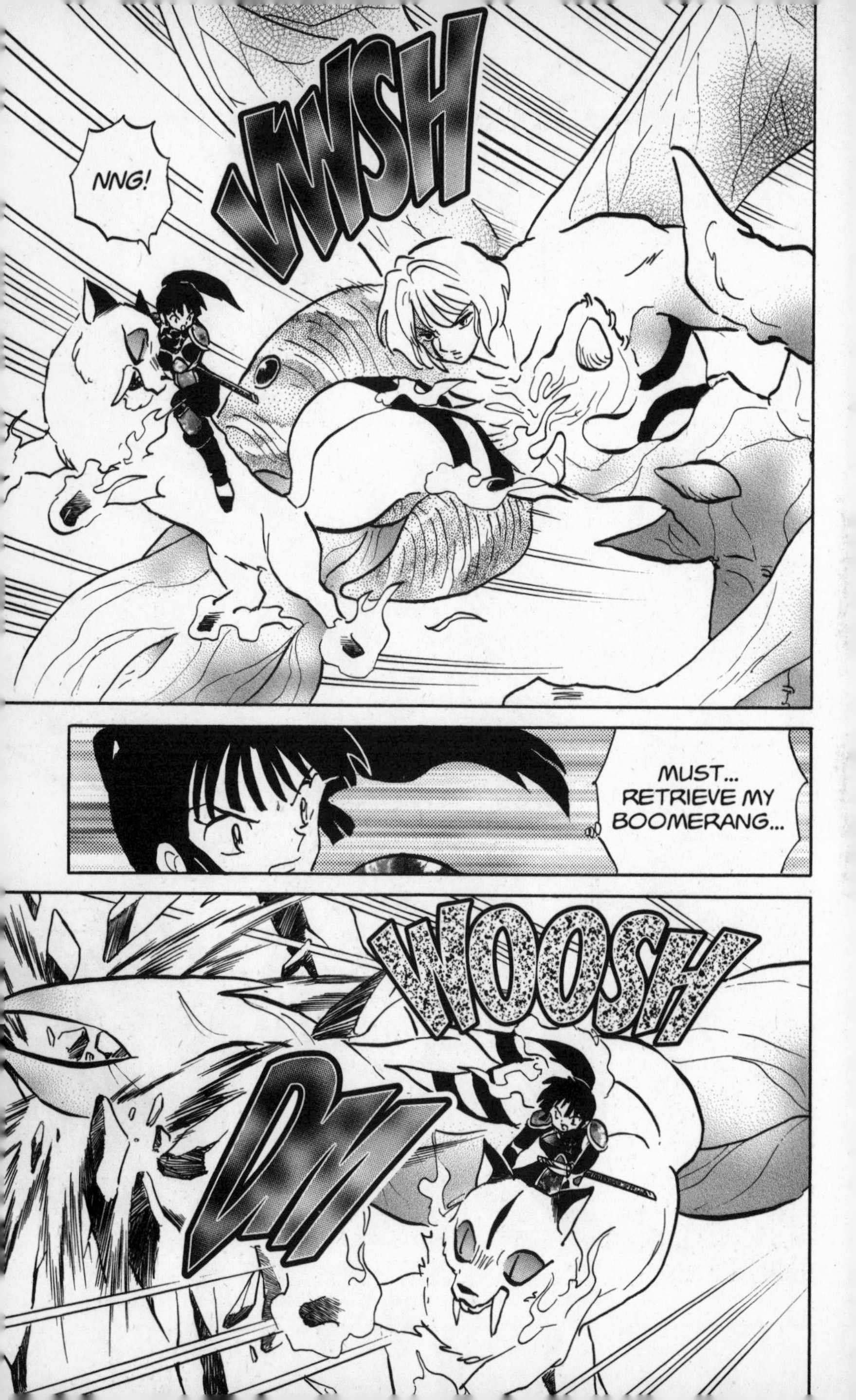
VWSH
NNG!
MUST... RETRIEVE MY BOOMERANG...
WOOSH

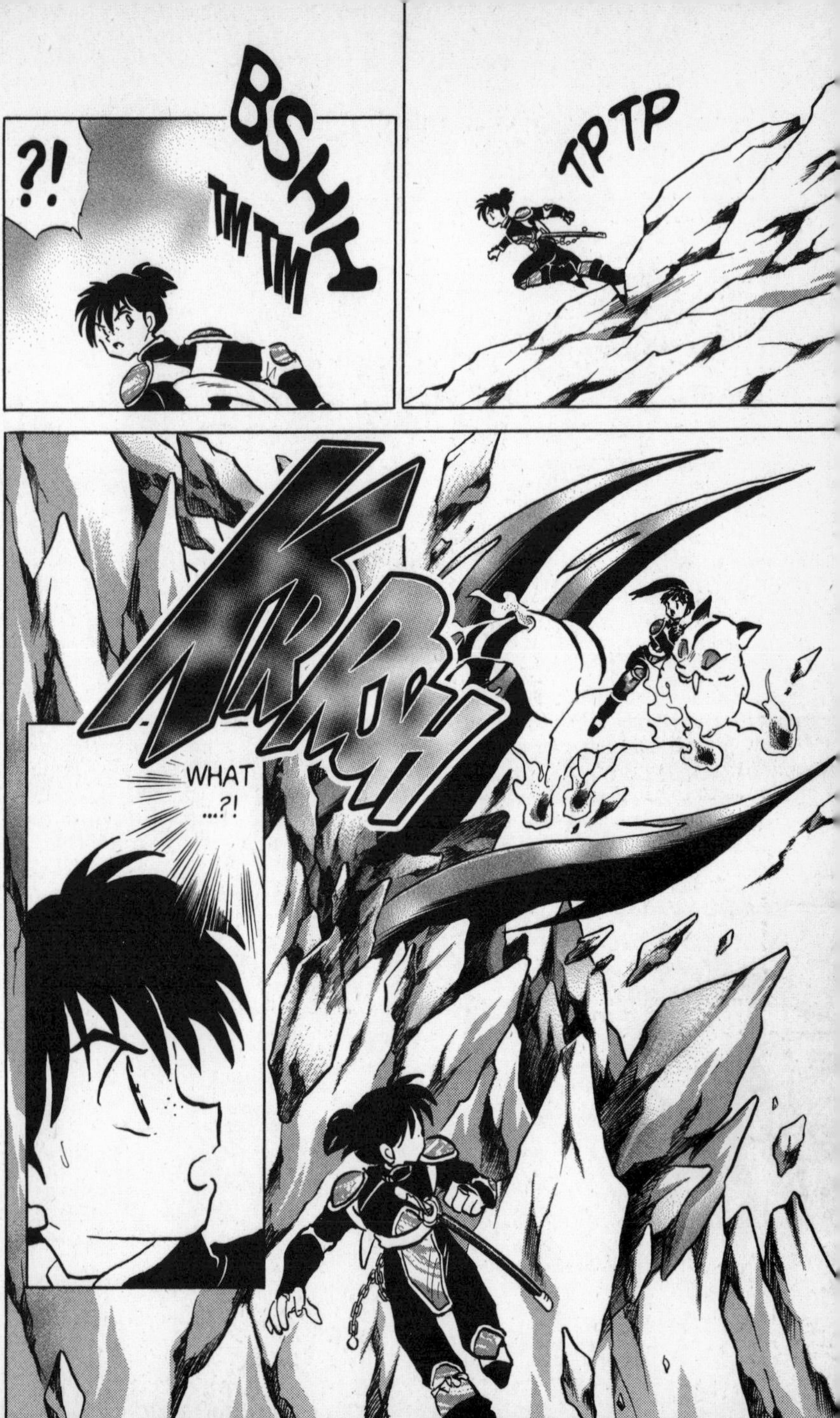
TPTP
BSHH
TM TM
?!
KRASH
WHAT ...?!

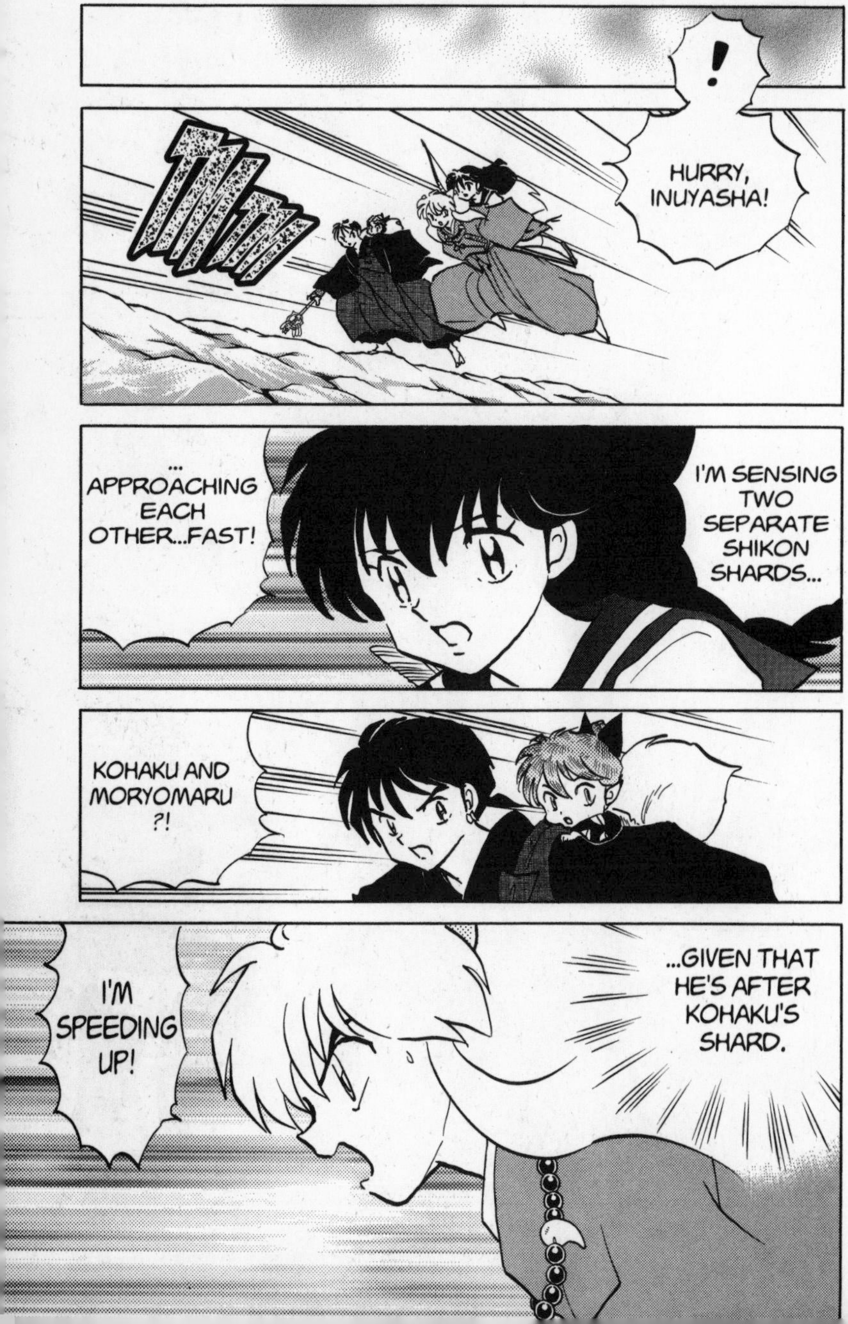
!
HURRY, INUYASHA!
I'M SENSING TWO SEPARATE SHIKON SHARDS...
...APPROACHING EACH OTHER...FAST!
KOHAKU AND MORYOMARU ?!
...GIVEN THAT HE'S AFTER KOHAKU'S SHARD.
I'M SPEEDING UP!

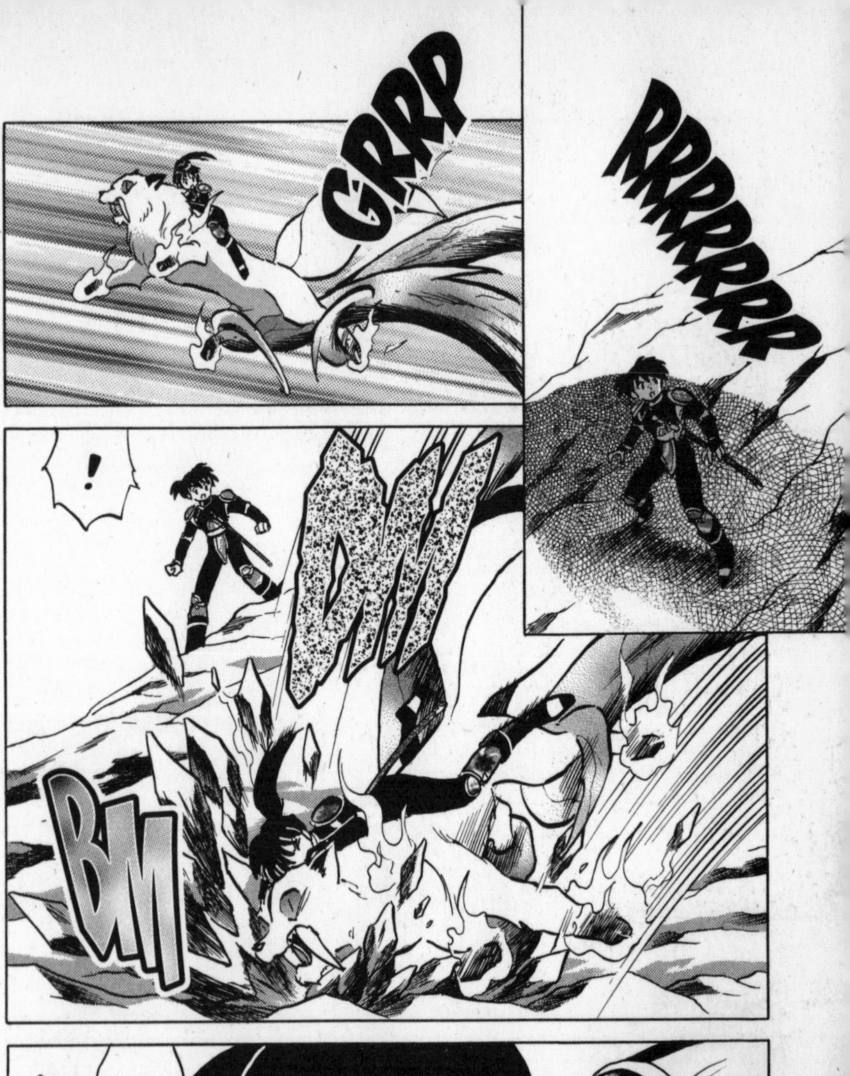
RRRRRRR
GRRP
!
DM
BM
UNH...
TM TM

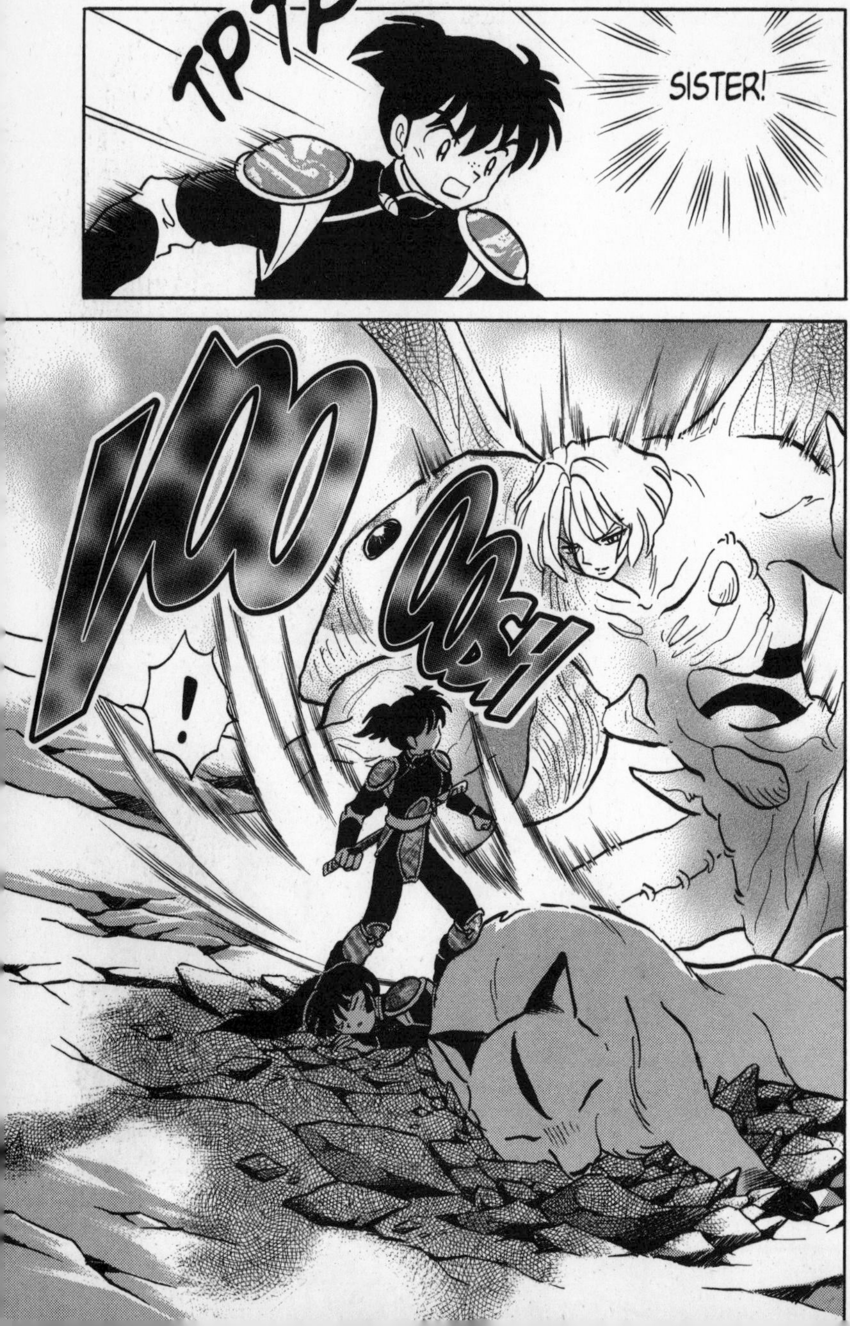
SISTER!
TPTP
!
WOOOSH

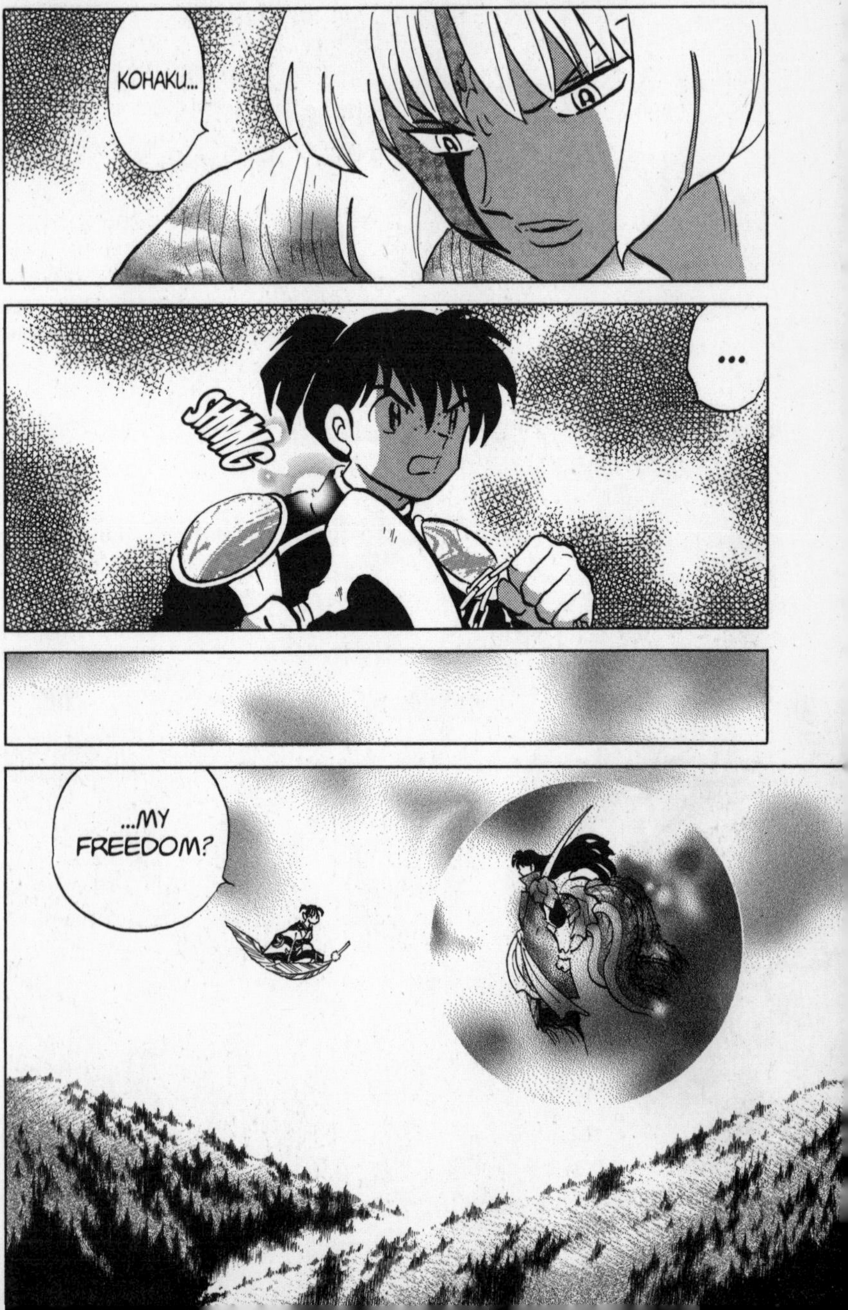
KOHAKU...
...
SHING
...MY FREEDOM?

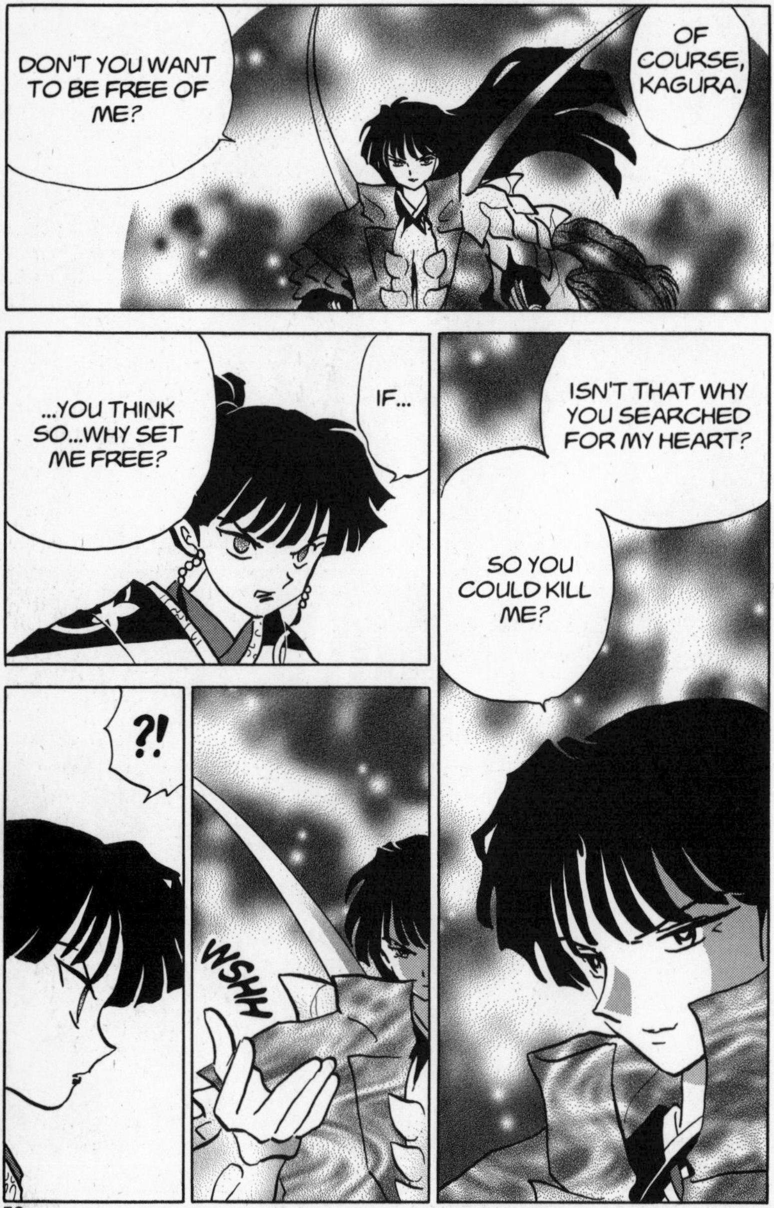
OF COURSE, KAGURA.
DON'T YOU WANT TO BE FREE OF ME?
ISN'T THAT WHY YOU SEARCHED FOR MY HEART?
SO YOU COULD KILL ME?
IF...
...YOU THINK SO...WHY SET ME FREE?
WSHH
?!

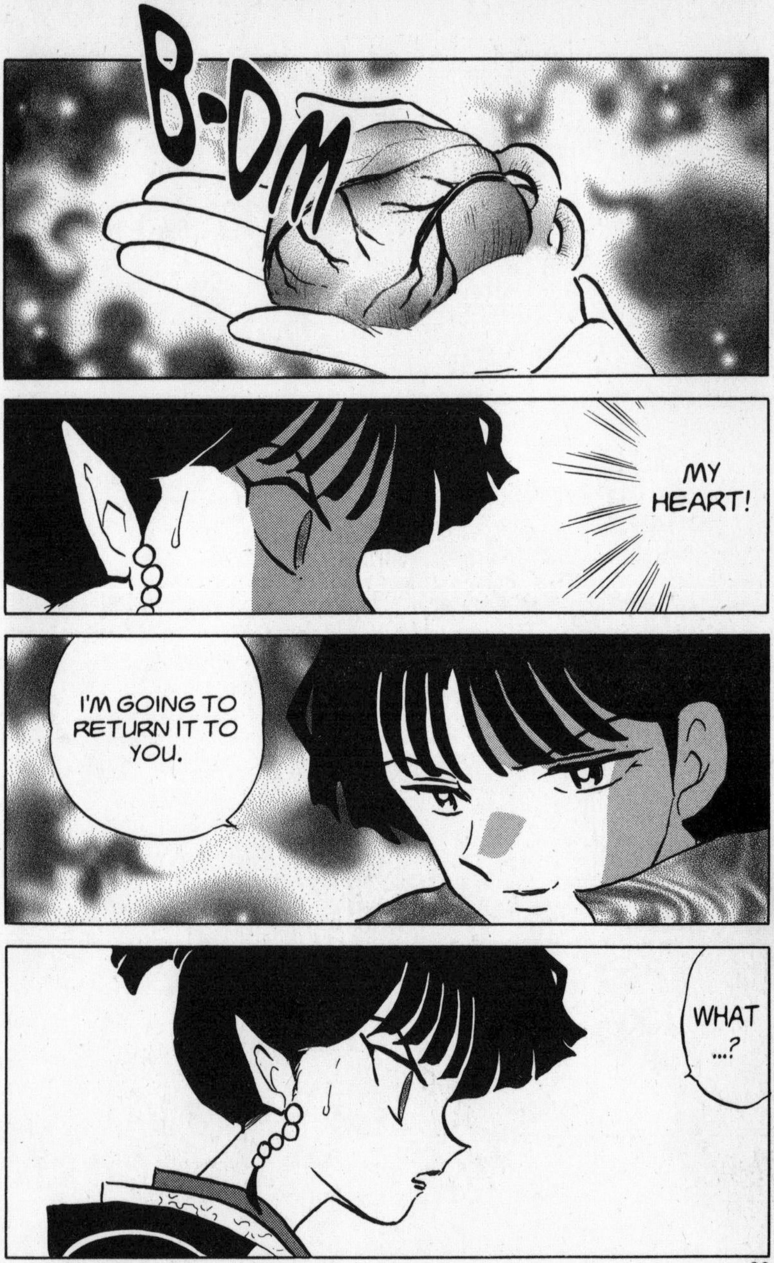
B-DM
MY HEART!
I'M GOING TO RETURN IT TO YOU.
WHAT ...?

SCROLL 4

PAIN WITHOUT END

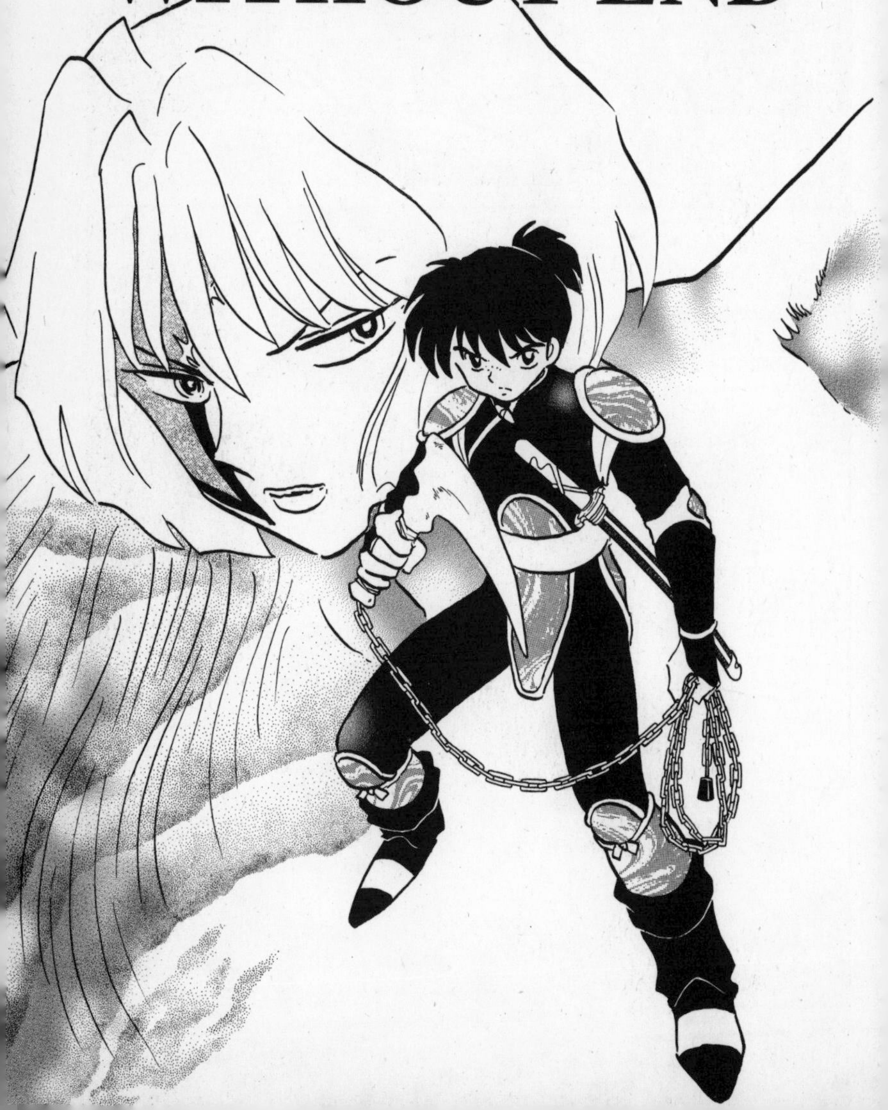

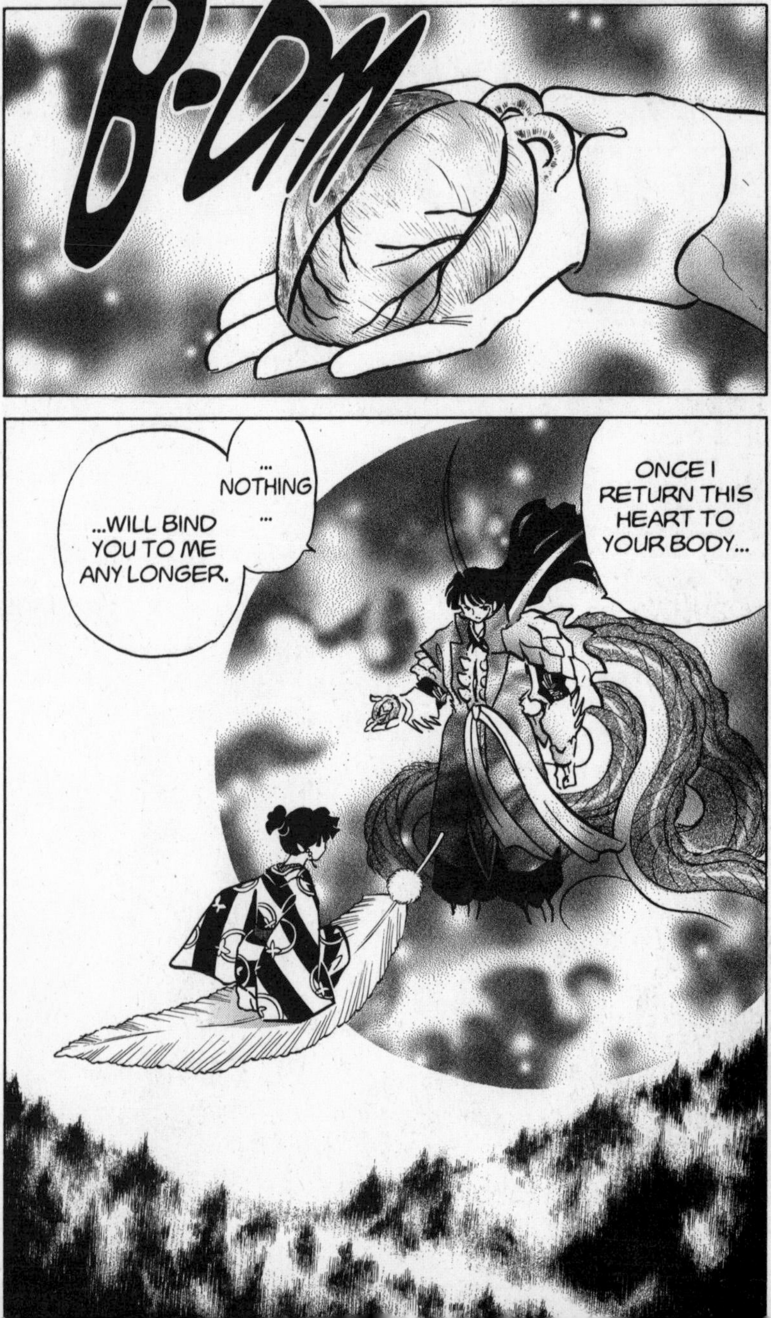
B-DM
ONCE I RETURN THIS HEART TO YOUR BODY...
... NOTHING ...
...WILL BIND YOU TO ME ANY LONGER.

YOU WILL BE FREE.

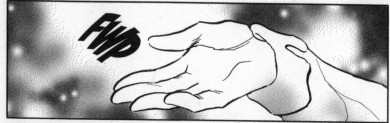

FWP

MY HEART... I HAVE MY HEART BACK!

BOOM

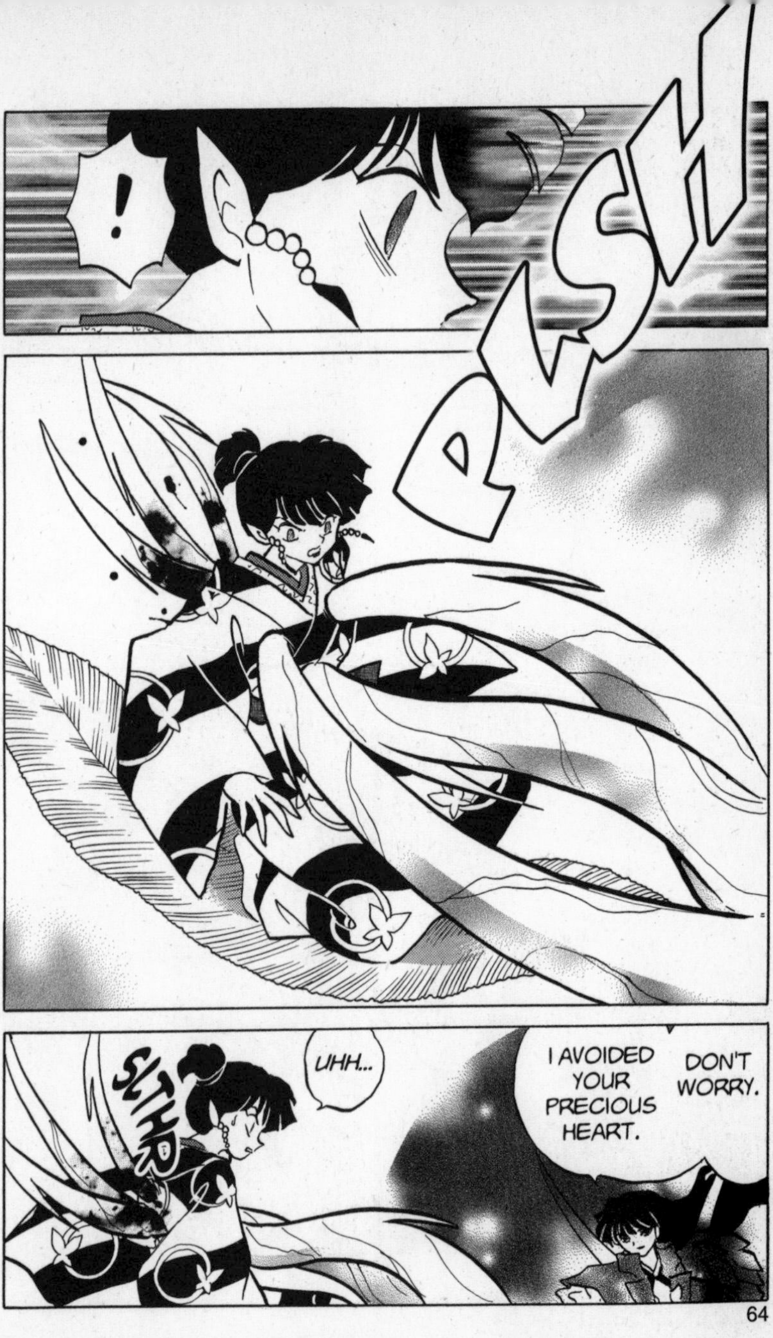
!
PLESH
DON'T WORRY.
I AVOIDED YOUR PRECIOUS HEART.
UHH...
SLITHR

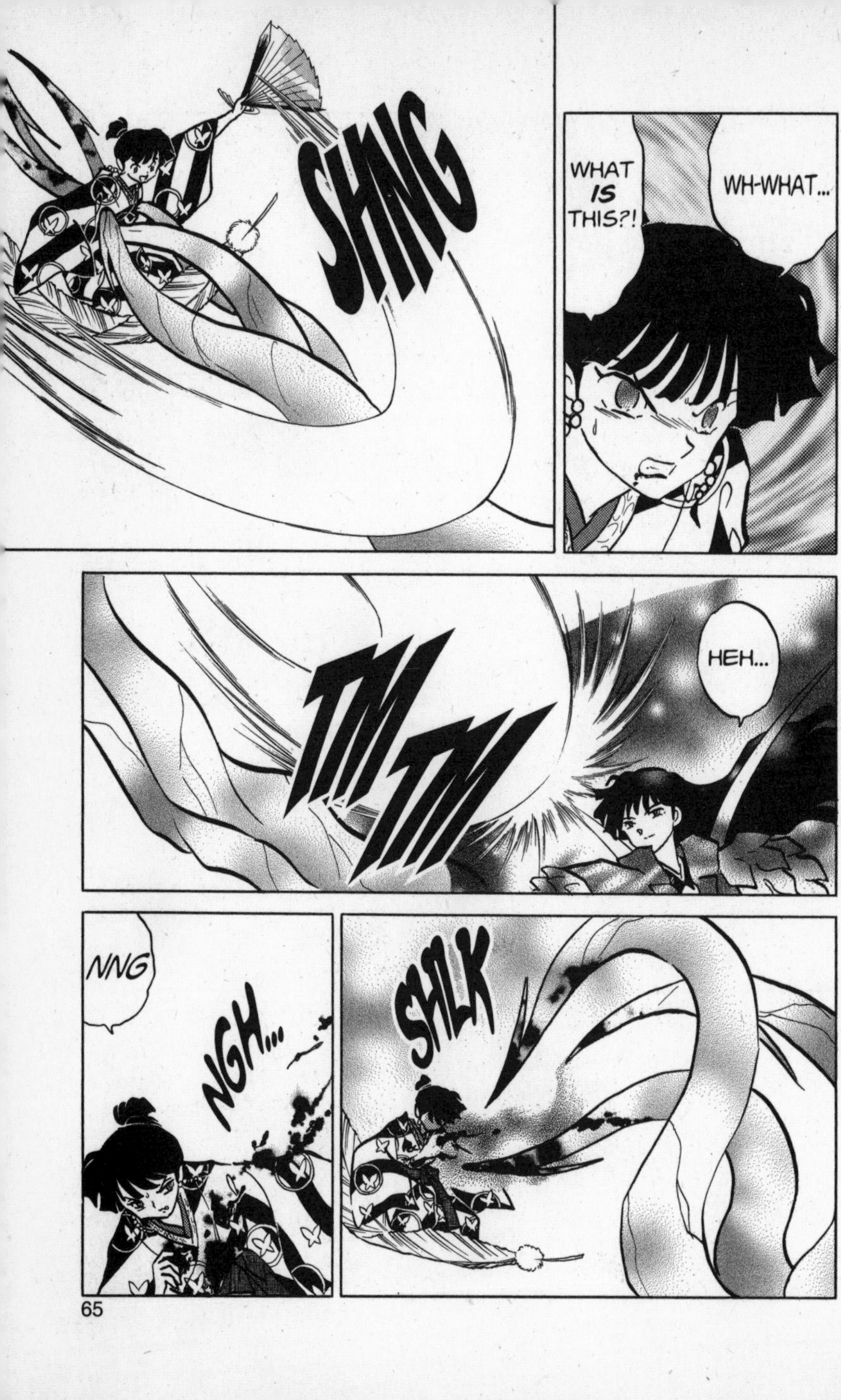
WH-WHAT...
WHAT IS THIS?!
SHING
HEH...
TM TM
SHLK
NNG
NGH...

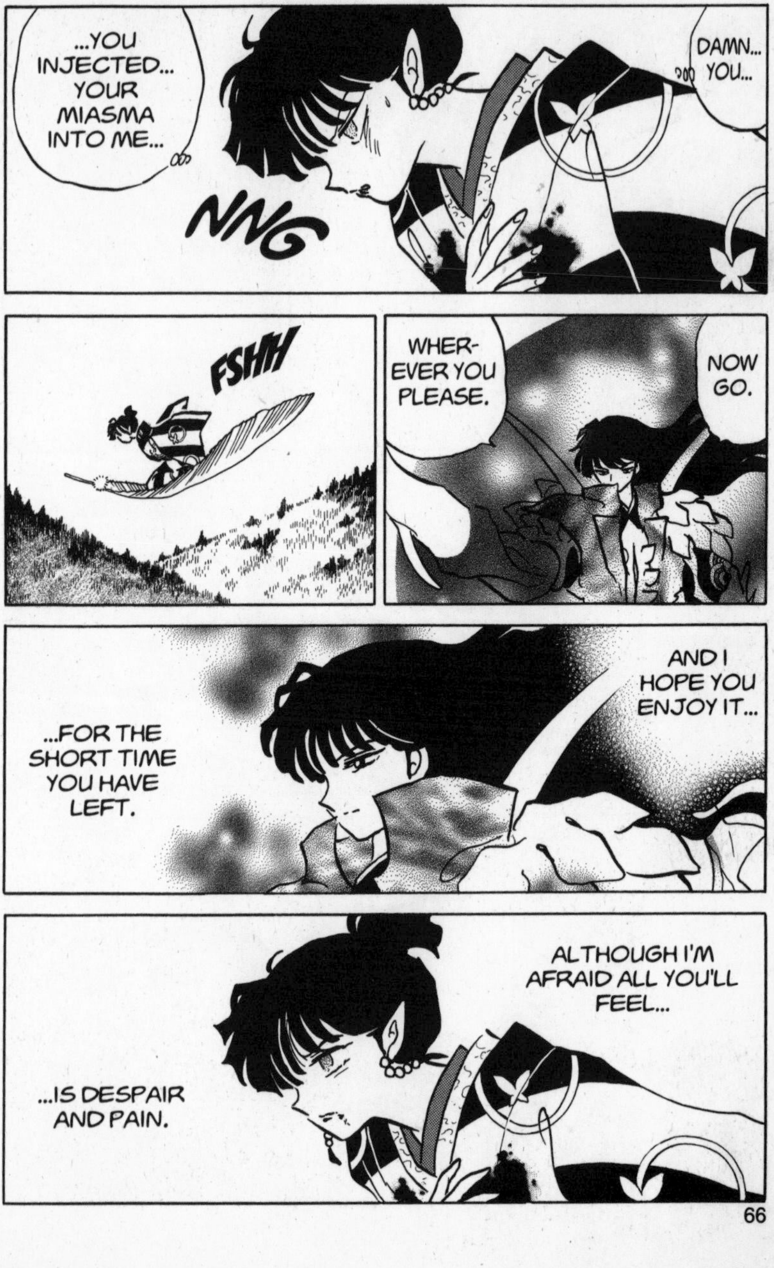
DAMN... YOU...
...YOU INJECTED... YOUR MIASMA INTO ME...
NNG
NOW GO.
WHER-EVER YOU PLEASE.
FSHH
AND I HOPE YOU ENJOY IT...
...FOR THE SHORT TIME YOU HAVE LEFT.
ALTHOUGH I'M AFRAID ALL YOU'LL FEEL...
...IS DESPAIR AND PAIN.

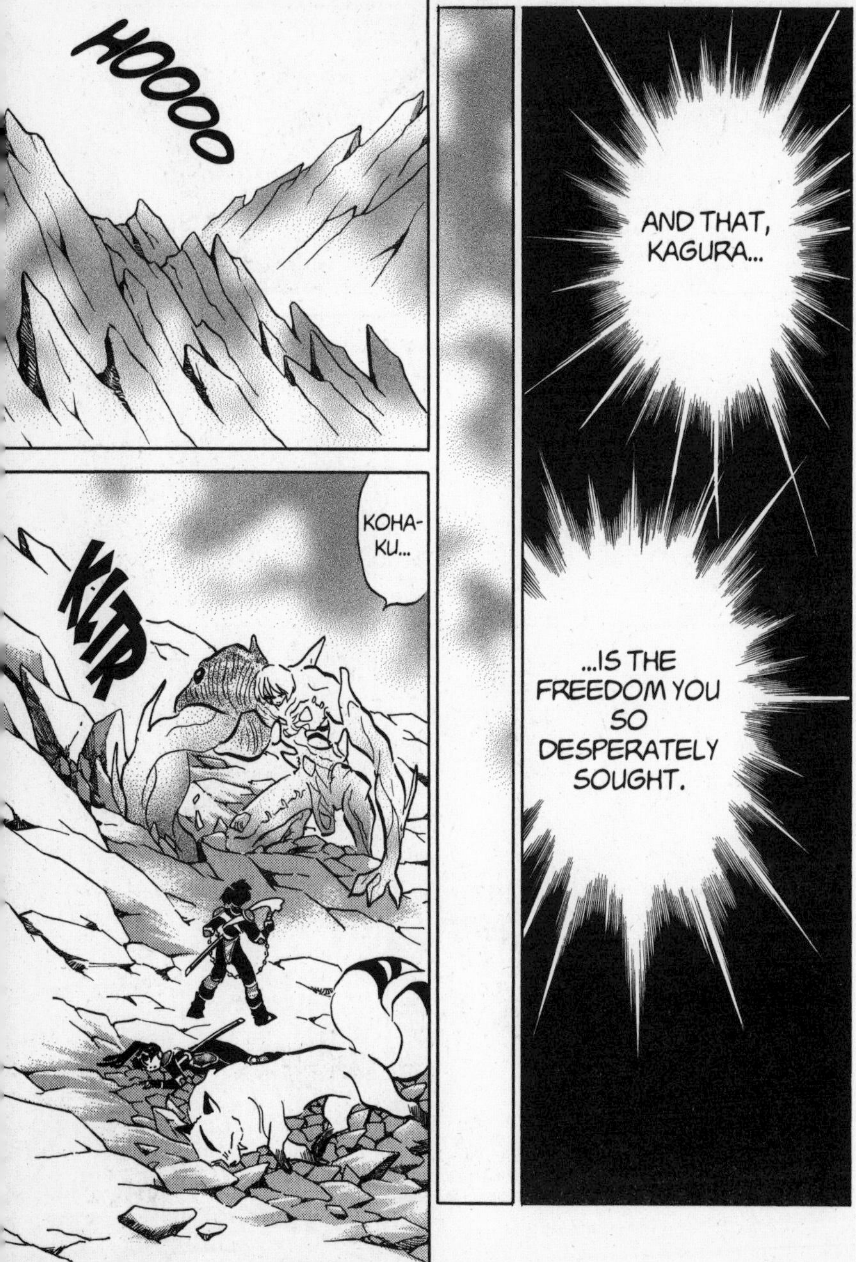
AND THAT, KAGURA...
...IS THE FREEDOM YOU SO DESPERATELY SOUGHT.
HOOOO
KOHA-KU...
KLTR

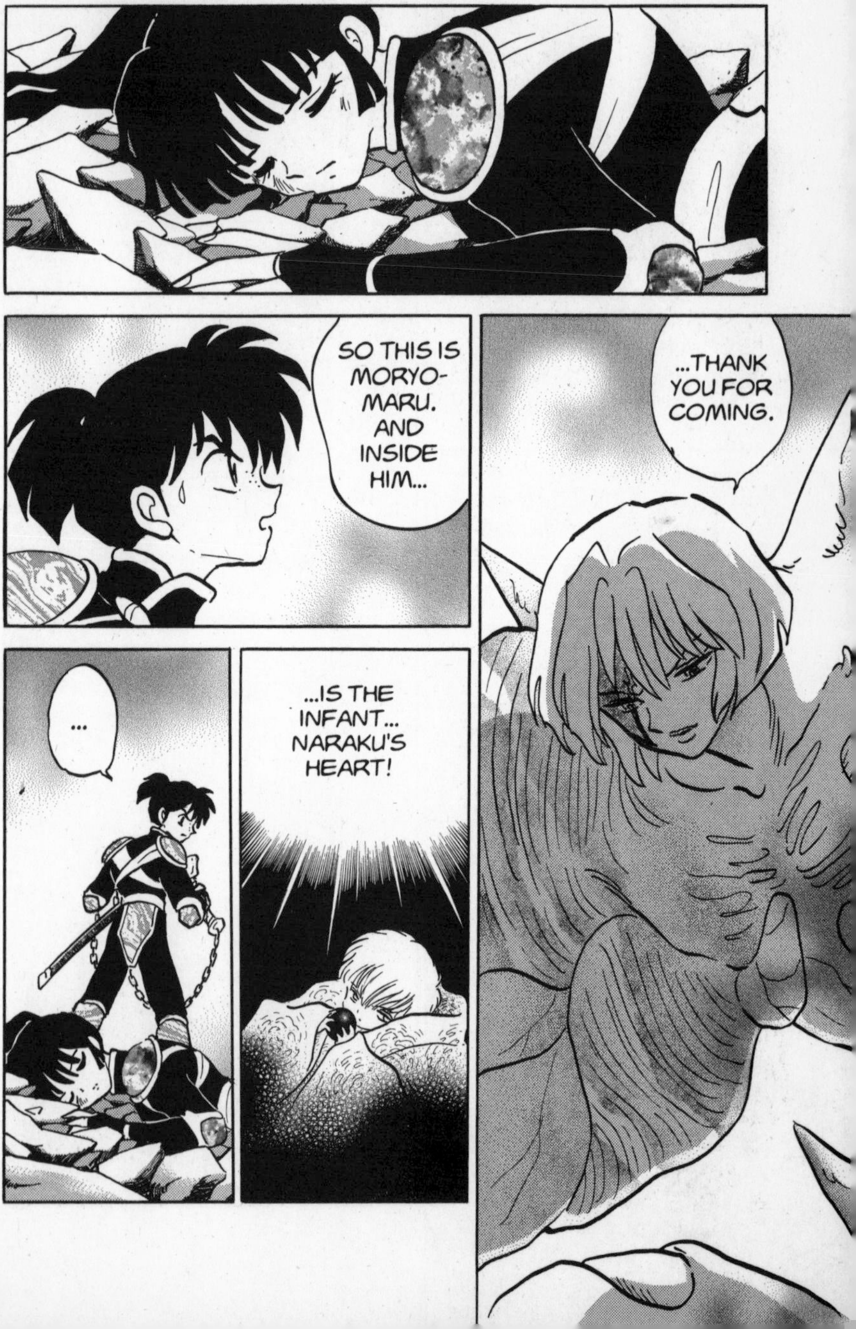
...THANK YOU FOR COMING.
SO THIS IS MORYO-MARU. AND INSIDE HIM...
...IS THE INFANT... NARAKU'S HEART!
...

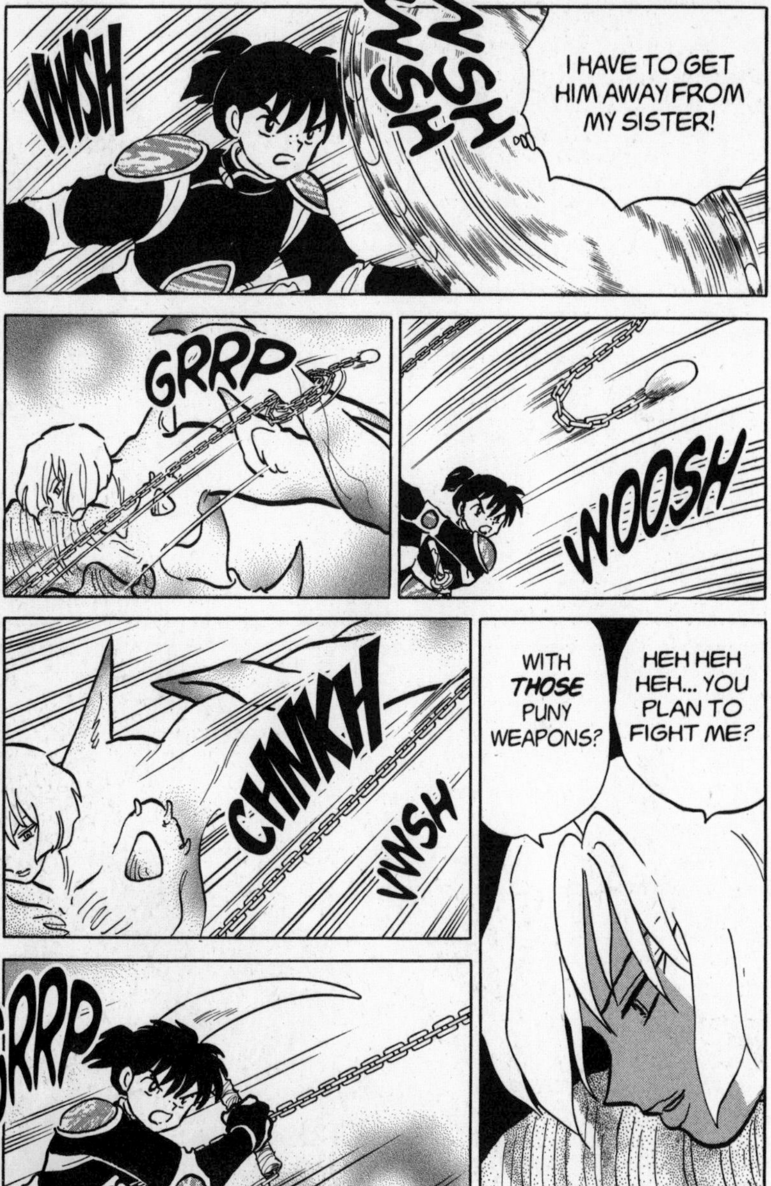
SWSH SWSH
I HAVE TO GET HIM AWAY FROM MY SISTER!
VWSH
WOOSH
GRRP
HEH HEH HEH... YOU PLAN TO FIGHT ME?
WITH *THOSE* PUNY WEAPONS?
CHNKH
VWSH
GRRP

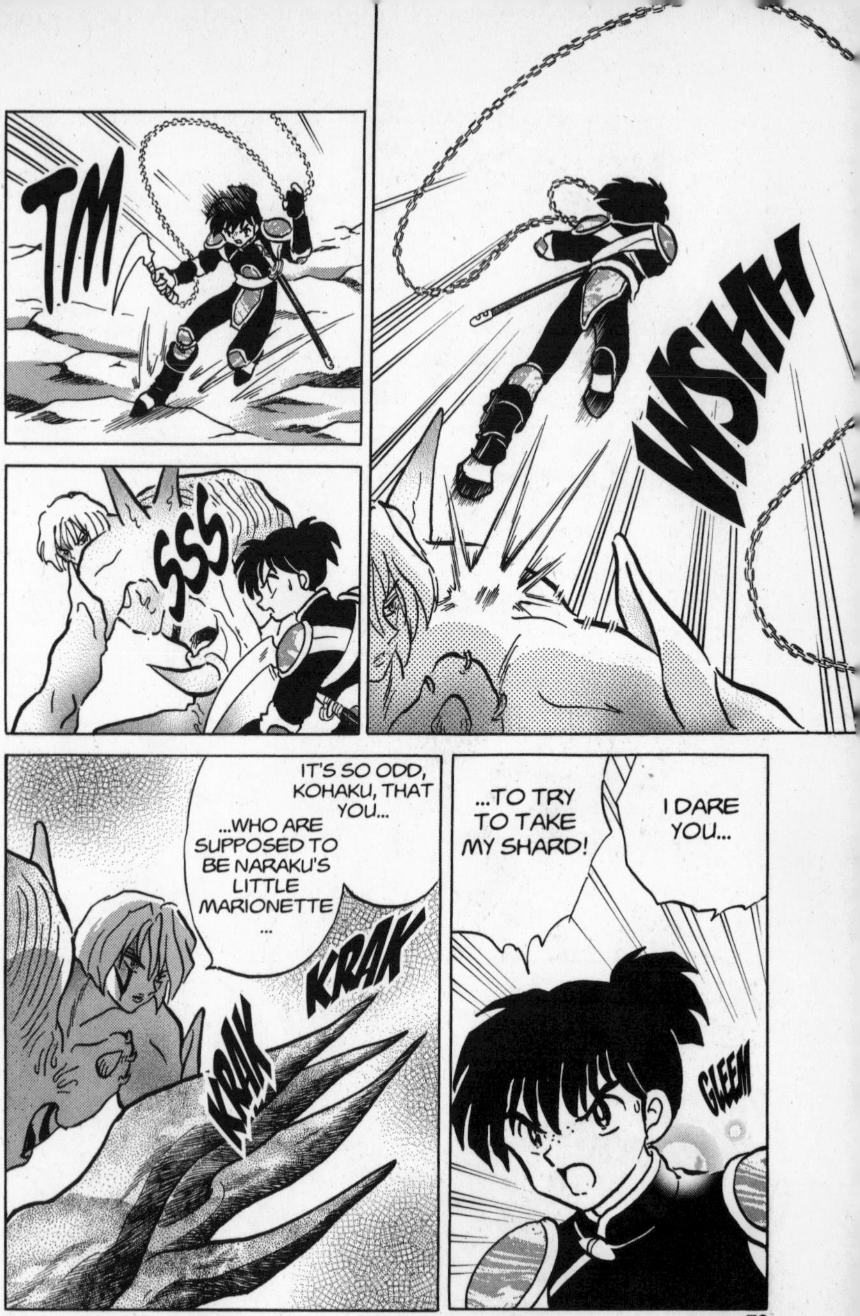
WSHH
TM
SSS
I DARE YOU...
...TO TRY TO TAKE MY SHARD!
GLEEM
IT'S SO ODD, KOHAKU, THAT YOU...
...WHO ARE SUPPOSED TO BE NARAKU'S LITTLE MARIONETTE ...
KRAK
KRAK

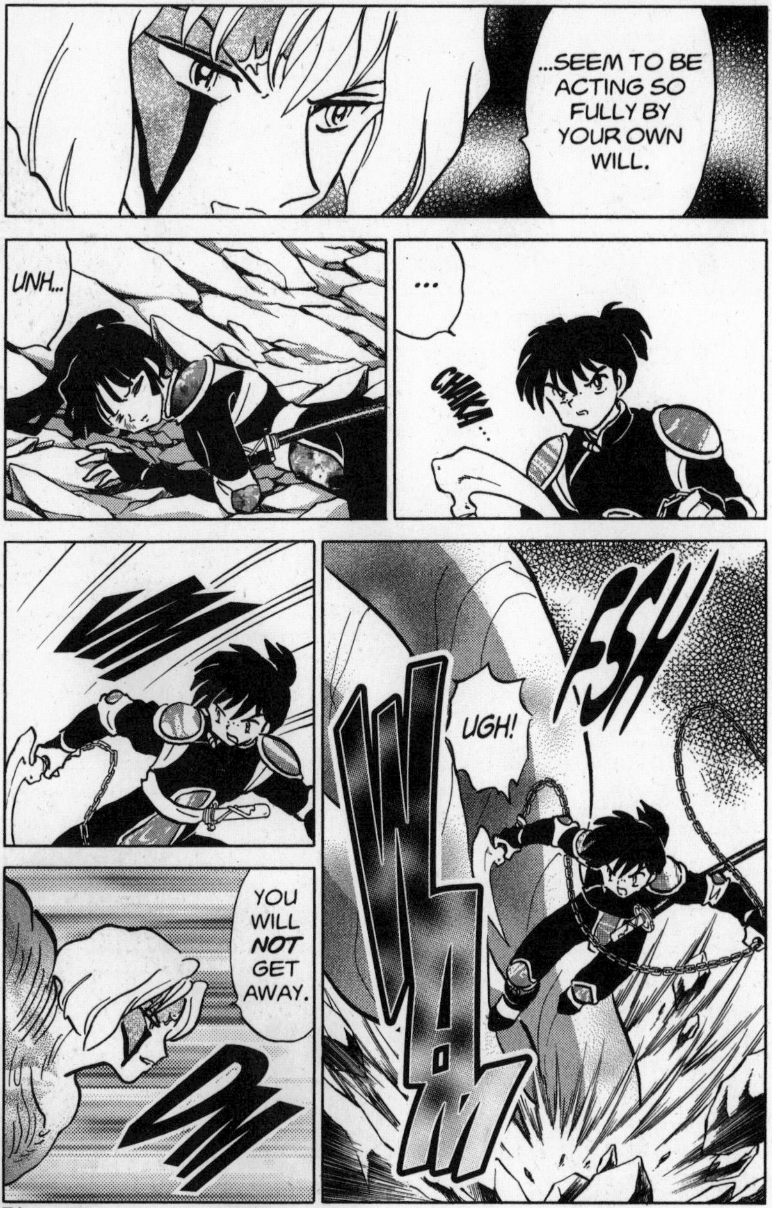
...SEEM TO BE ACTING SO FULLY BY YOUR OWN WILL.
...
CHAKA...
UNH...
FSH
UGH!
YOU WILL NOT GET AWAY.

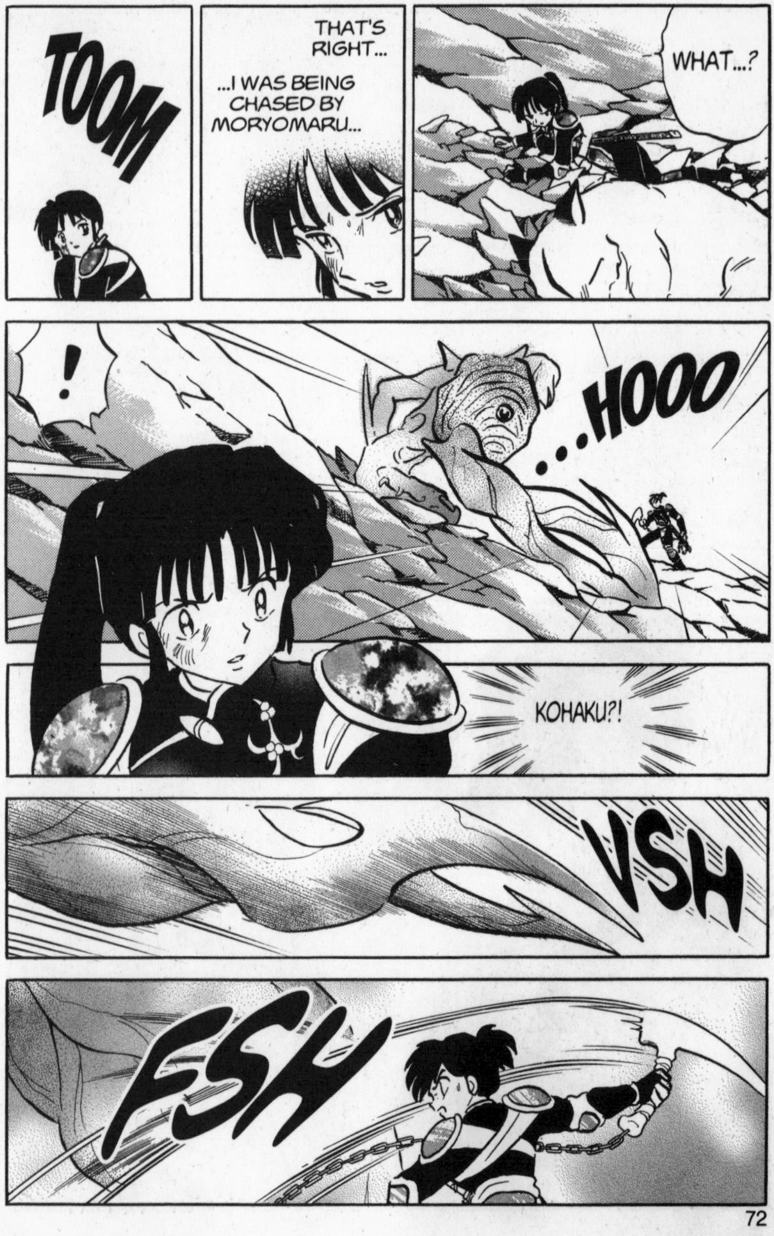
WHAT...?
THAT'S RIGHT...
...I WAS BEING CHASED BY MORYOMARU...
TOOM
...HOOO
!
KOHAKU?!
VSH
FSH

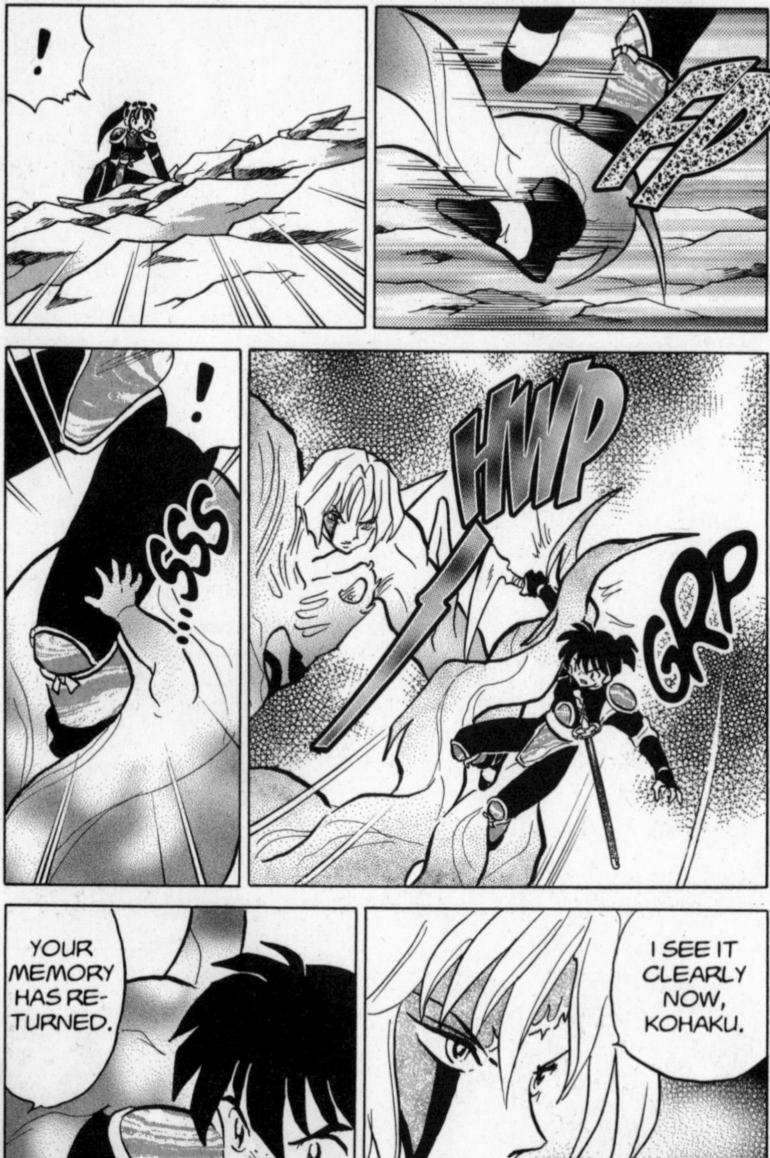
FP
!
HWP
GRP
!
SSS...
I SEE IT CLEARLY NOW, KOHAKU.
YOUR MEMORY HAS RE-TURNED.

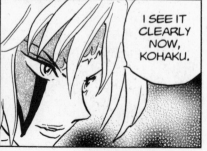

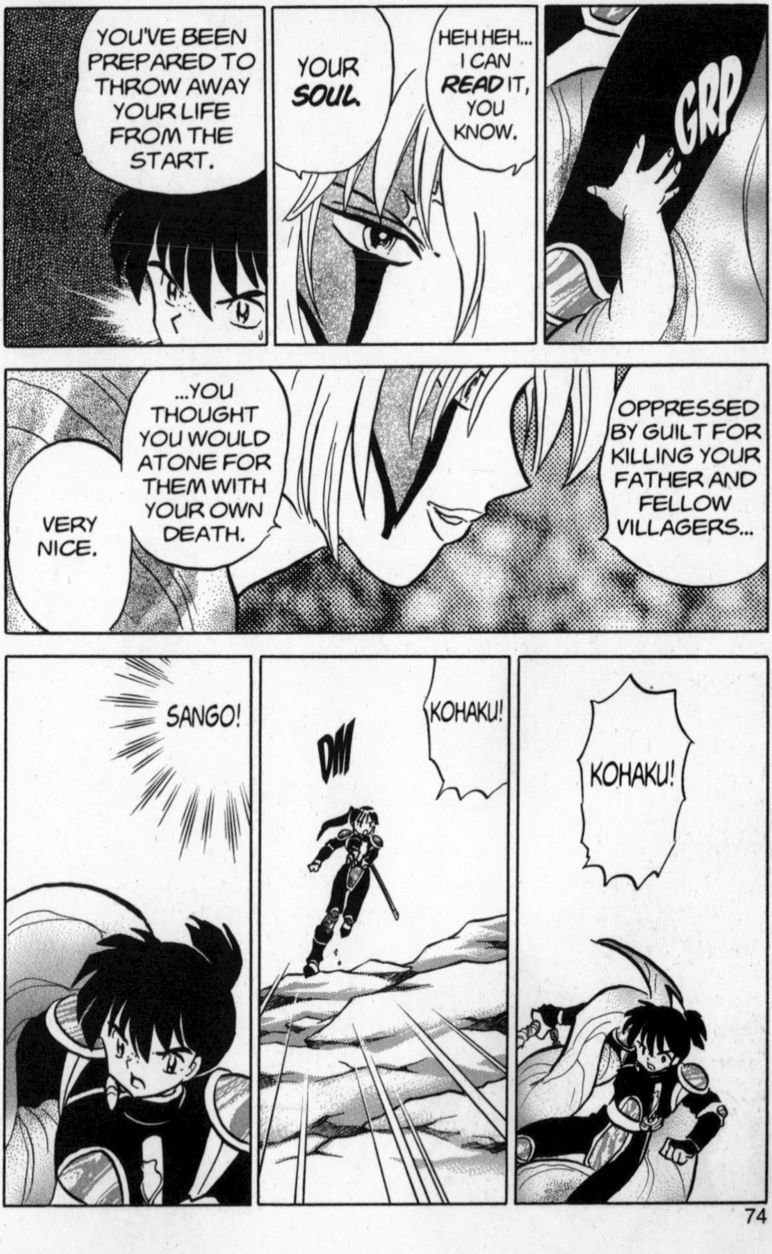
GRP
HEH HEH... I CAN READ IT, YOU KNOW.
YOUR SOUL.
YOU'VE BEEN PREPARED TO THROW AWAY YOUR LIFE FROM THE START.
OPPRESSED BY GUILT FOR KILLING YOUR FATHER AND FELLOW VILLAGERS...
...YOU THOUGHT YOU WOULD ATONE FOR THEM WITH YOUR OWN DEATH.
VERY NICE.
KOHAKU!
KOHAKU!
DM
SANGO!

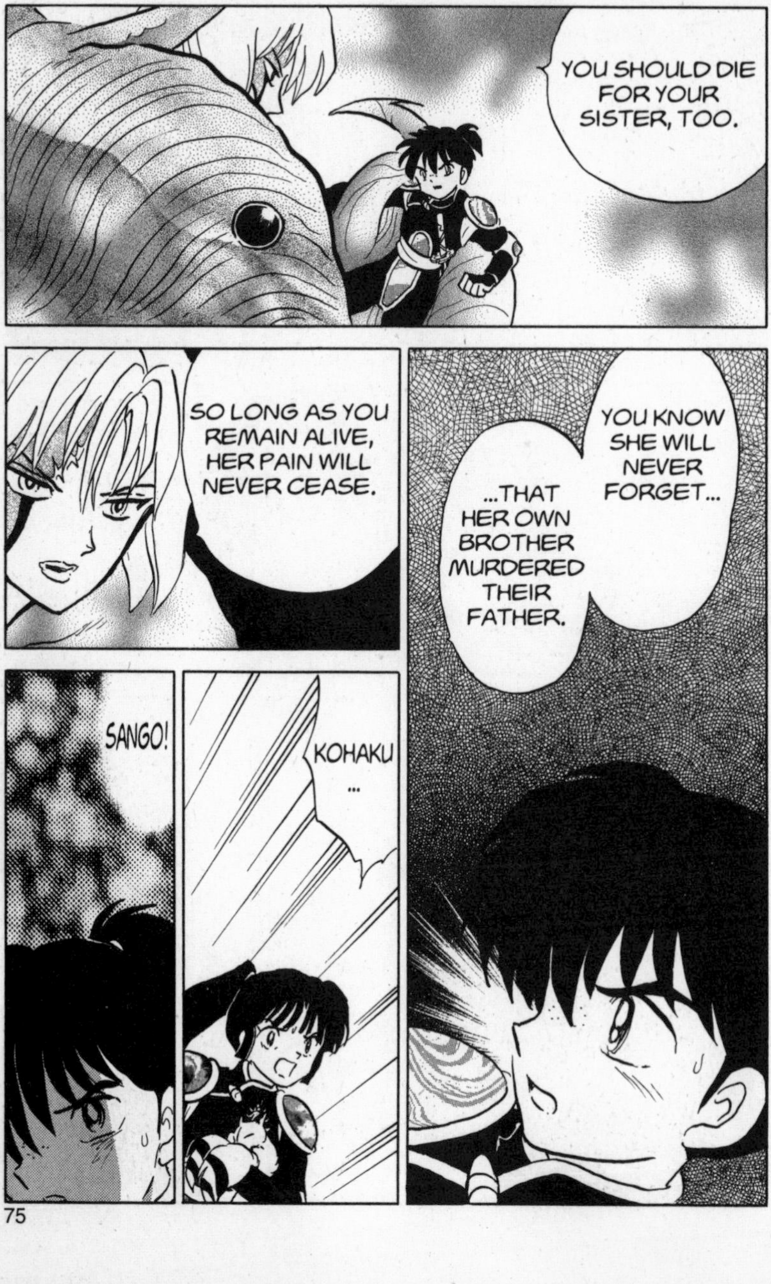
YOU SHOULD DIE FOR YOUR SISTER, TOO.
YOU KNOW SHE WILL NEVER FORGET...
...THAT HER OWN BROTHER MURDERED THEIR FATHER.
SO LONG AS YOU REMAIN ALIVE, HER PAIN WILL NEVER CEASE.
KOHAKU ...
SANGO!

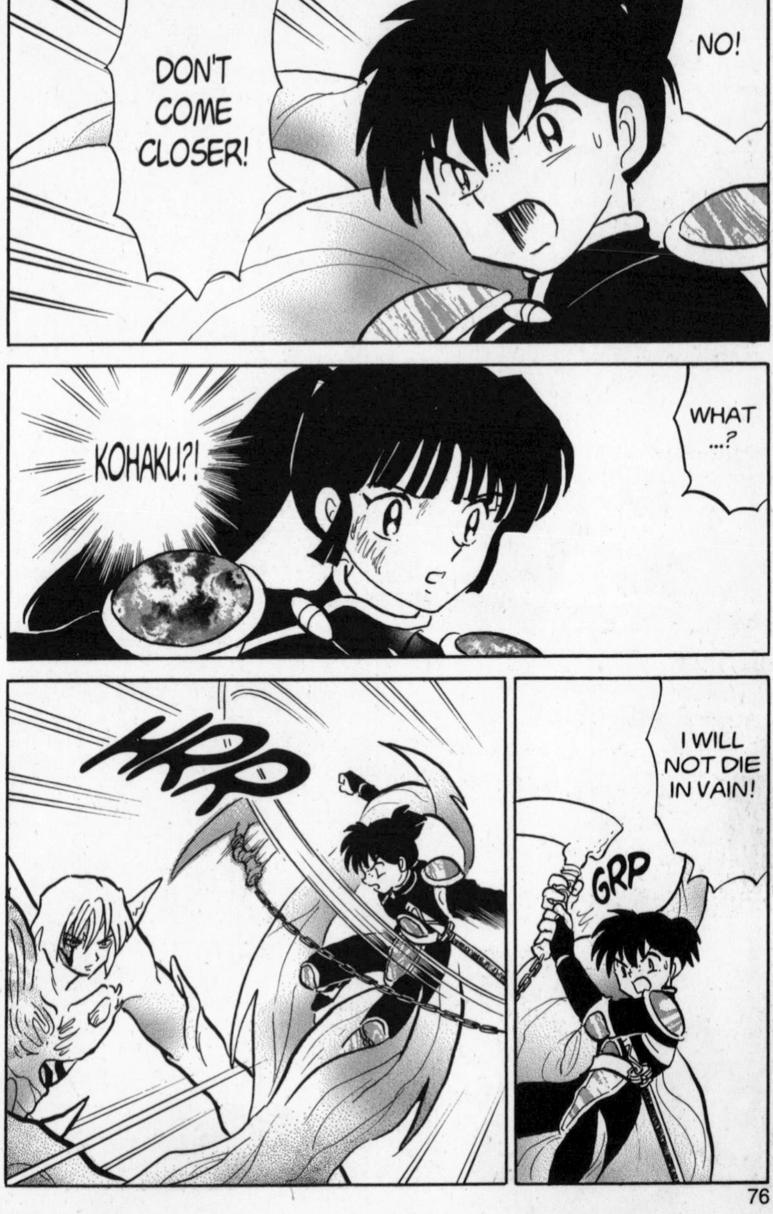
NO!
DON'T COME CLOSER!
WHAT ...?
KOHAKU?!
I WILL NOT DIE IN VAIN!
GRP
HRR

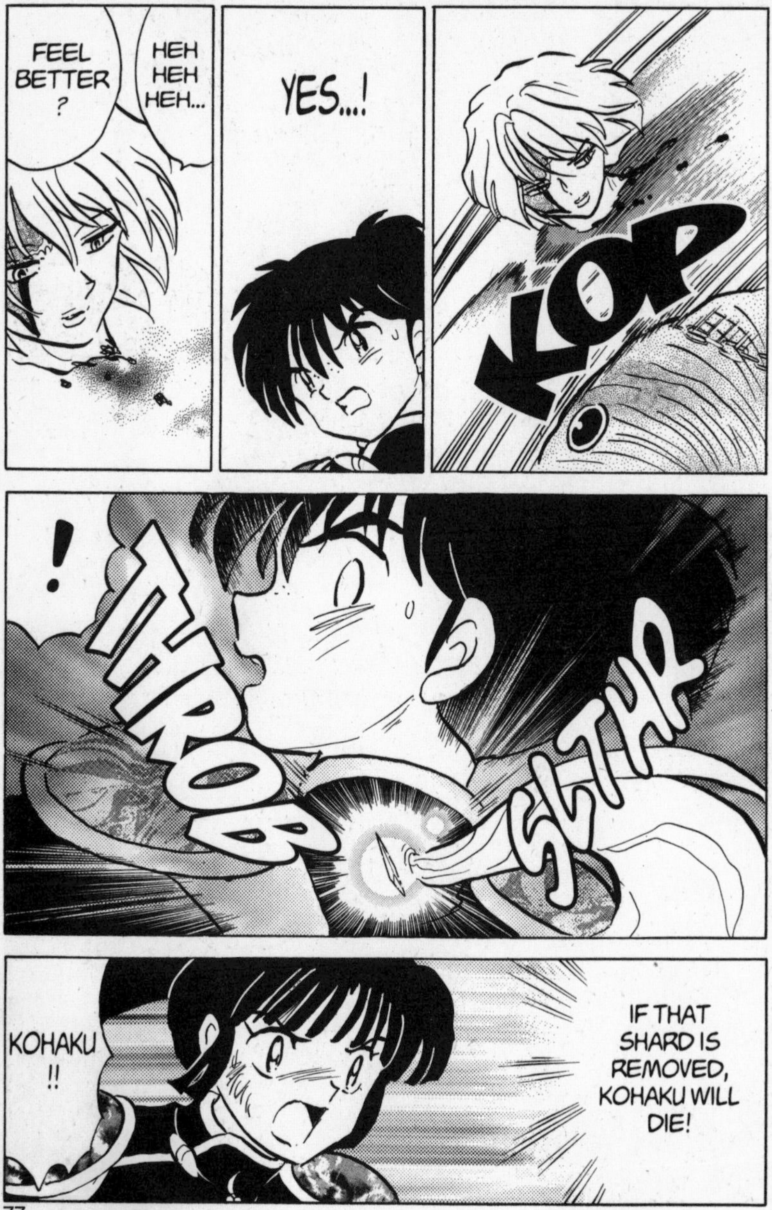
KOP
YES...!
HEH HEH HEH...
FEEL BETTER ?
SLTHR
THROB
!
IF THAT SHARD IS REMOVED, KOHAKU WILL DIE!
KOHAKU !!

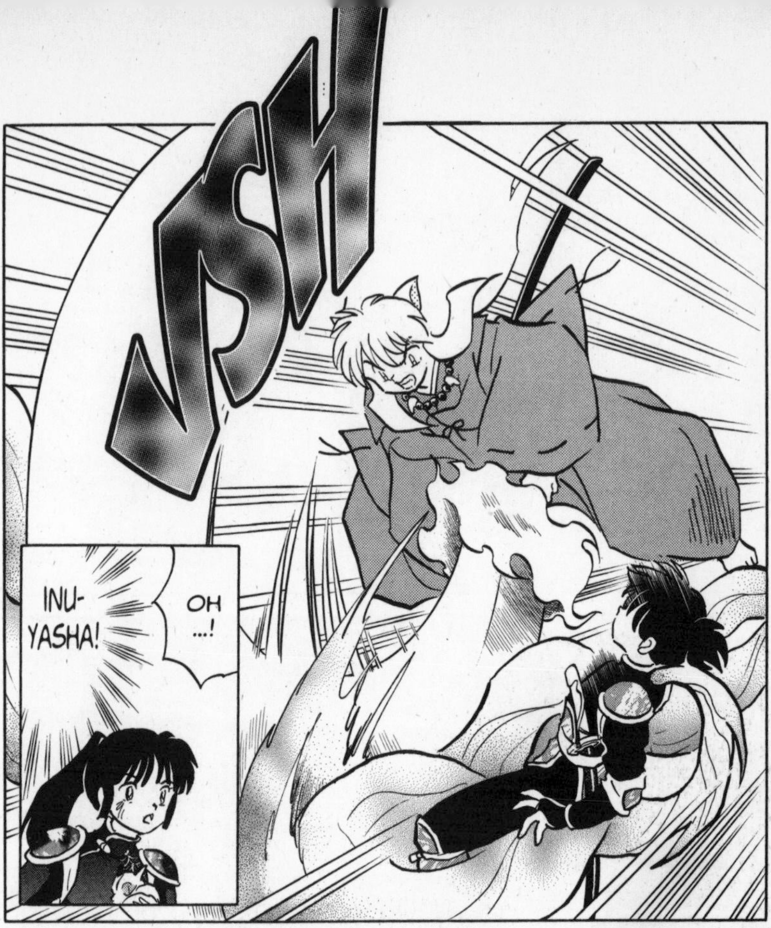
VSH
OH ...!
INU-YASHA!
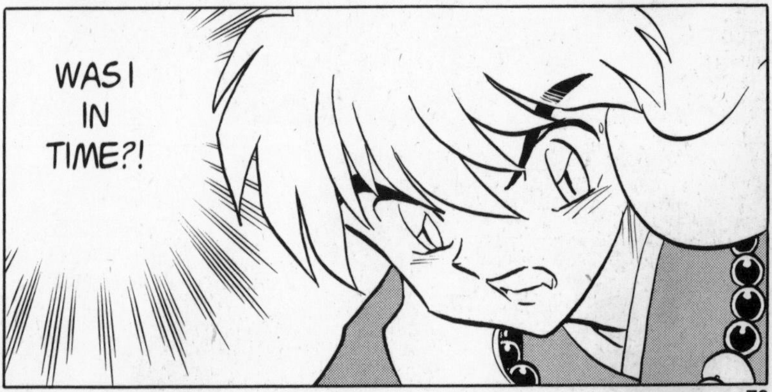
WAS I IN TIME?!

SCROLL 5
SIBLINGS

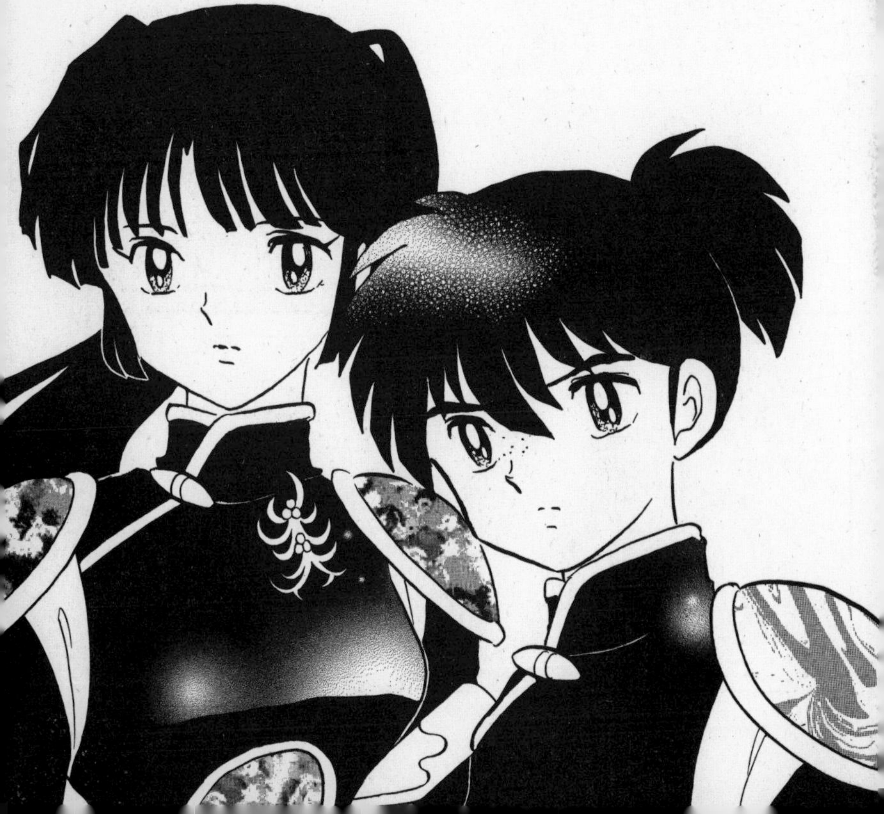

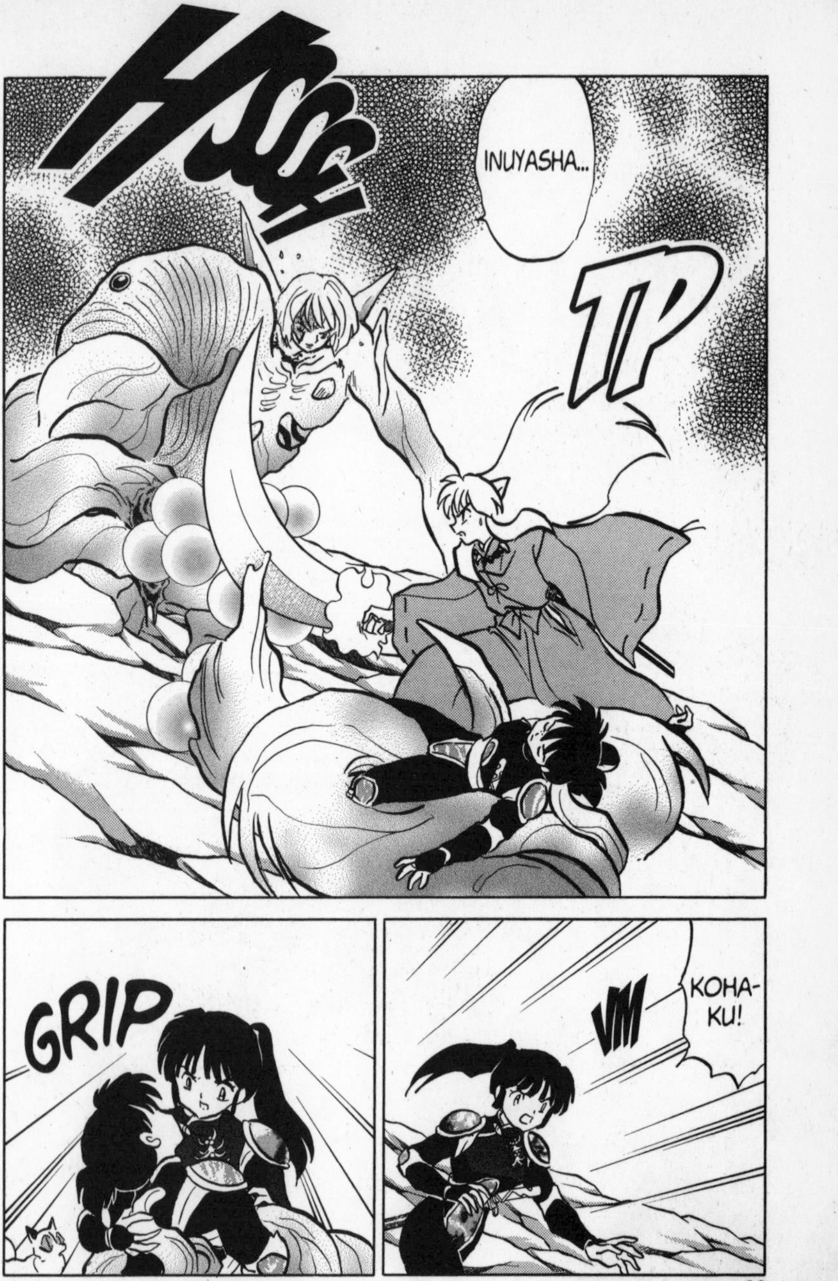
INUYASHA...
TP
KOHA-KU!
VM
GRIP

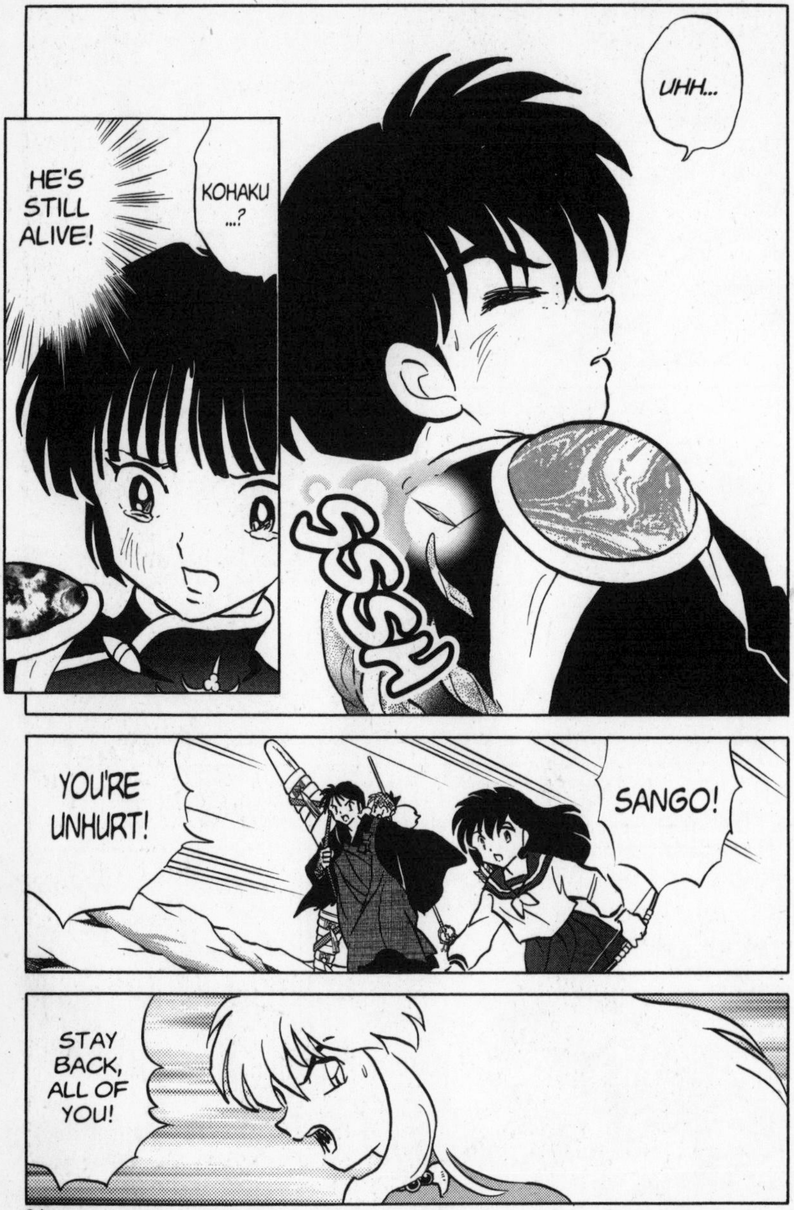
UHH...
SSSH
KOHAKU ...?
HE'S STILL ALIVE!
SANGO!
YOU'RE UNHURT!
STAY BACK, ALL OF YOU!

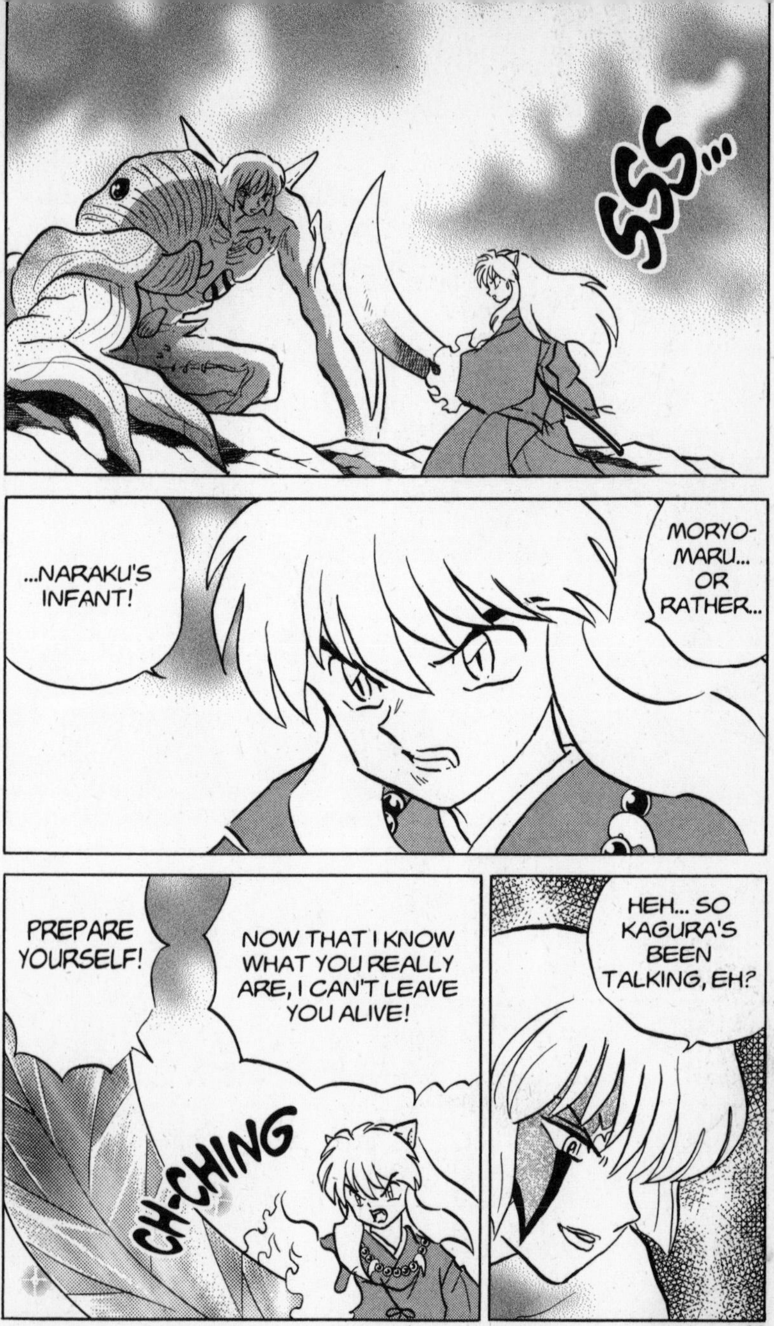
SSS...
MORYO-MARU... OR RATHER...
...NARAKU'S INFANT!
HEH... SO KAGURA'S BEEN TALKING, EH?
NOW THAT I KNOW WHAT YOU REALLY ARE, I CAN'T LEAVE YOU ALIVE!
PREPARE YOURSELF!
CH-CHING

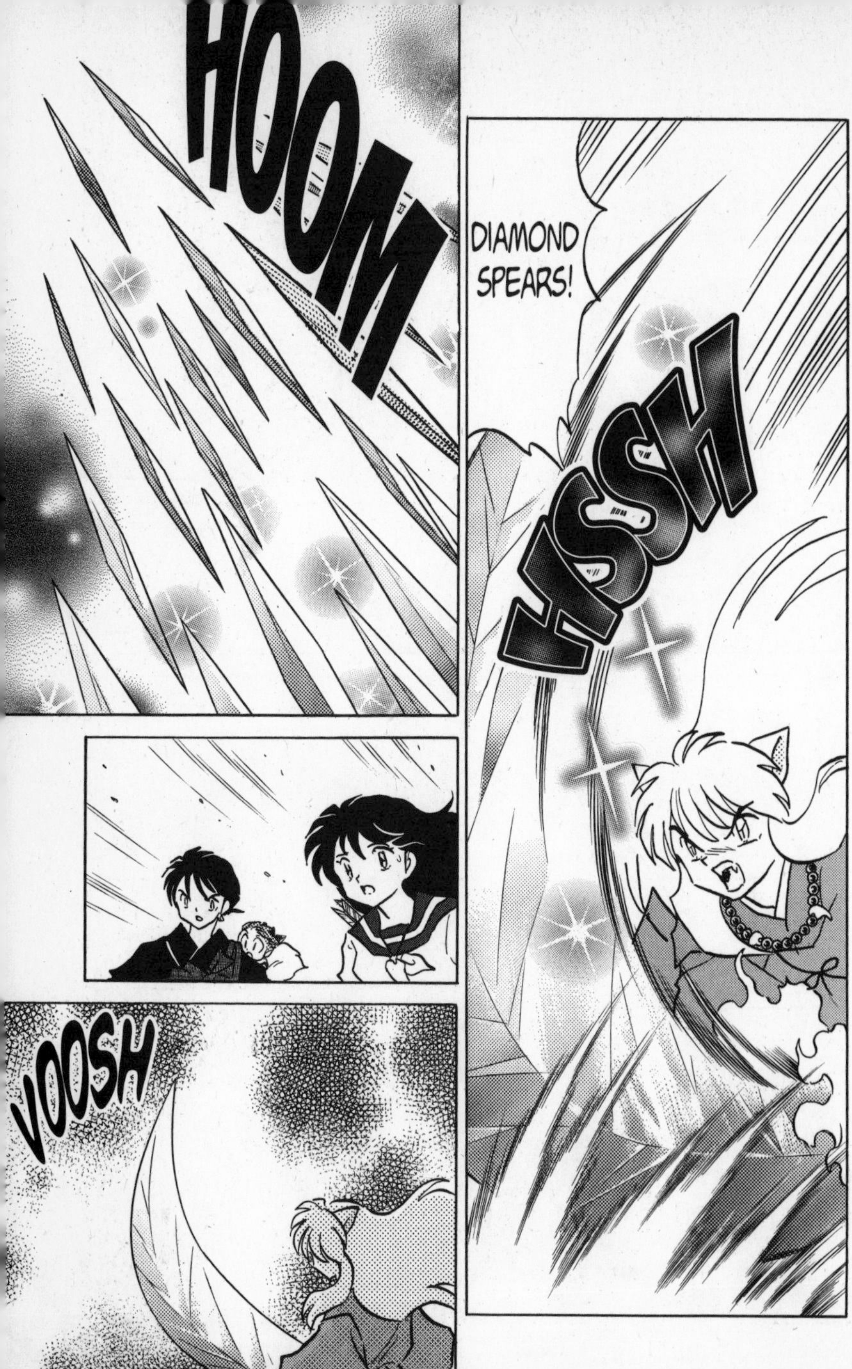
DIAMOND SPEARS!
HISSH
HOOM
VOOSH

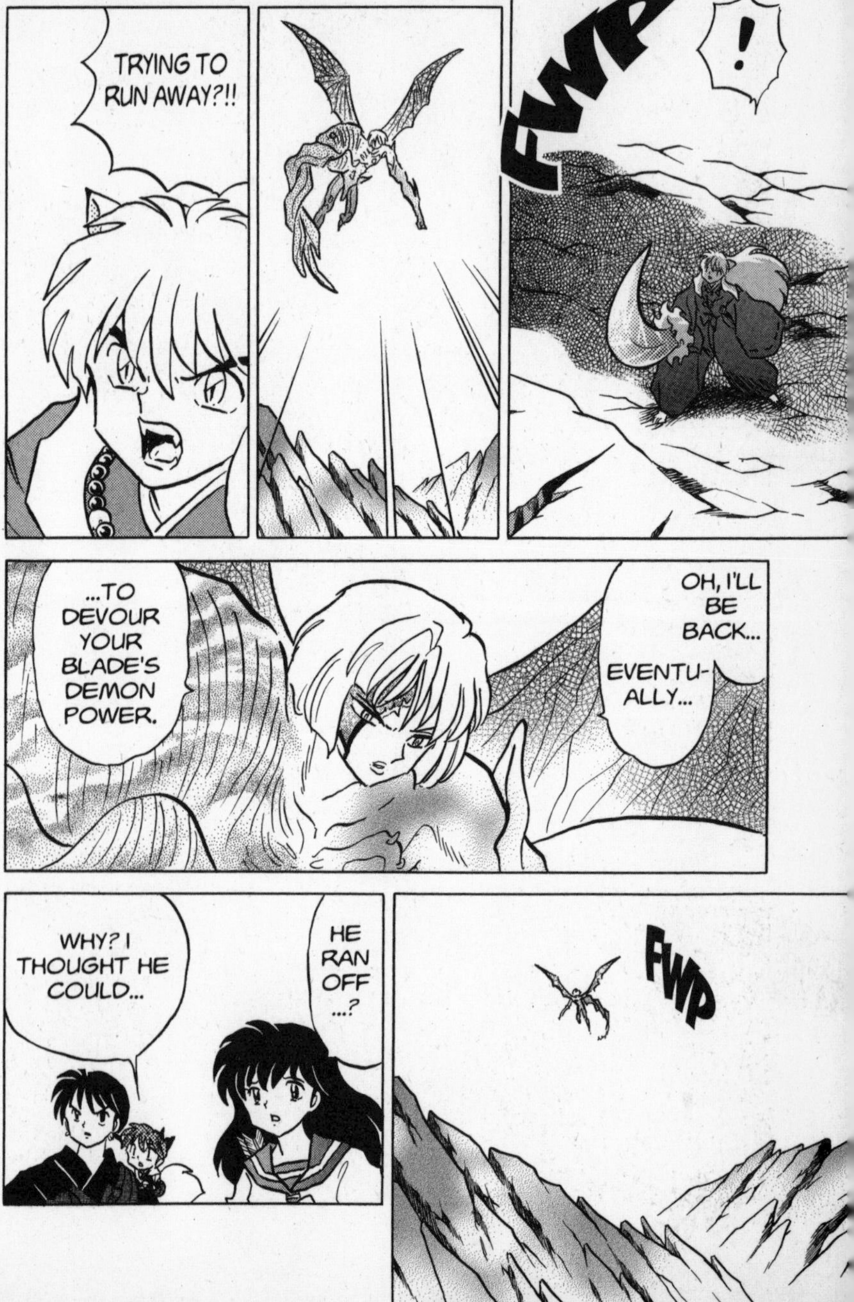
FWP
!
TRYING TO RUN AWAY?!!
OH, I'LL BE BACK... EVENTU-ALLY...
...TO DEVOUR YOUR BLADE'S DEMON POWER.
FWP
HE RAN OFF ...?
WHY? I THOUGHT HE COULD...

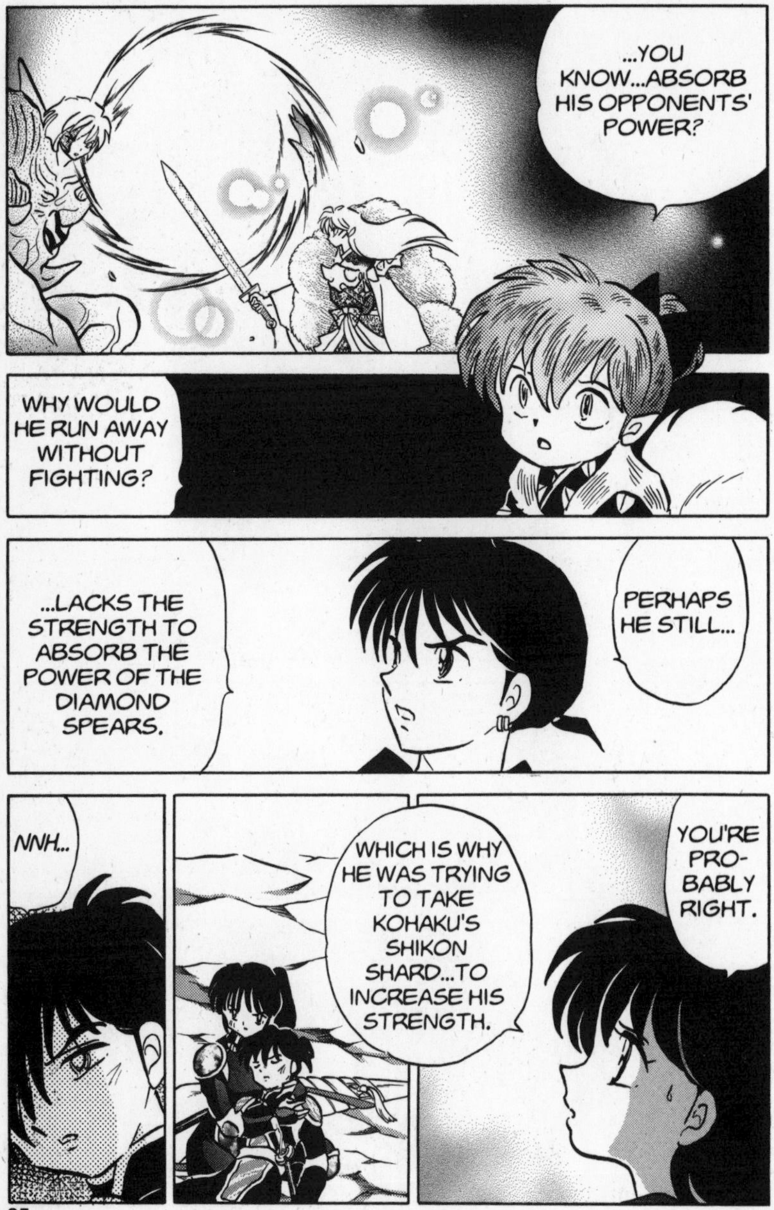
...YOU KNOW...ABSORB HIS OPPONENTS' POWER?
WHY WOULD HE RUN AWAY WITHOUT FIGHTING?
PERHAPS HE STILL...
...LACKS THE STRENGTH TO ABSORB THE POWER OF THE DIAMOND SPEARS.
YOU'RE PRO-BABLY RIGHT.
WHICH IS WHY HE WAS TRYING TO TAKE KOHAKU'S SHIKON SHARD...TO INCREASE HIS STRENGTH.
NNH...

!
KOHAKU ...
HE'S AWAKE?
VM
OH...!
DON'T GO, KOHAKU!

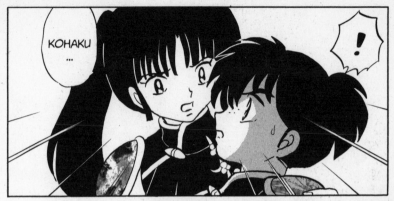

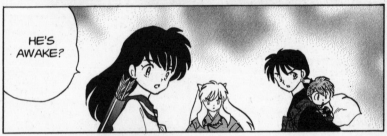

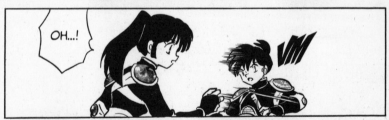

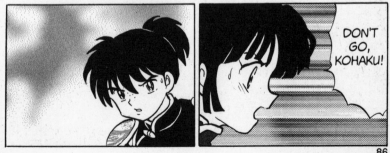

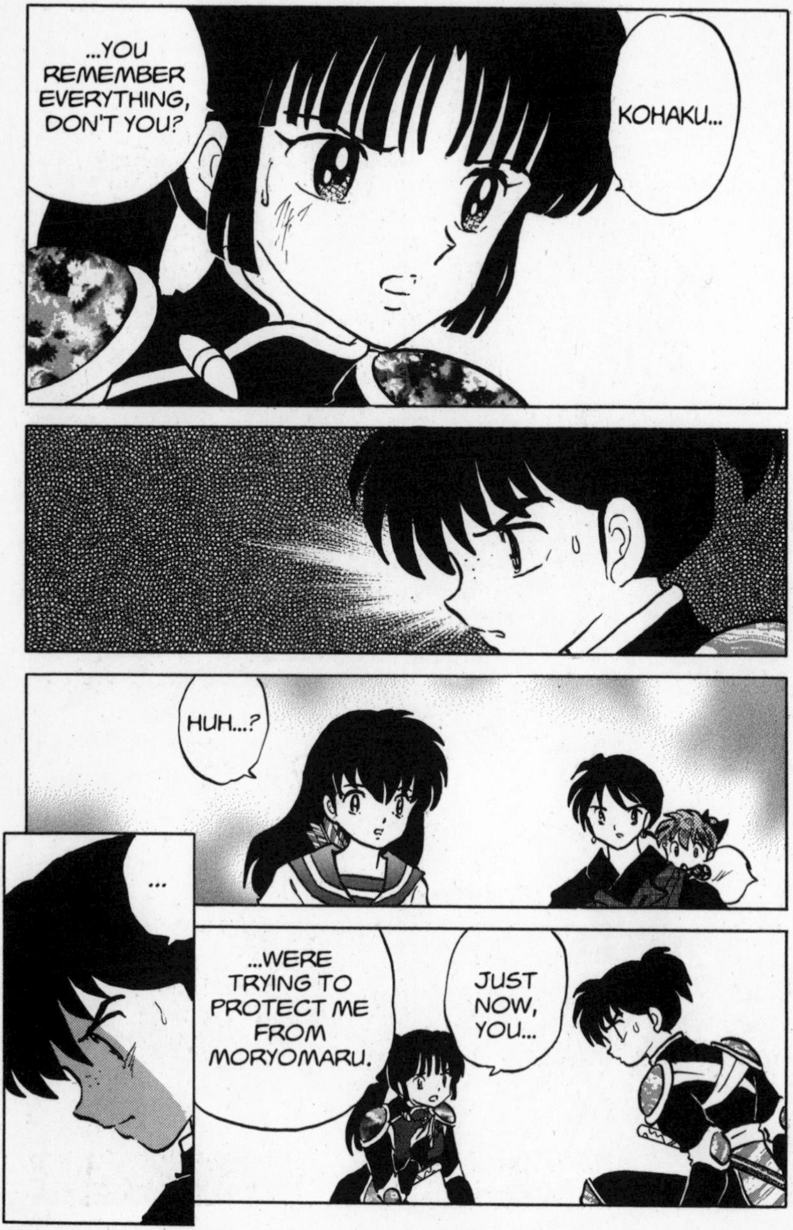
KOHAKU...
...YOU REMEMBER EVERYTHING, DON'T YOU?
HUH...?
JUST NOW, YOU...
...WERE TRYING TO PROTECT ME FROM MORYOMARU.
...

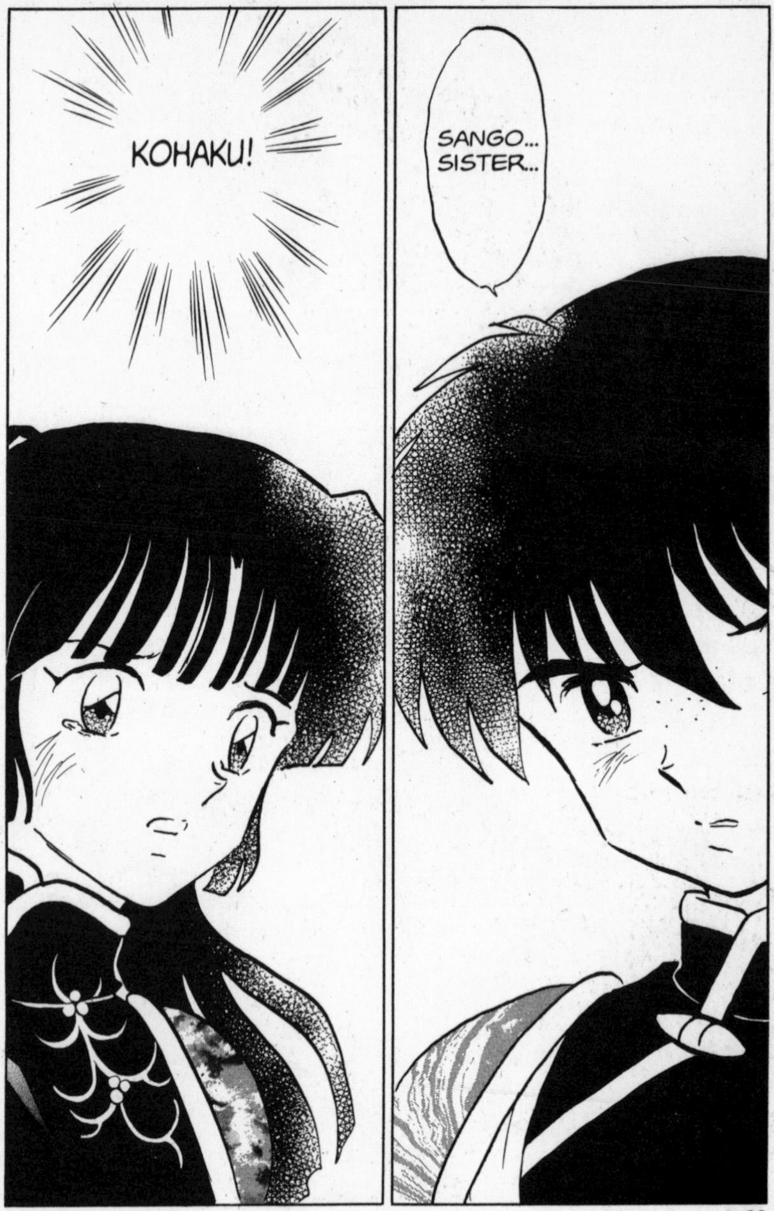
SANGO...
SISTER...
KOHAKU!

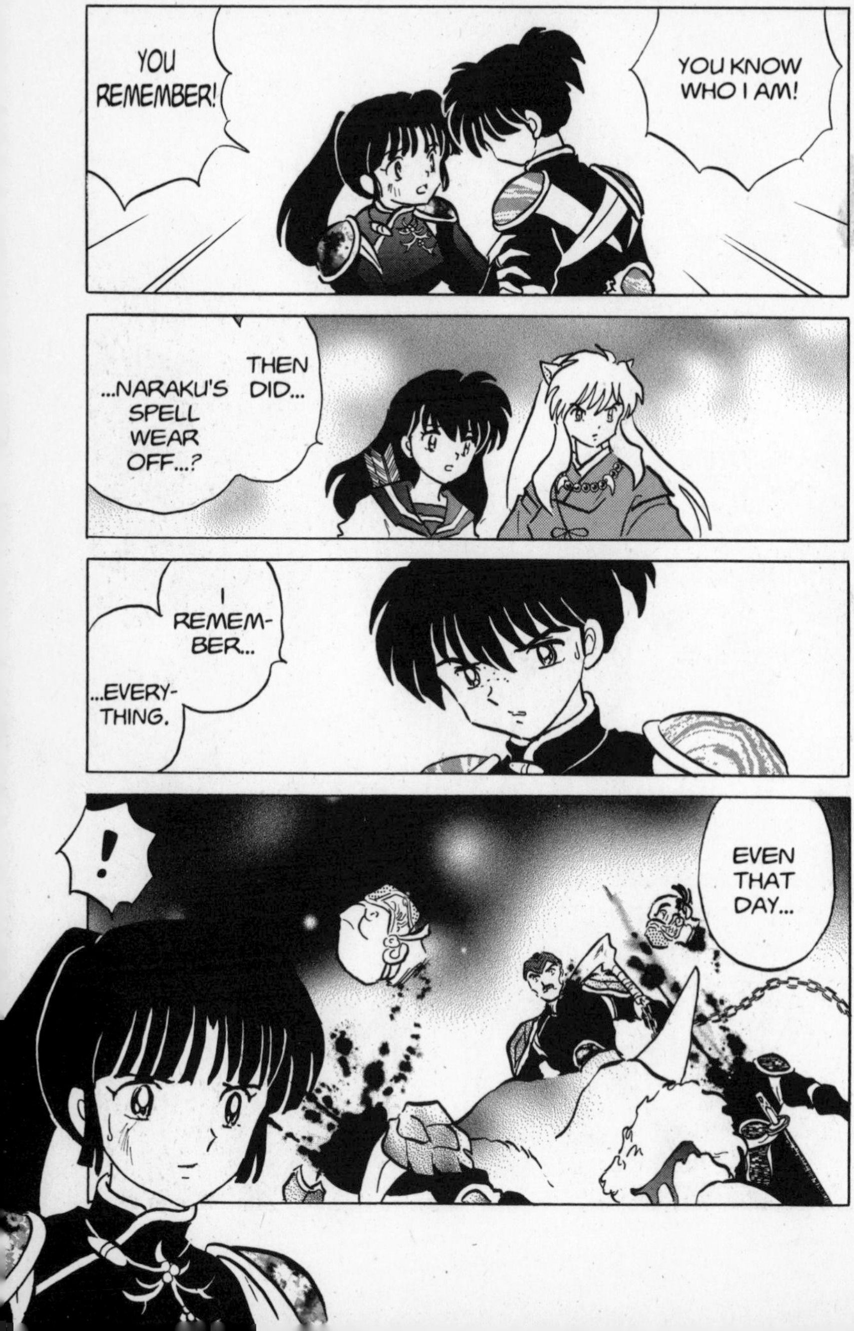
YOU KNOW WHO I AM!
YOU REMEMBER!
THEN DID...
...NARAKU'S SPELL WEAR OFF...?
I REMEMBER...
...EVERYTHING.
EVEN THAT DAY...
!

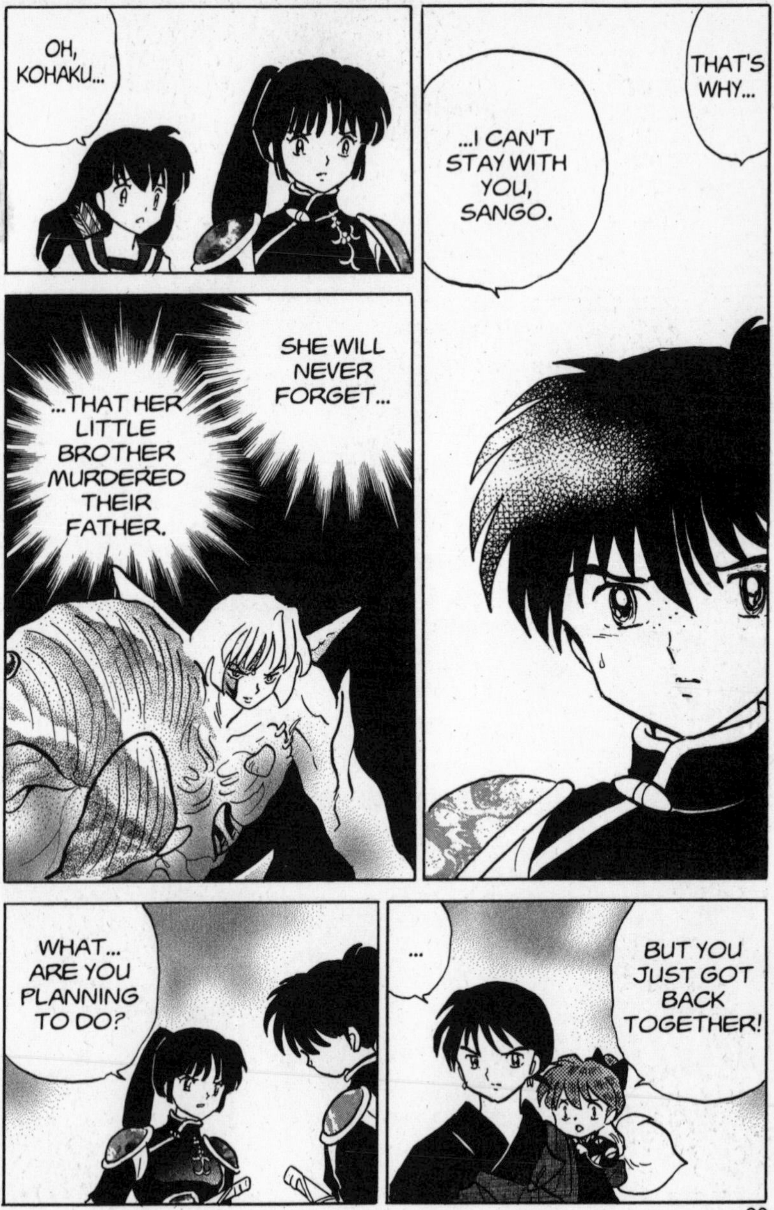
THAT'S WHY...
...I CAN'T STAY WITH YOU, SANGO.
OH, KOHAKU...
SHE WILL NEVER FORGET...
...THAT HER LITTLE BROTHER MURDERED THEIR FATHER.
BUT YOU JUST GOT BACK TOGETHER!
...
WHAT... ARE YOU PLANNING TO DO?

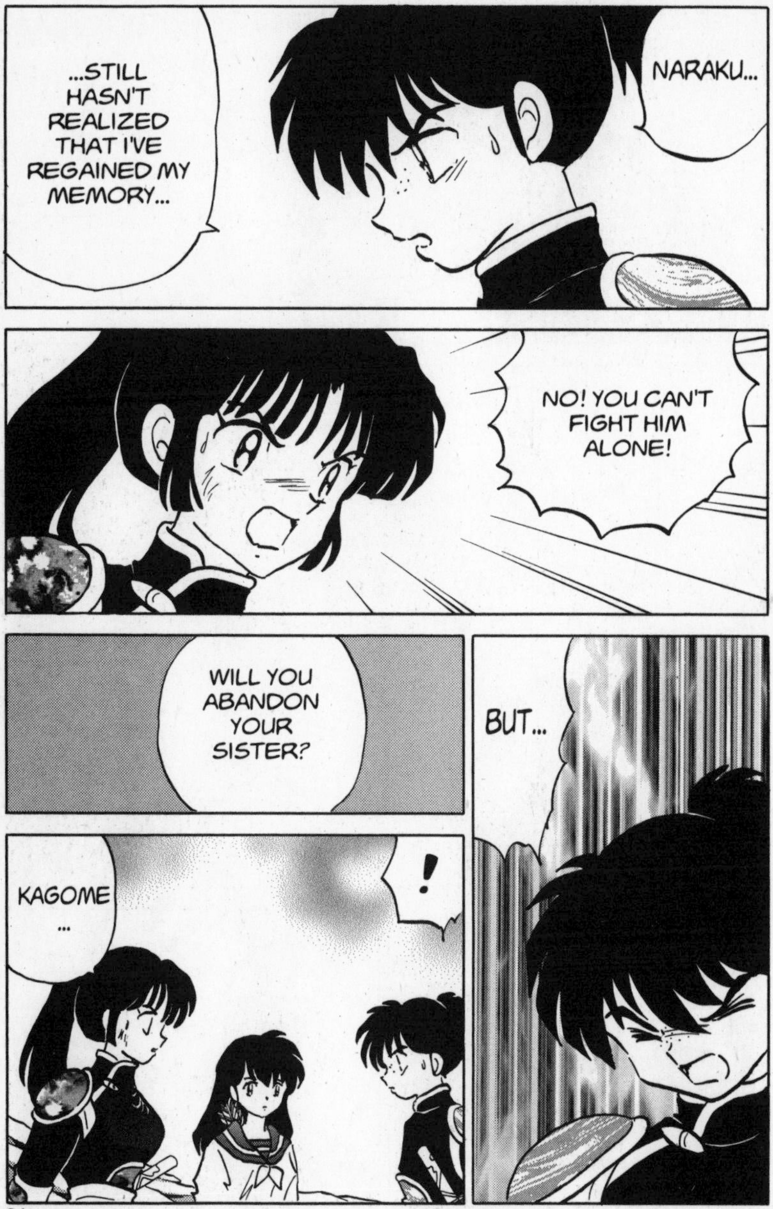
NARAKU...
...STILL HASN'T REALIZED THAT I'VE REGAINED MY MEMORY...
NO! YOU CAN'T FIGHT HIM ALONE!
BUT...
WILL YOU ABANDON YOUR SISTER?
!
KAGOME ...

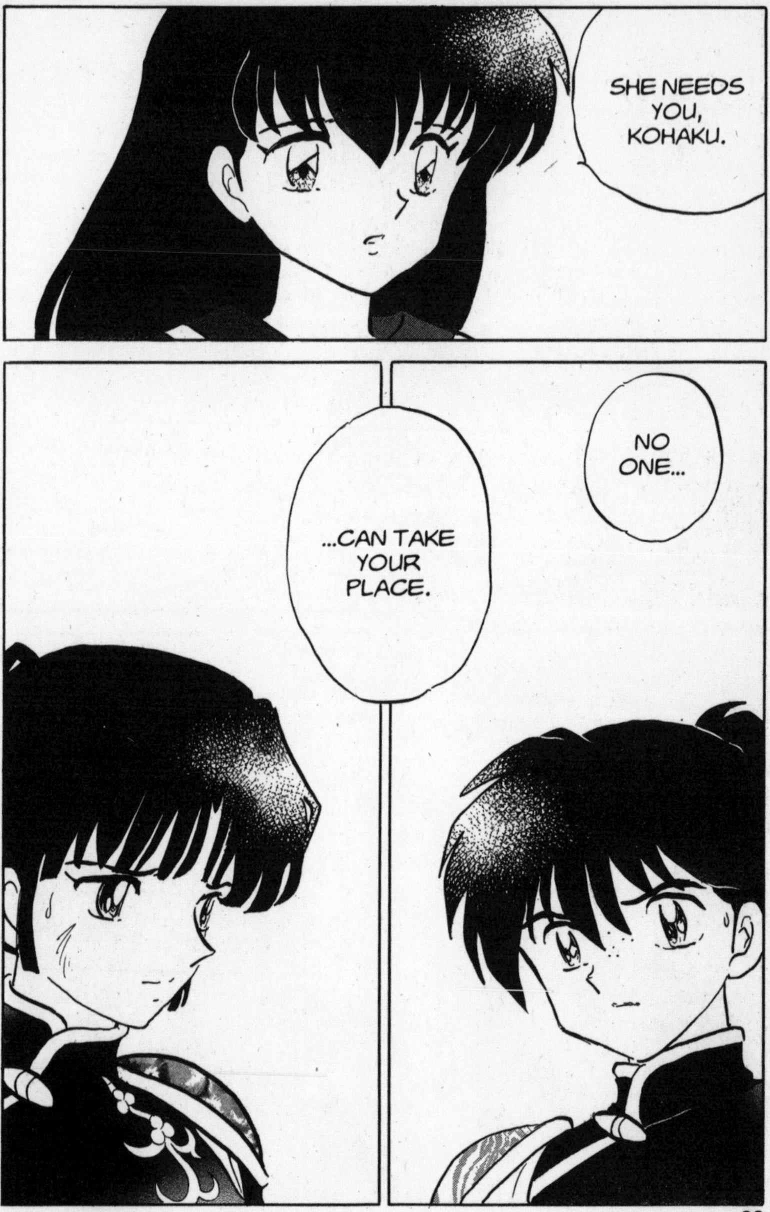
SHE NEEDS YOU, KOHAKU.
NO ONE...
...CAN TAKE YOUR PLACE.

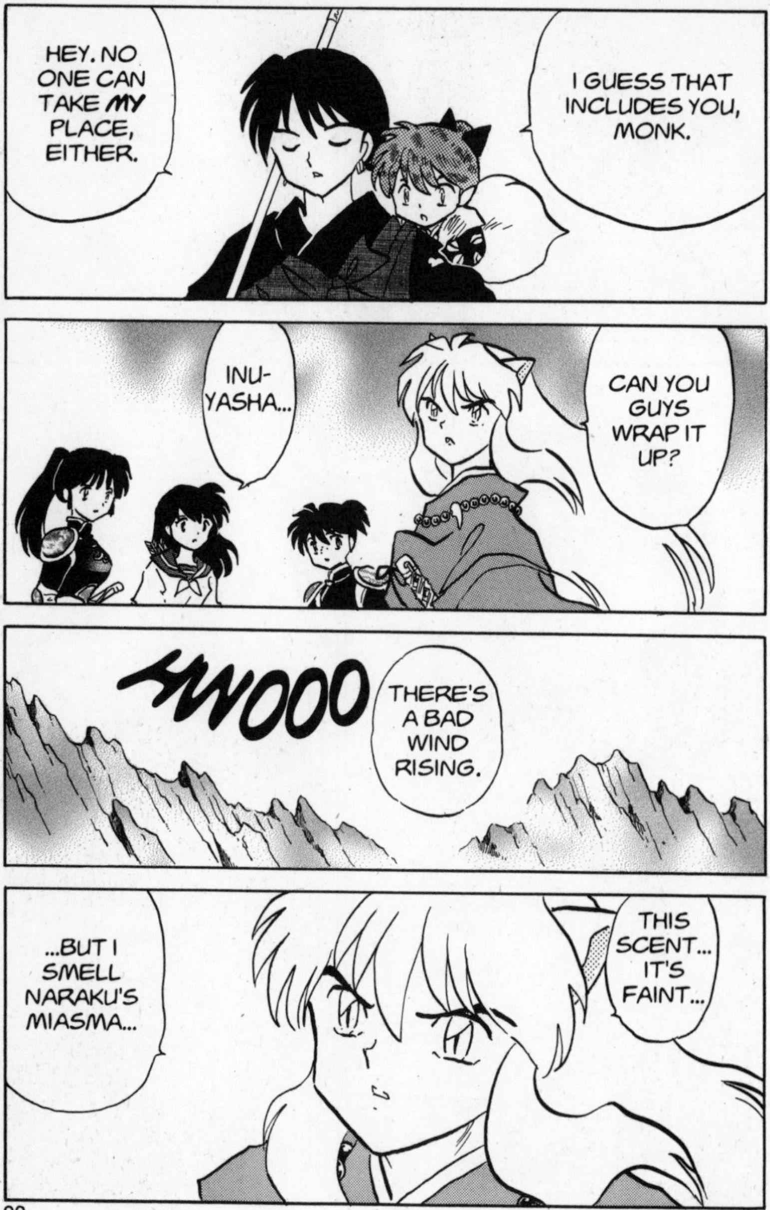
I GUESS THAT INCLUDES YOU, MONK.
HEY. NO ONE CAN TAKE *MY* PLACE, EITHER.
CAN YOU GUYS WRAP IT UP?
INU-YASHA...
THERE'S A BAD WIND RISING.
HWOOO
THIS SCENT... IT'S FAINT...
...BUT I SMELL NARAKU'S MIASMA...

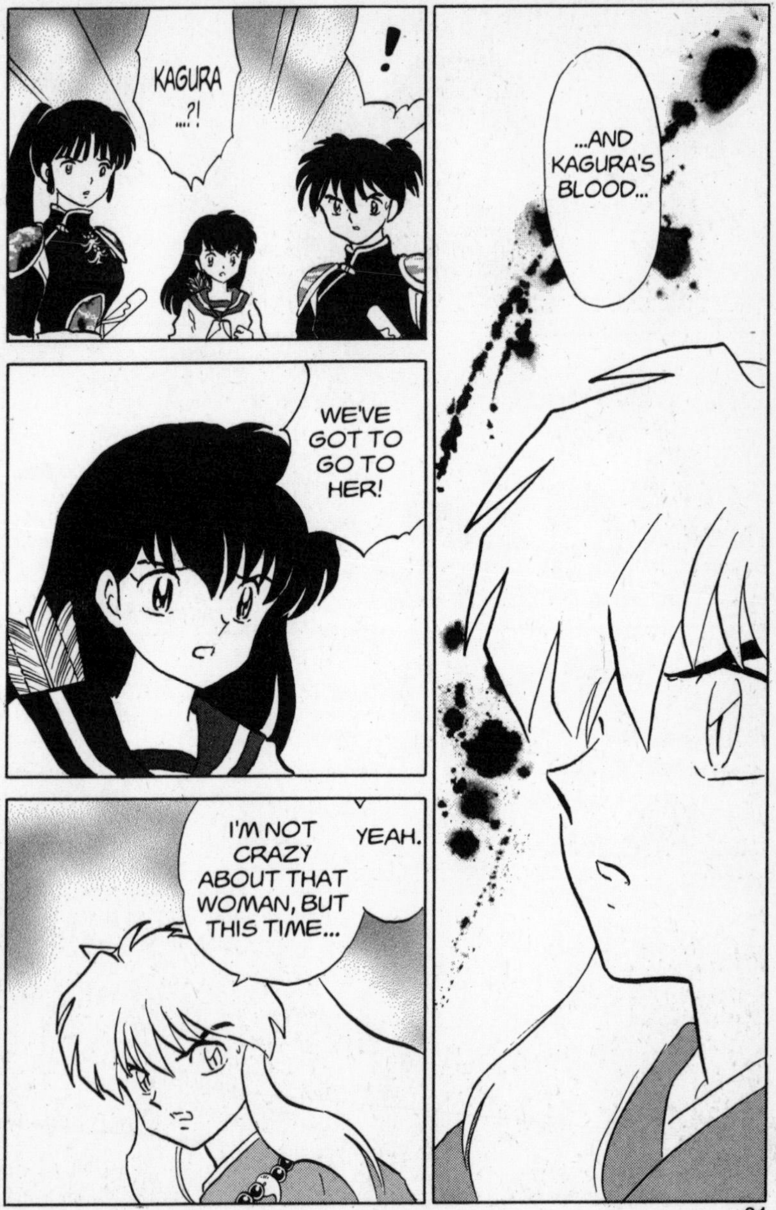
...AND KAGURA'S BLOOD...
!
KAGURA ...?!
WE'VE GOT TO GO TO HER!
YEAH.
I'M NOT CRAZY ABOUT THAT WOMAN, BUT THIS TIME...

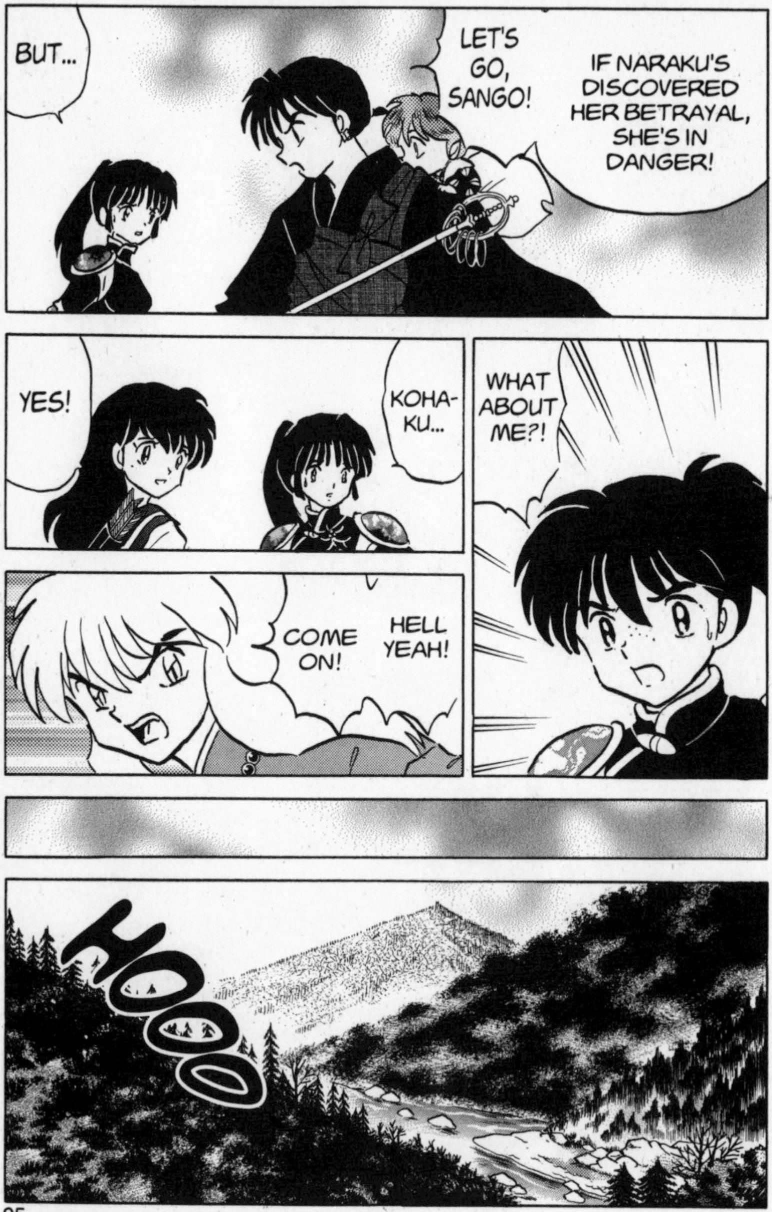
IF NARAKU'S DISCOVERED HER BETRAYAL, SHE'S IN DANGER!
LET'S GO, SANGO!
BUT...
WHAT ABOUT ME?!
KOHA-KU...
YES!
HELL YEAH!
COME ON!
HOOO

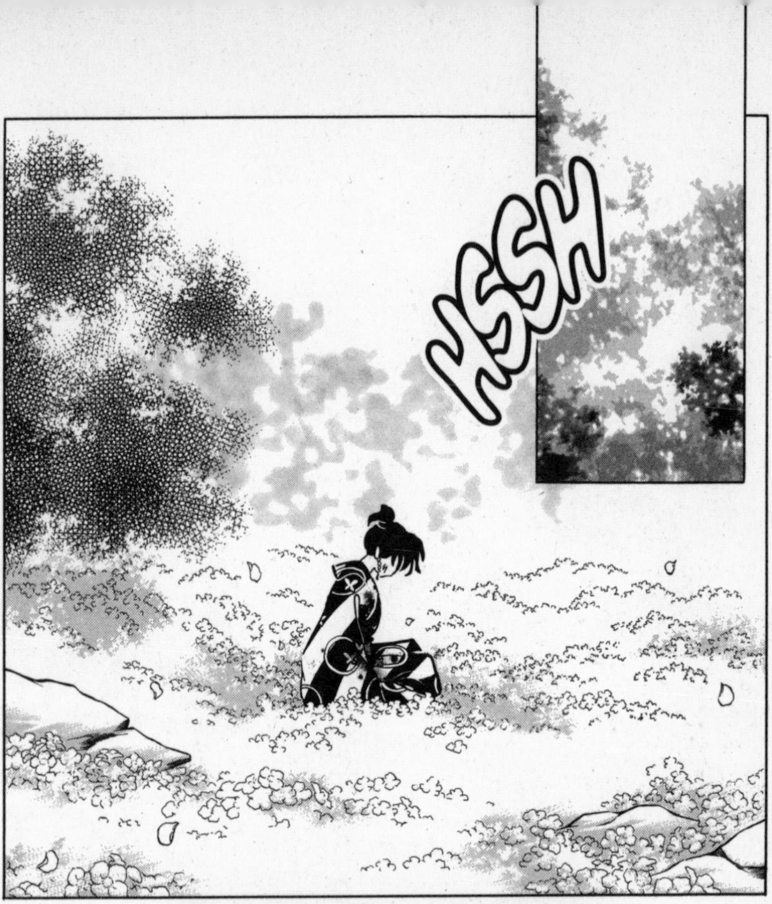
HSSH

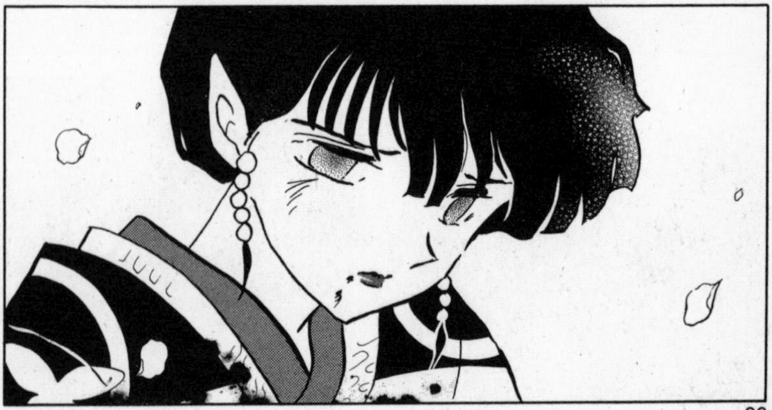

SCROLL 6
THE WIND

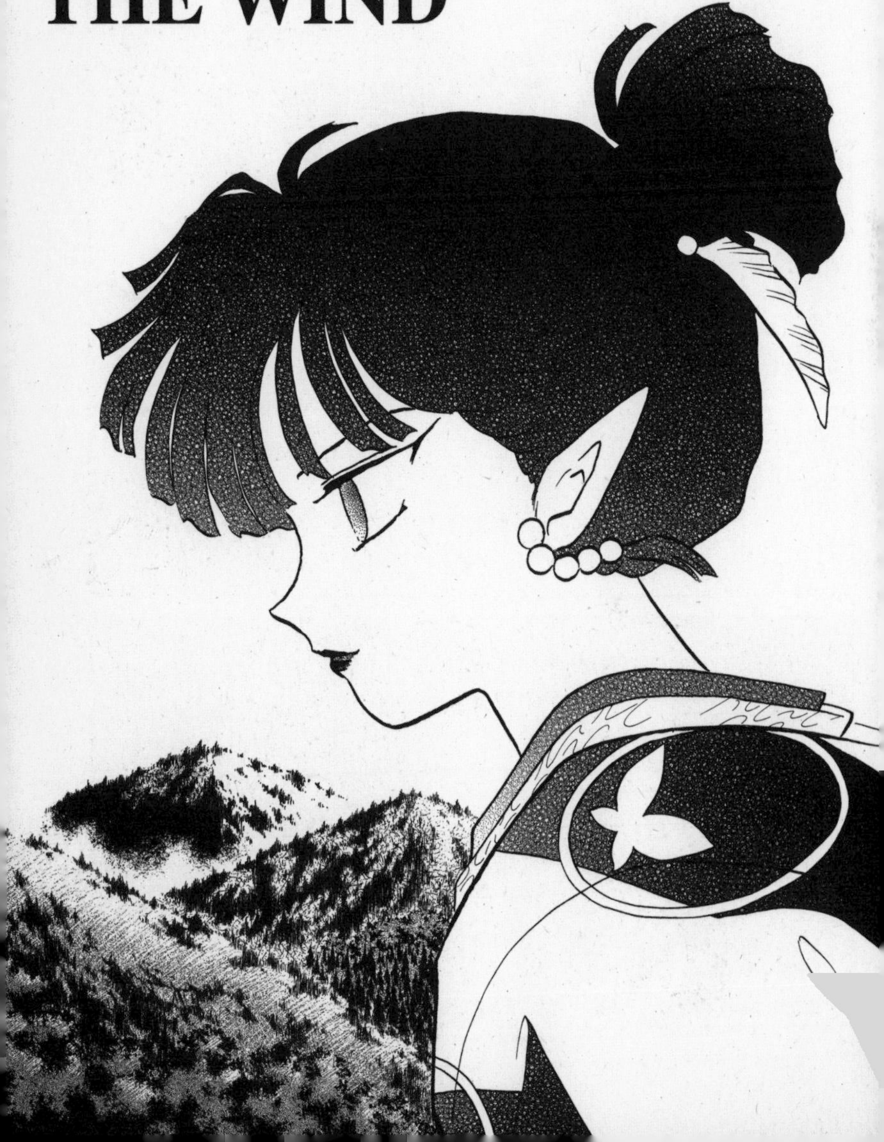

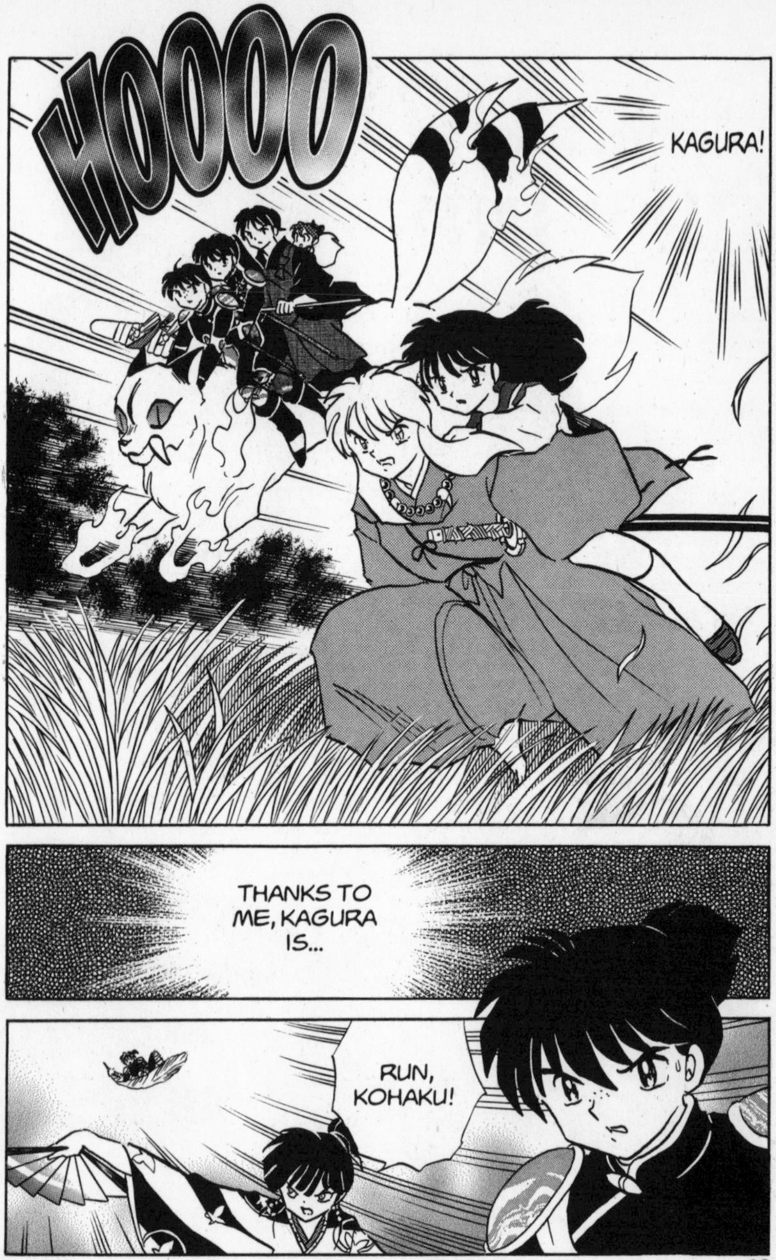
HOOOO
KAGURA!
THANKS TO ME, KAGURA IS...
RUN, KOHAKU!

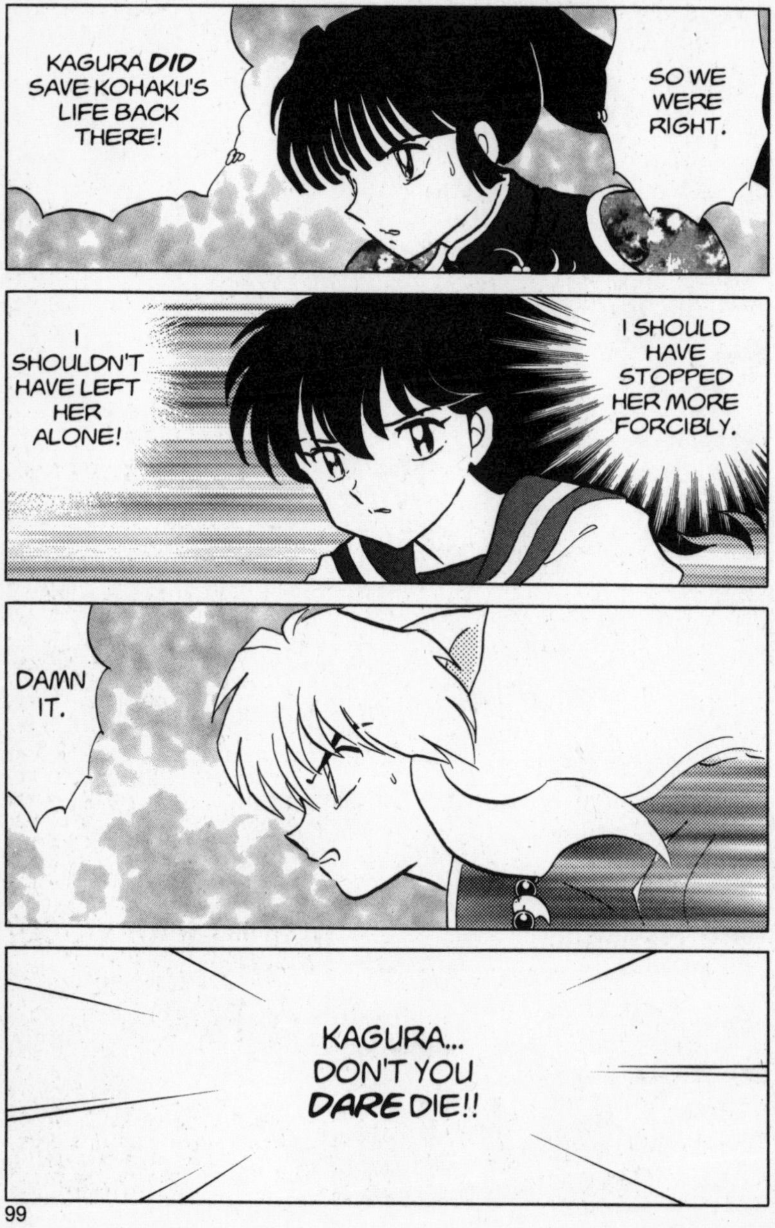
SO WE WERE RIGHT.
KAGURA DID SAVE KOHAKU'S LIFE BACK THERE!
I SHOULD HAVE STOPPED HER MORE FORCIBLY.
I SHOULDN'T HAVE LEFT HER ALONE!
DAMN IT.
KAGURA... DON'T YOU DARE DIE!!

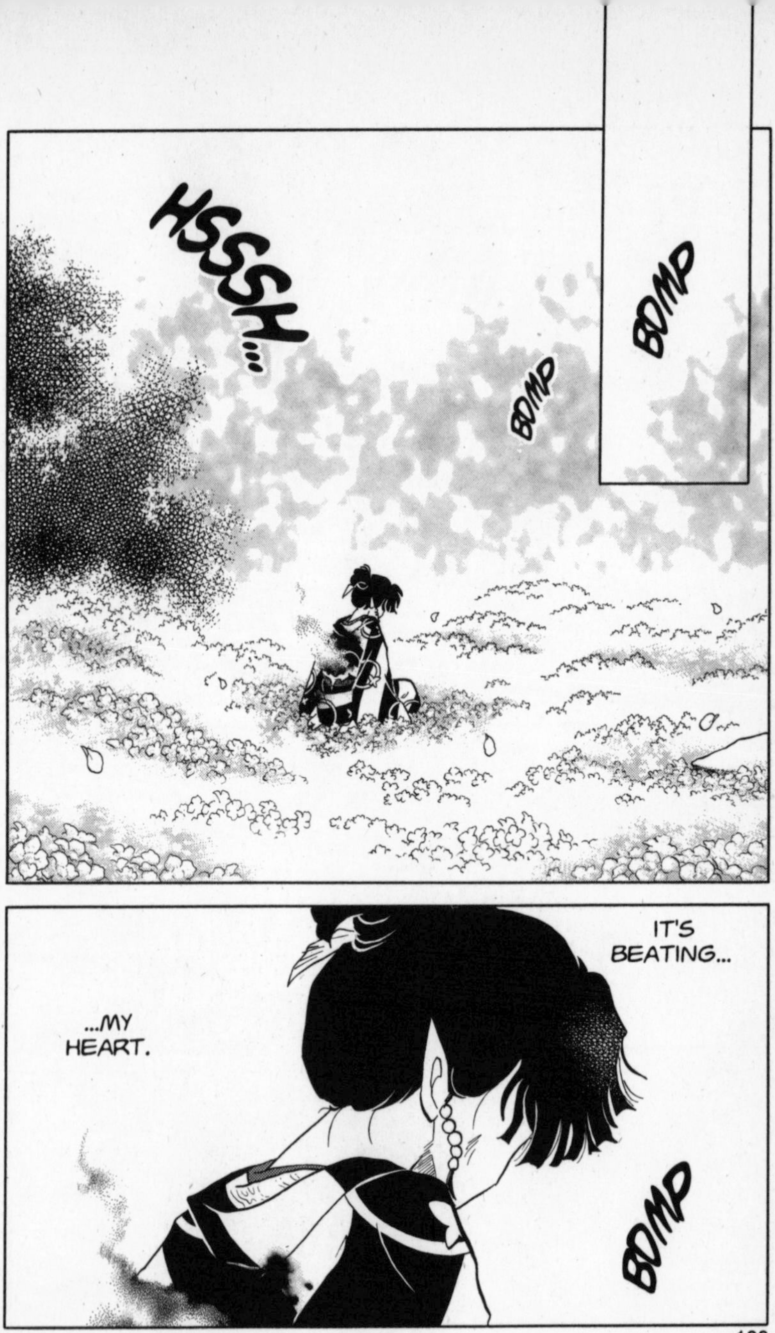
BDMP
HSSSH...
BDMP
IT'S BEATING...
...MY HEART.
BDMP

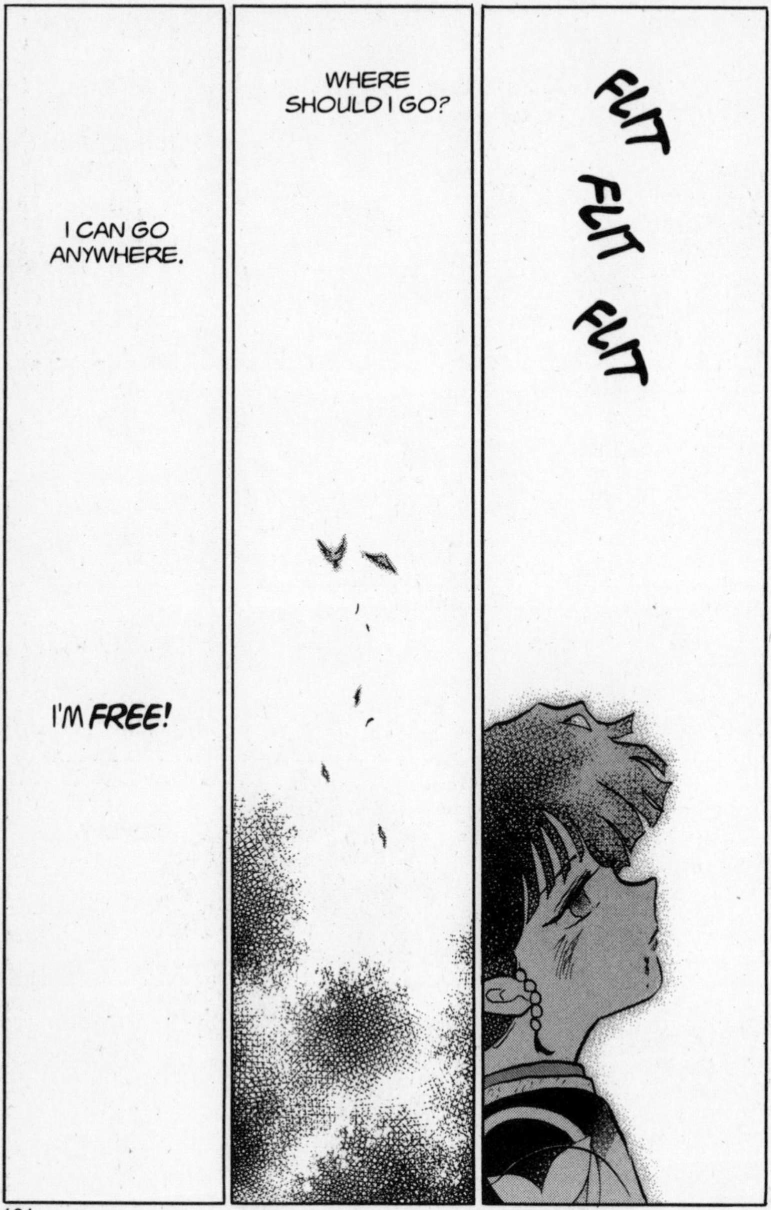
FLIT FLIT FLIT
WHERE SHOULD I GO?
I CAN GO ANYWHERE.
I'M **FREE!**

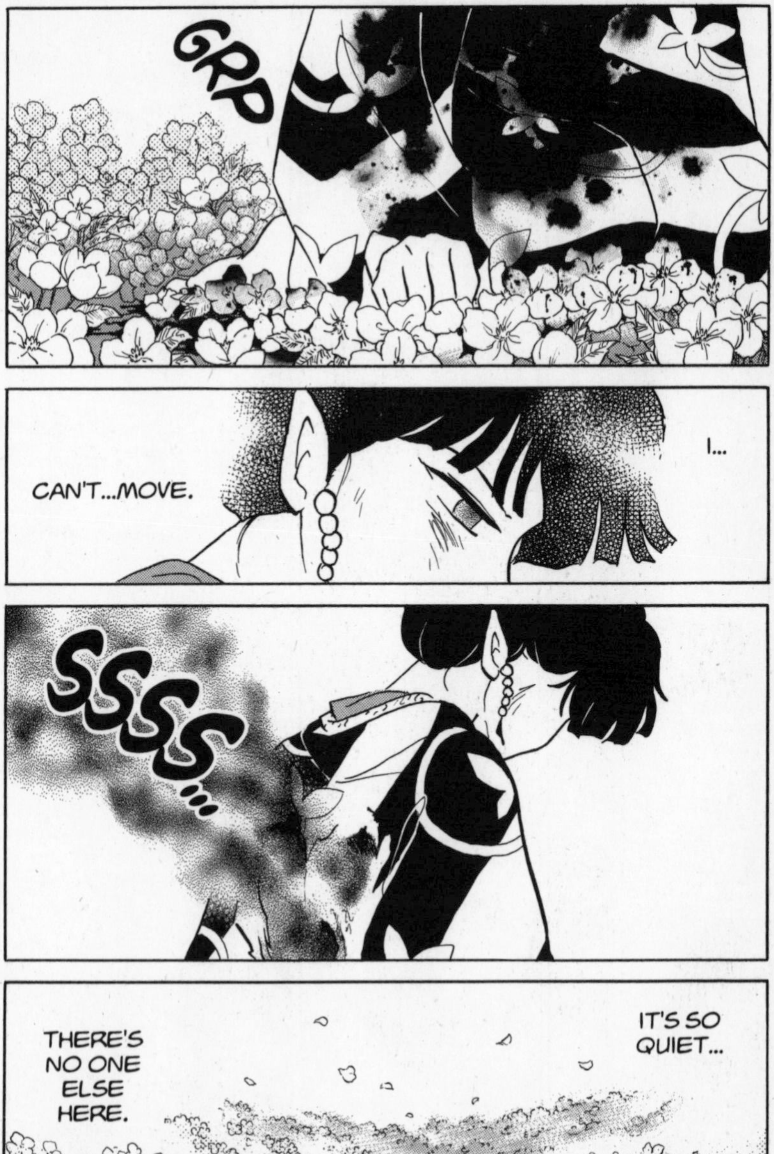
GRP
I...
CAN'T...MOVE.
SSSS...
IT'S SO QUIET...
THERE'S NO ONE ELSE HERE.

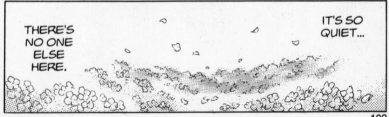

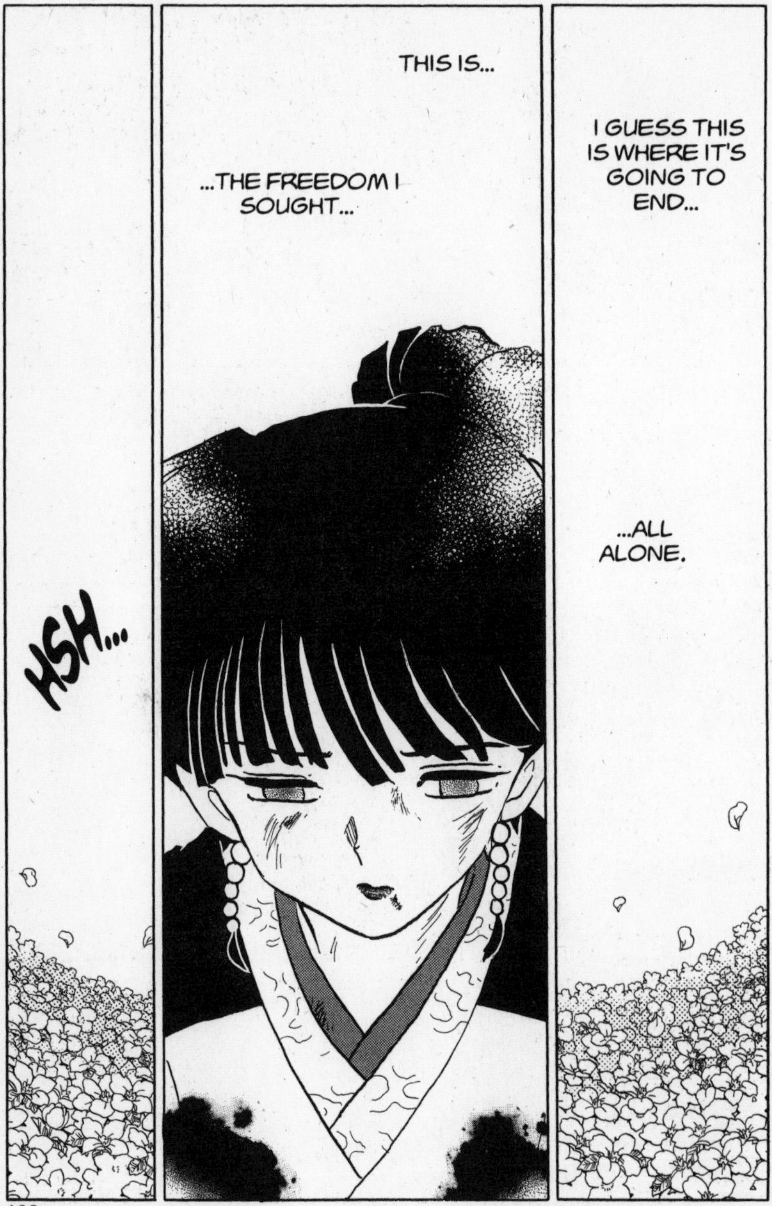
I GUESS THIS IS WHERE IT'S GOING TO END...
...ALL ALONE.
THIS IS...
...THE FREEDOM I SOUGHT...
HSH...

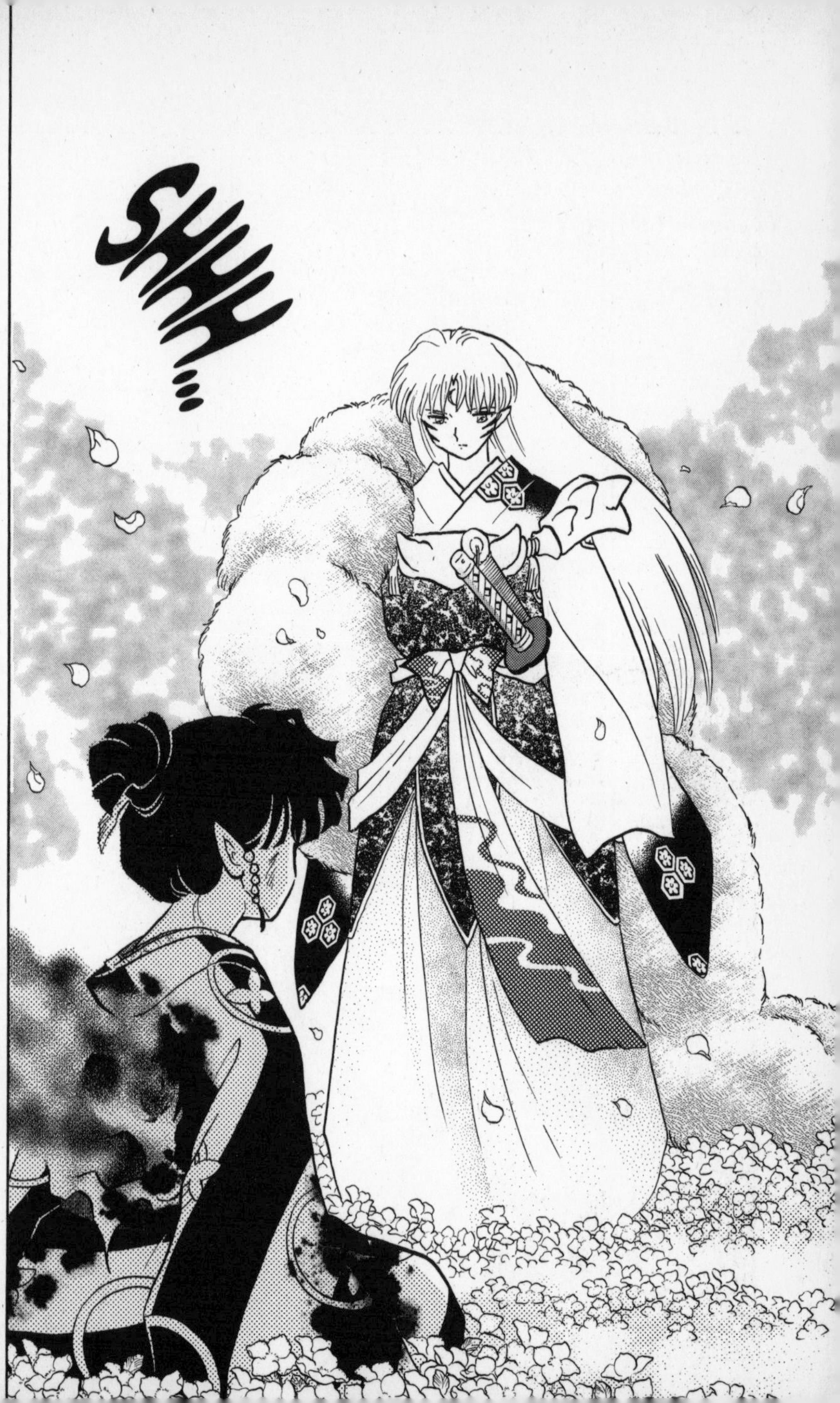
SHHH...

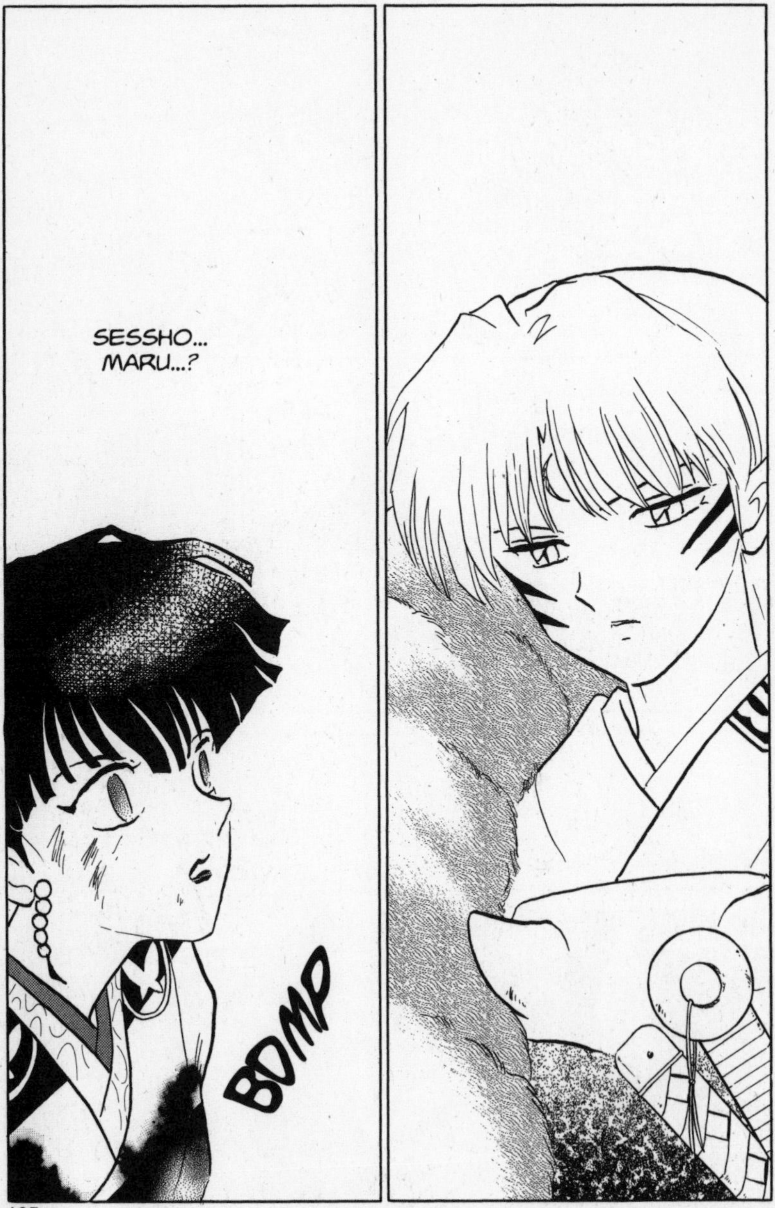
SESSHO...
MARU...?
BDMP

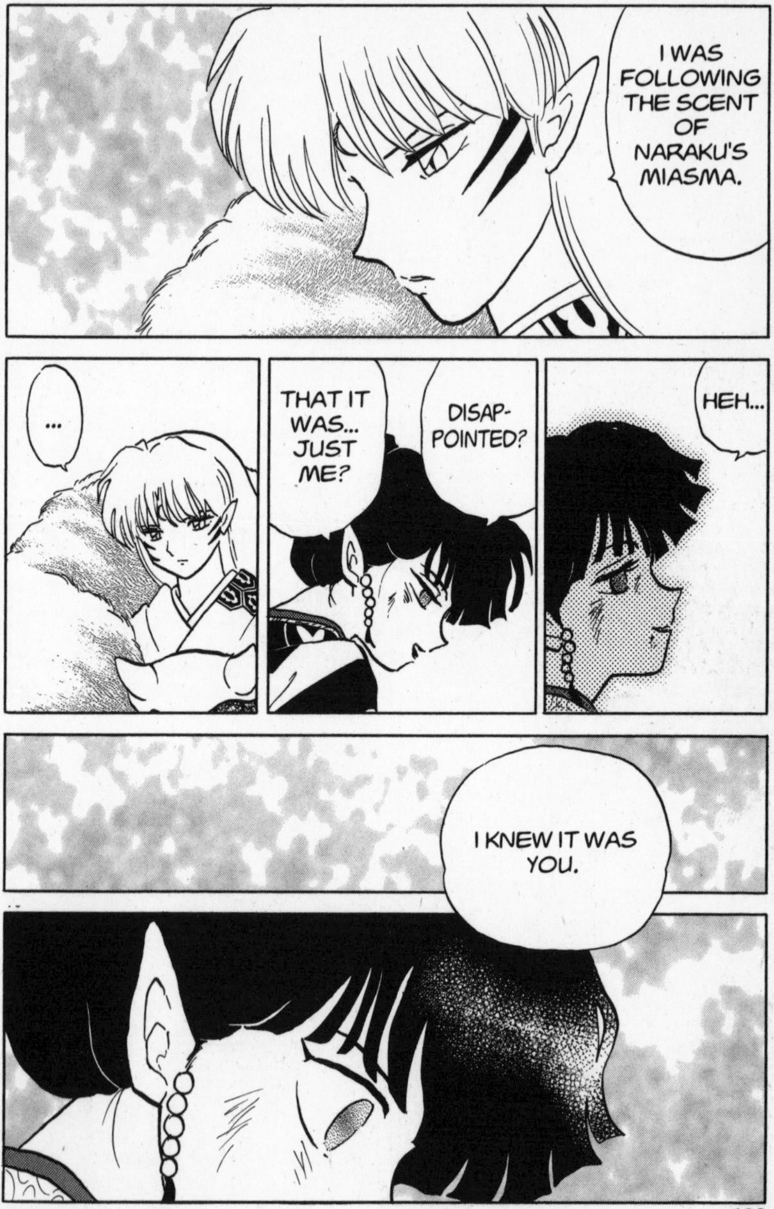
I WAS FOLLOWING THE SCENT OF NARAKU'S MIASMA.
HEH...
DISAP-POINTED?
THAT IT WAS... JUST ME?
...
I KNEW IT WAS YOU.

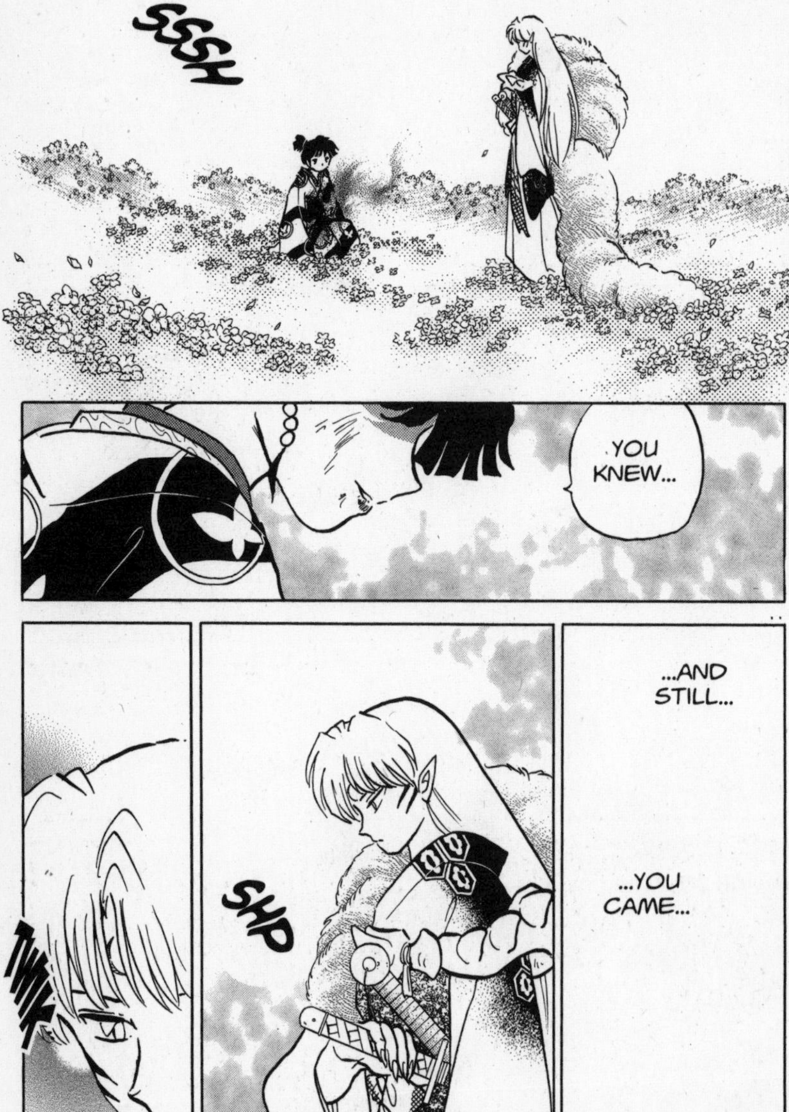
SSSH
YOU KNEW...
...AND STILL...
...YOU CAME...
SHP
TWIK

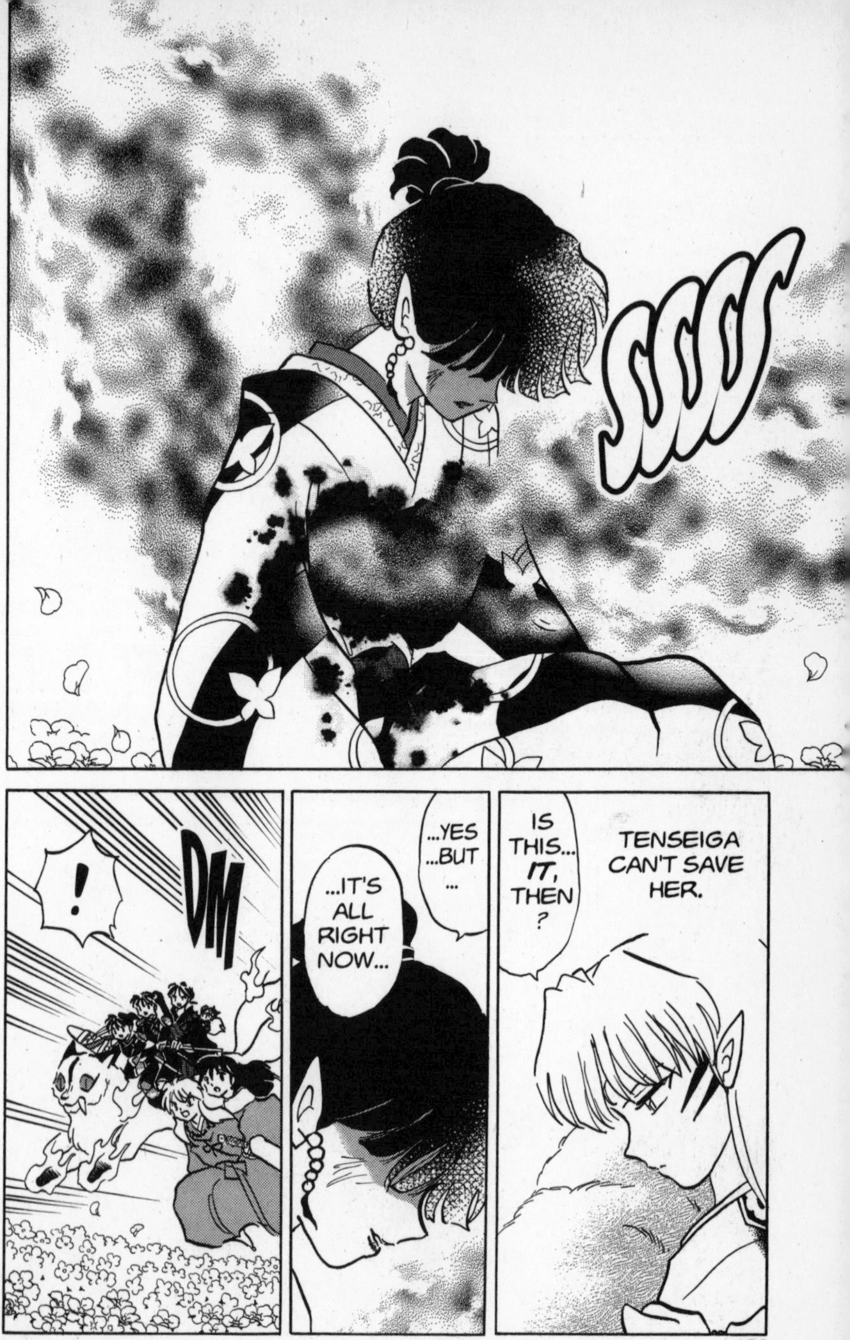
SSSS
TENSEIGA CAN'T SAVE HER.
IS THIS... *IT*, THEN?
...YES ...BUT ...
...IT'S ALL RIGHT NOW...
DM
!

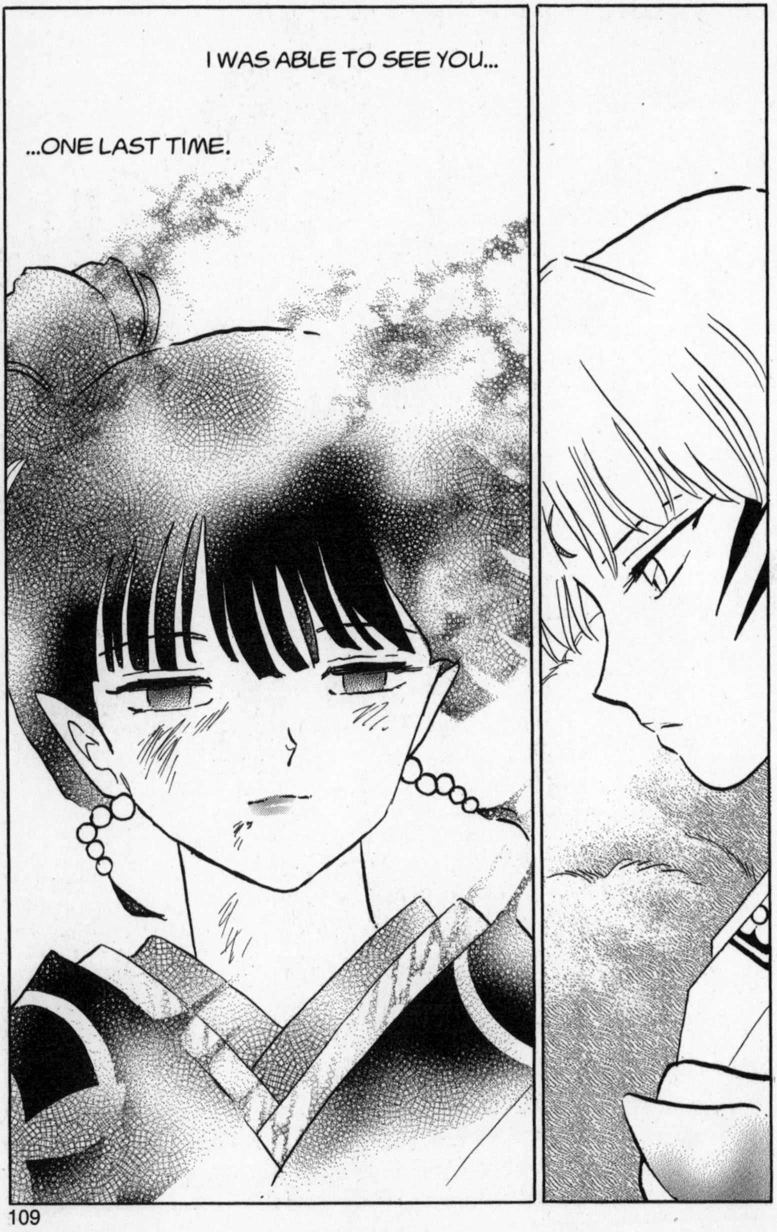
I WAS ABLE TO SEE YOU...
...ONE LAST TIME.

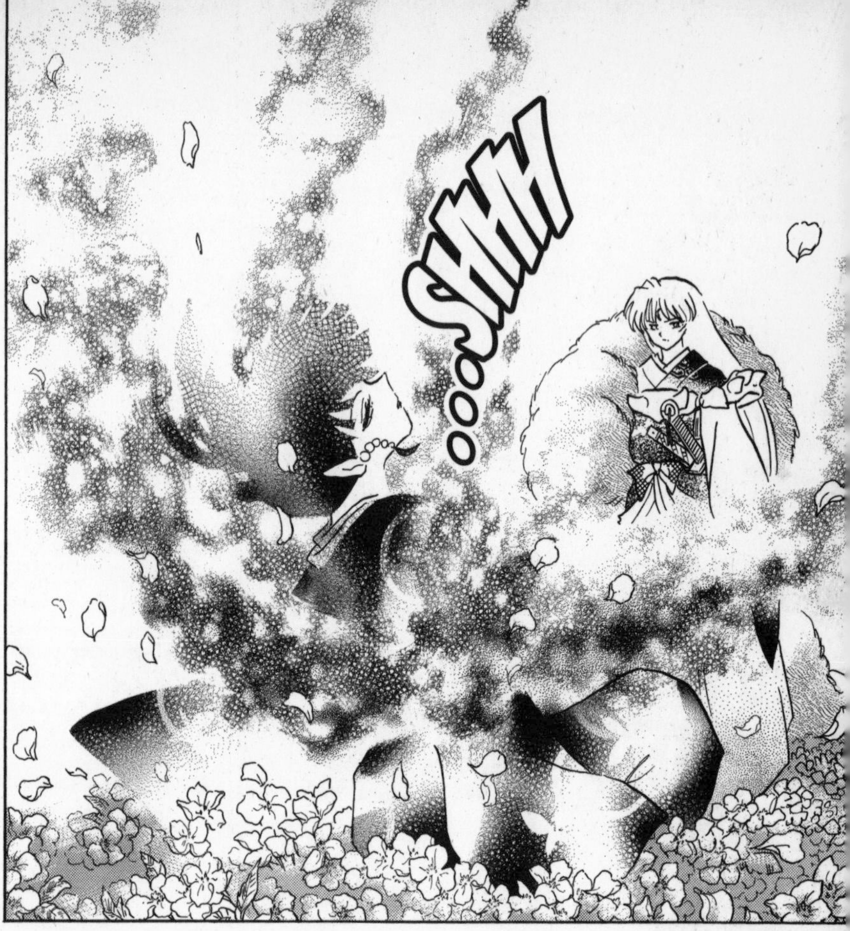
OOOSHHH

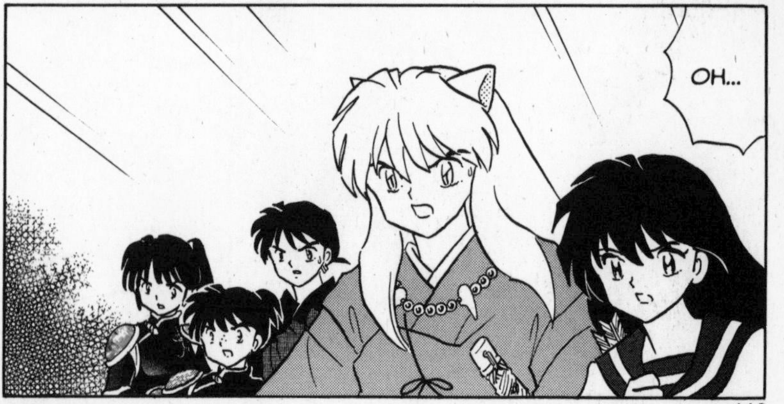
OH...

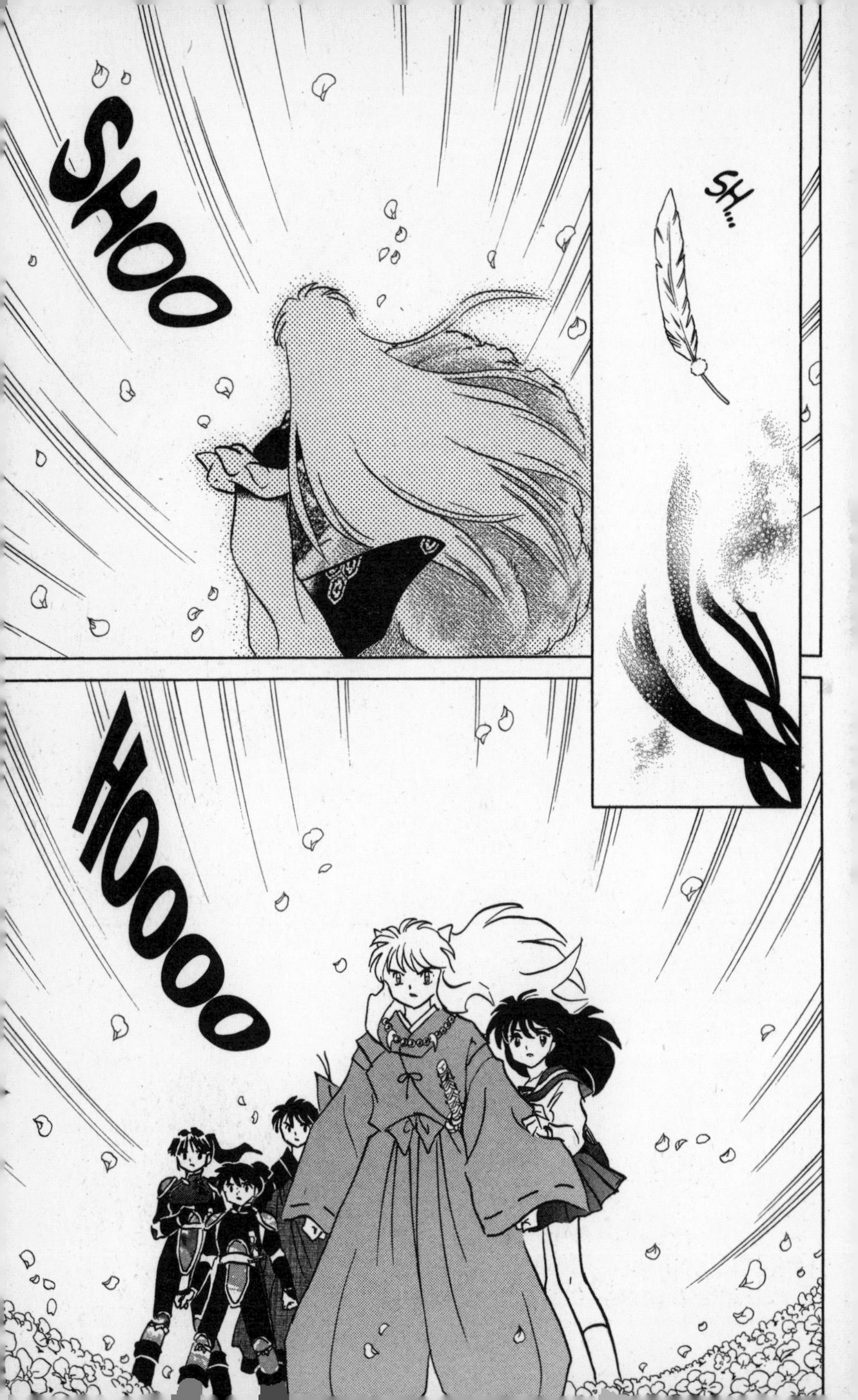
SH...
SHOOO
HOOOOO

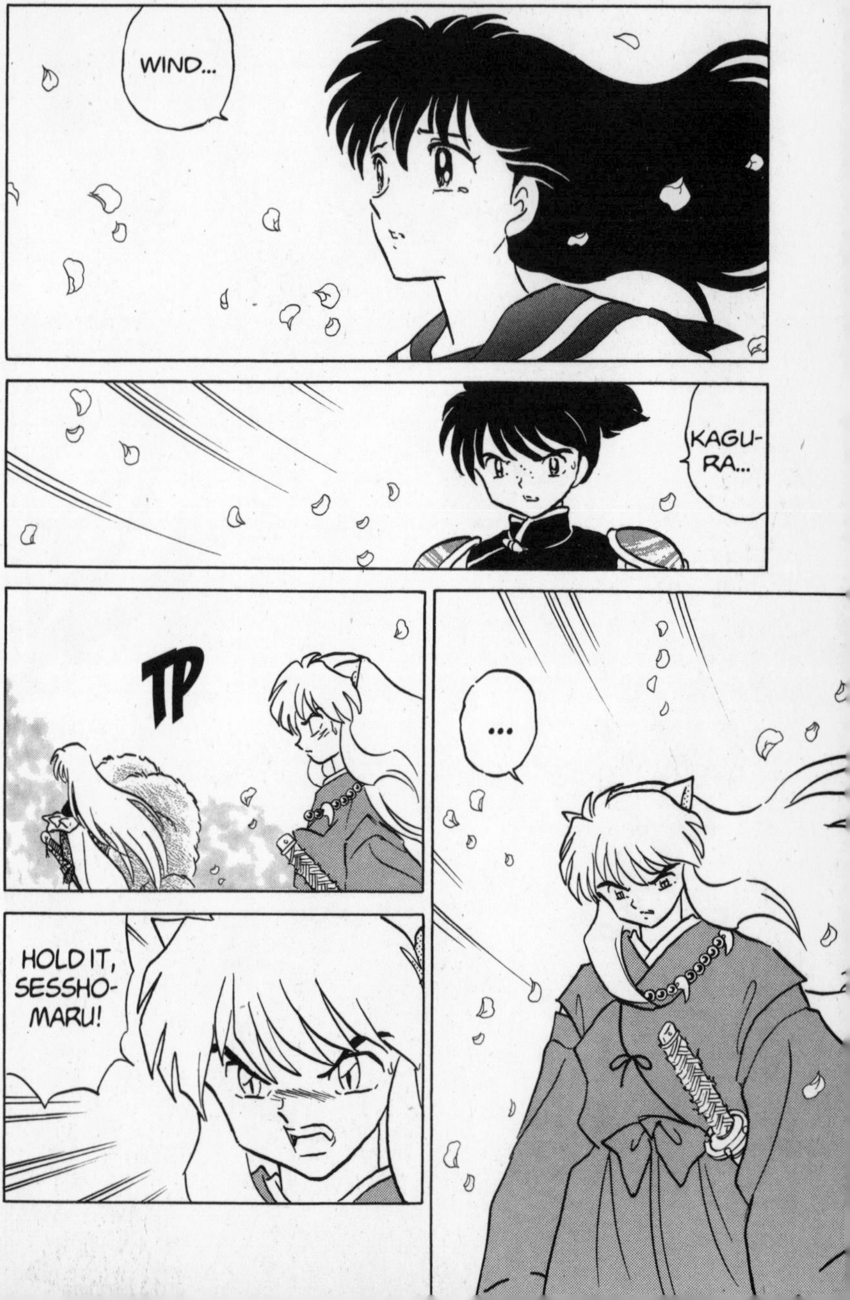
WIND...
KAGU-
RA...
...
TP
HOLD IT,
SESSHO-
MARU!

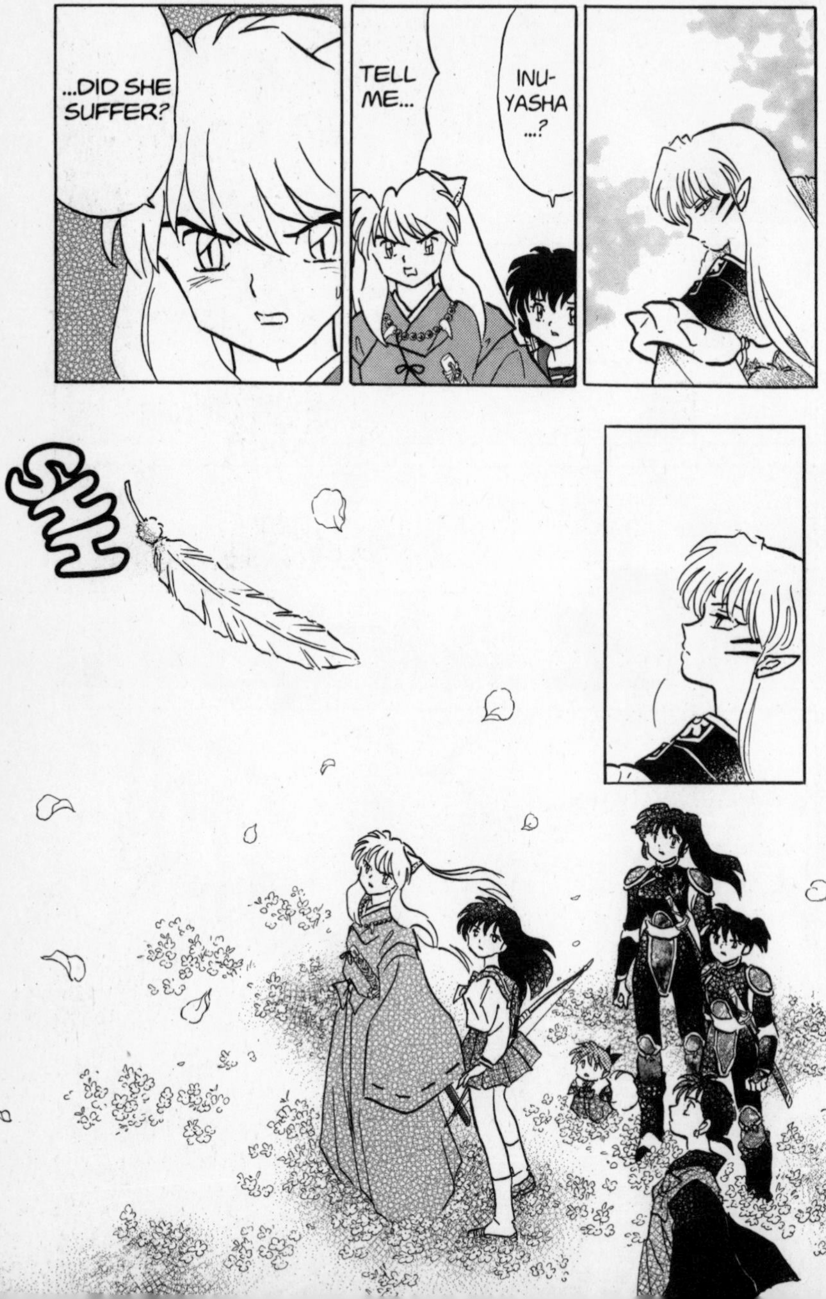
INU-YASHA ...?
TELL ME...
...DID SHE SUFFER?
SHH

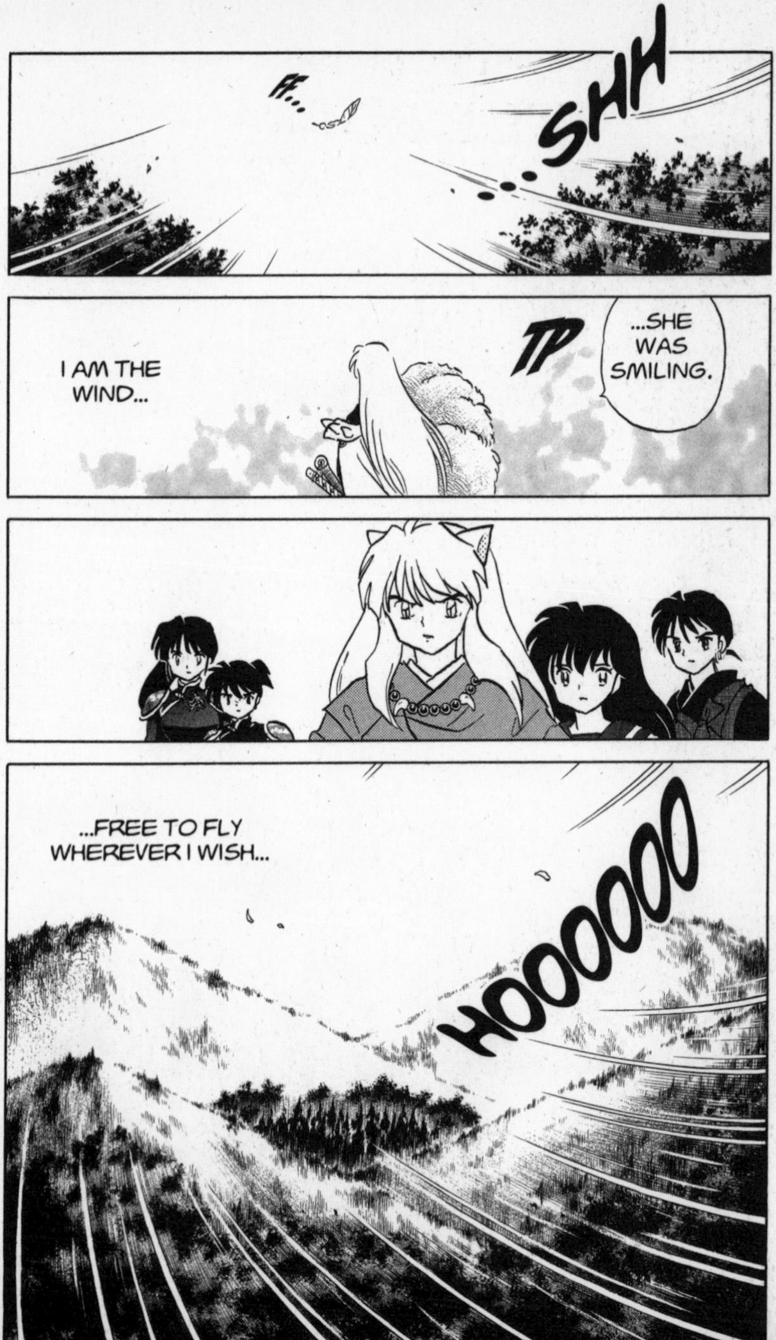
FF...
SHH
...SHE WAS SMILING.
TP
I AM THE WIND...
...FREE TO FLY WHEREVER I WISH...
HOOOOOO

SCROLL 7

THE HOLE IN HER CHEST

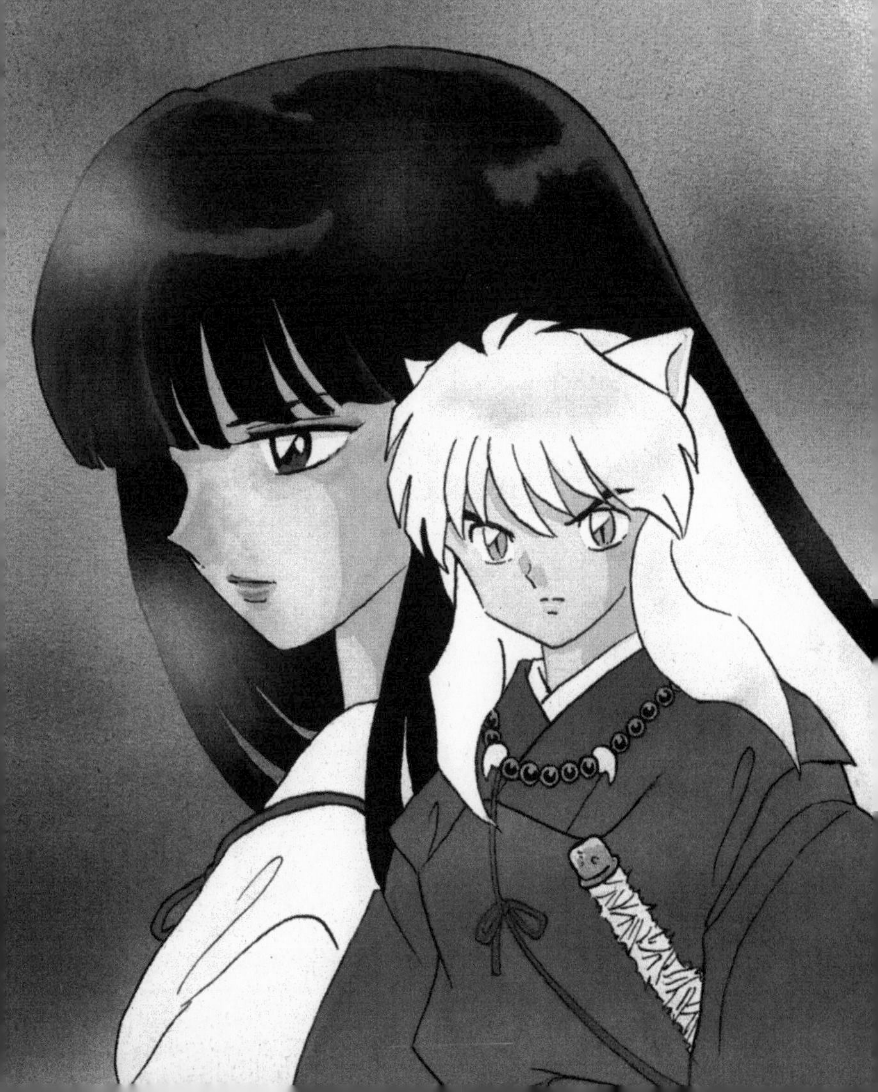

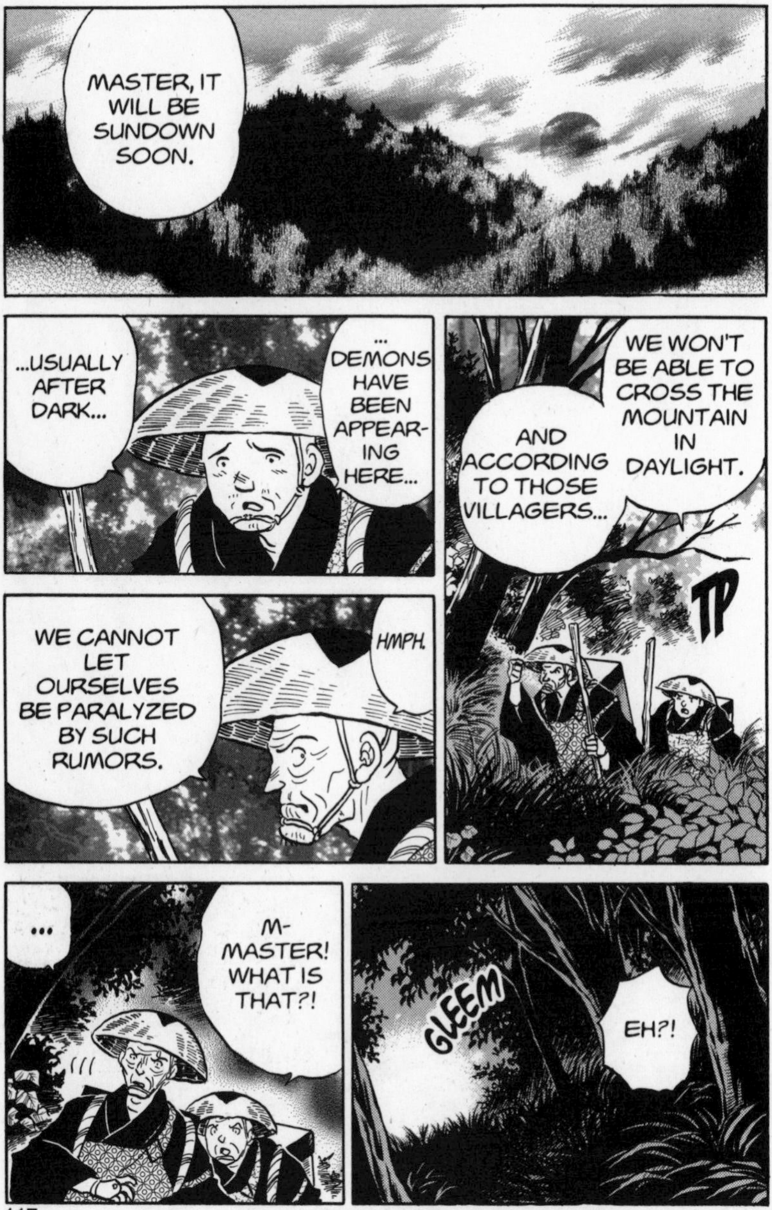
MASTER, IT WILL BE SUNDOWN SOON.
WE WON'T BE ABLE TO CROSS THE MOUNTAIN IN DAYLIGHT.
AND ACCORDING TO THOSE VILLAGERS...
TP
...DEMONS HAVE BEEN APPEARING HERE...
...USUALLY AFTER DARK...
HMPH.
WE CANNOT LET OURSELVES BE PARALYZED BY SUCH RUMORS.
GLEEM
EH?!
M-MASTER! WHAT IS THAT?!
...

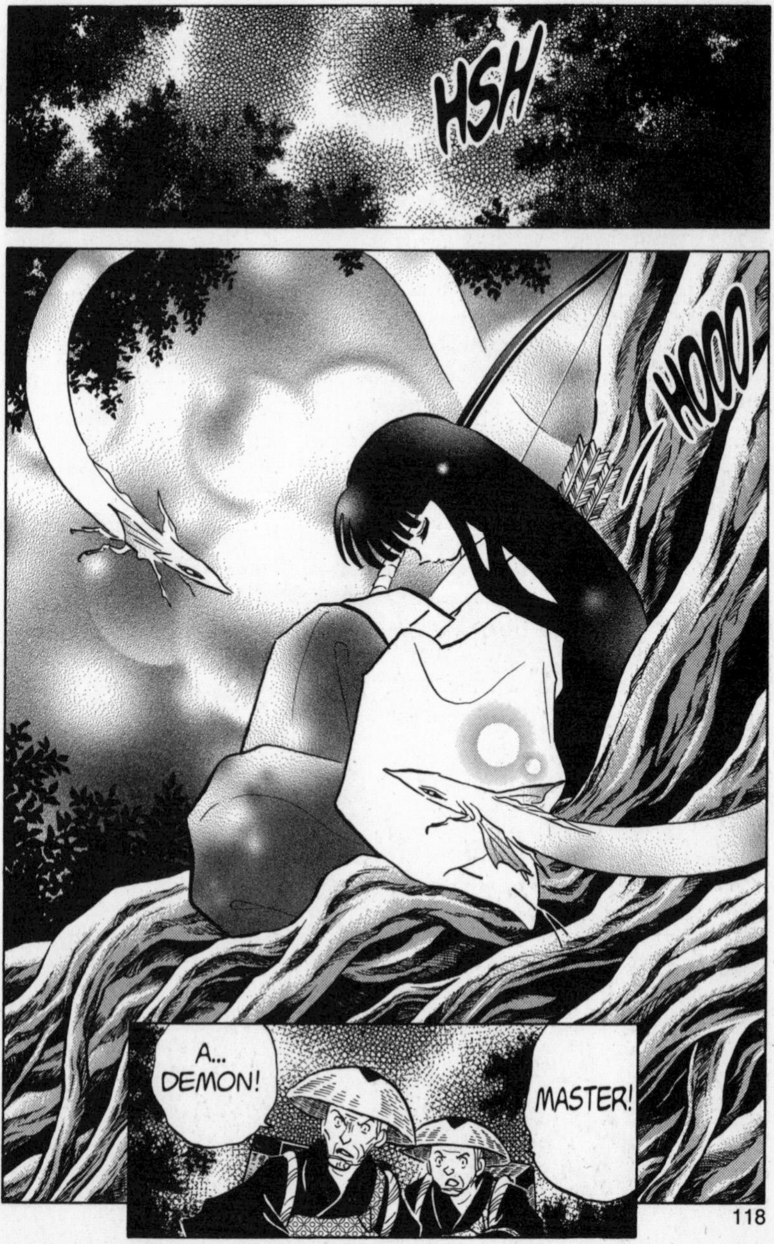
HSH
HOOO
MASTER!
A... DEMON!

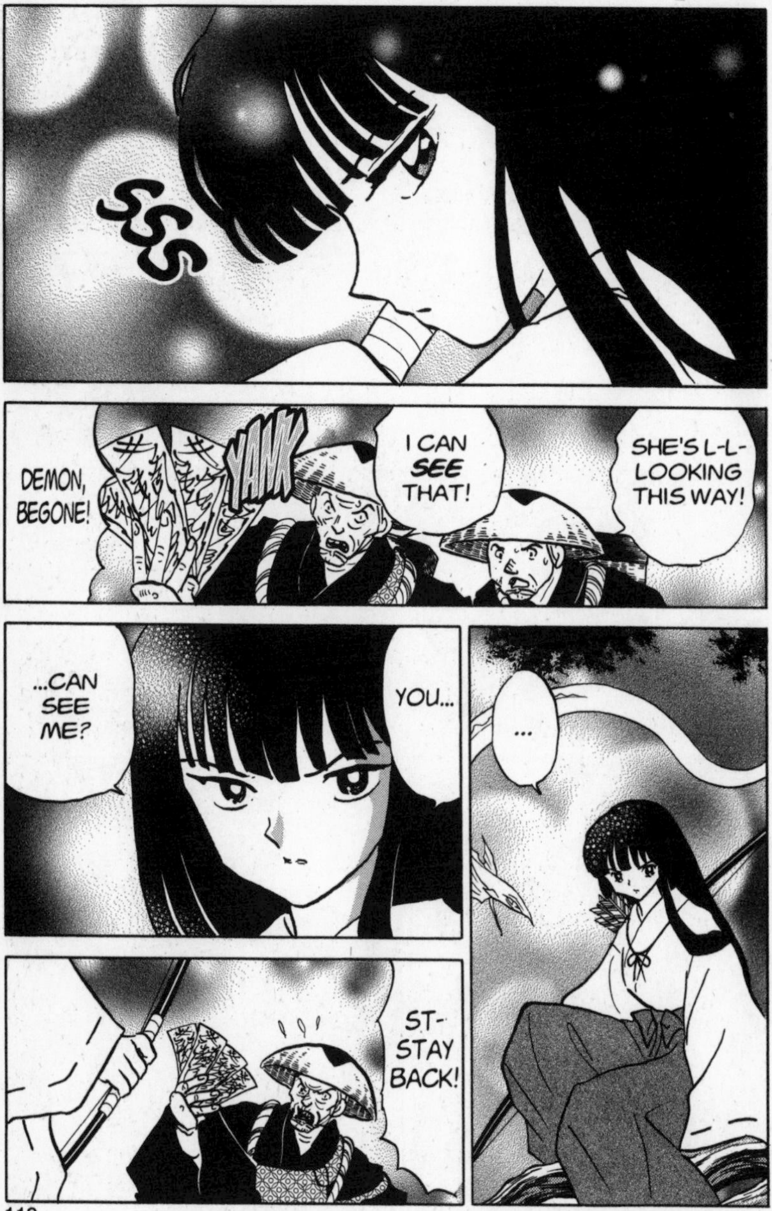
SSS
SHE'S L-L-LOOKING THIS WAY!
I CAN SEE THAT!
YANK
DEMON, BEGONE!
...
YOU...
...CAN SEE ME?
ST-STAY BACK!

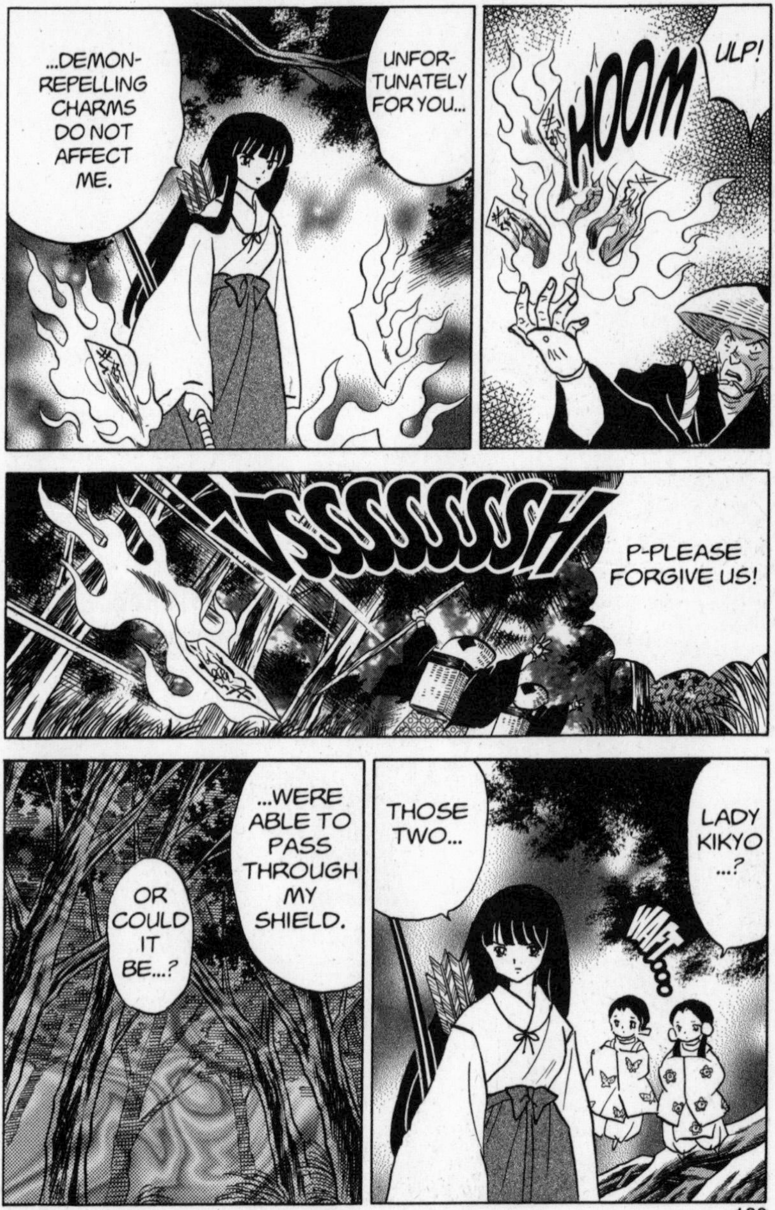
ULP!
HOOM
UNFORTUNATELY FOR YOU...
...DEMON-REPELLING CHARMS DO NOT AFFECT ME.
P-PLEASE FORGIVE US!
VSSSSSSH
LADY KIKYO ...?
WAFT
THOSE TWO...
...WERE ABLE TO PASS THROUGH MY SHIELD.
OR COULD IT BE...?

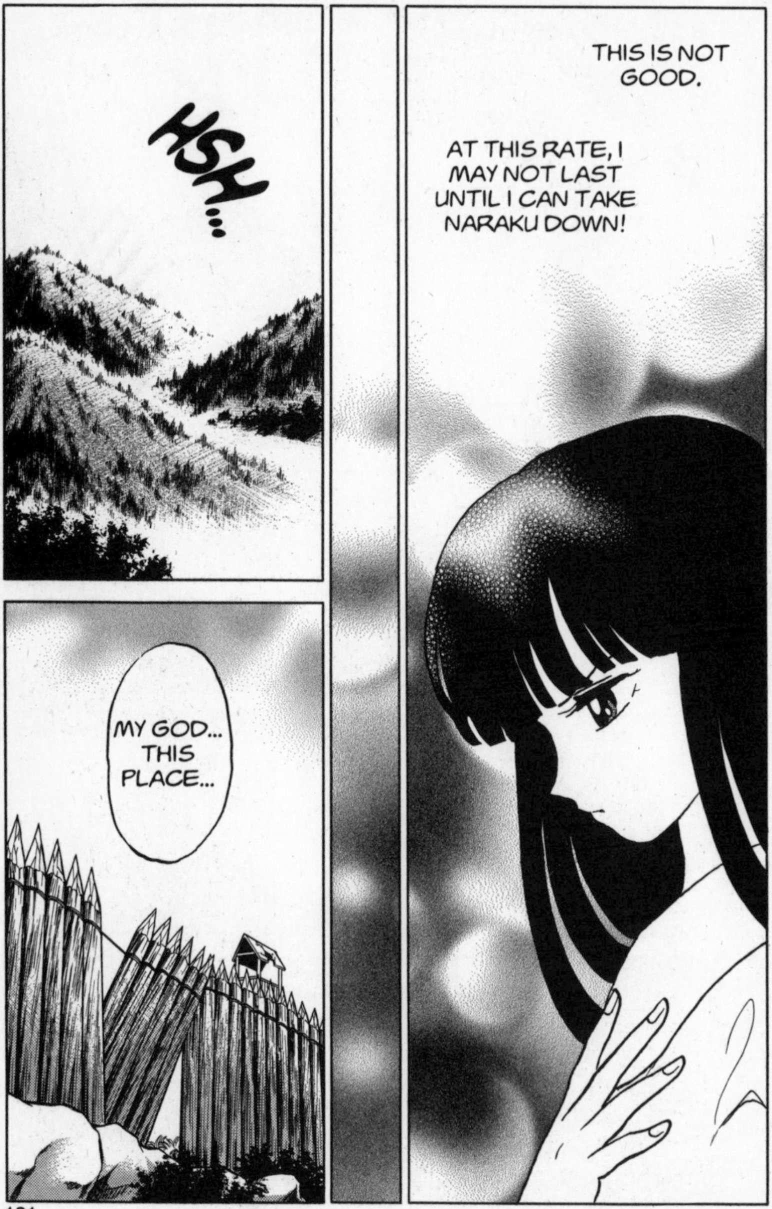
THIS IS NOT GOOD.
AT THIS RATE, I MAY NOT LAST UNTIL I CAN TAKE NARAKU DOWN!
HSH...
MY GOD... THIS PLACE...

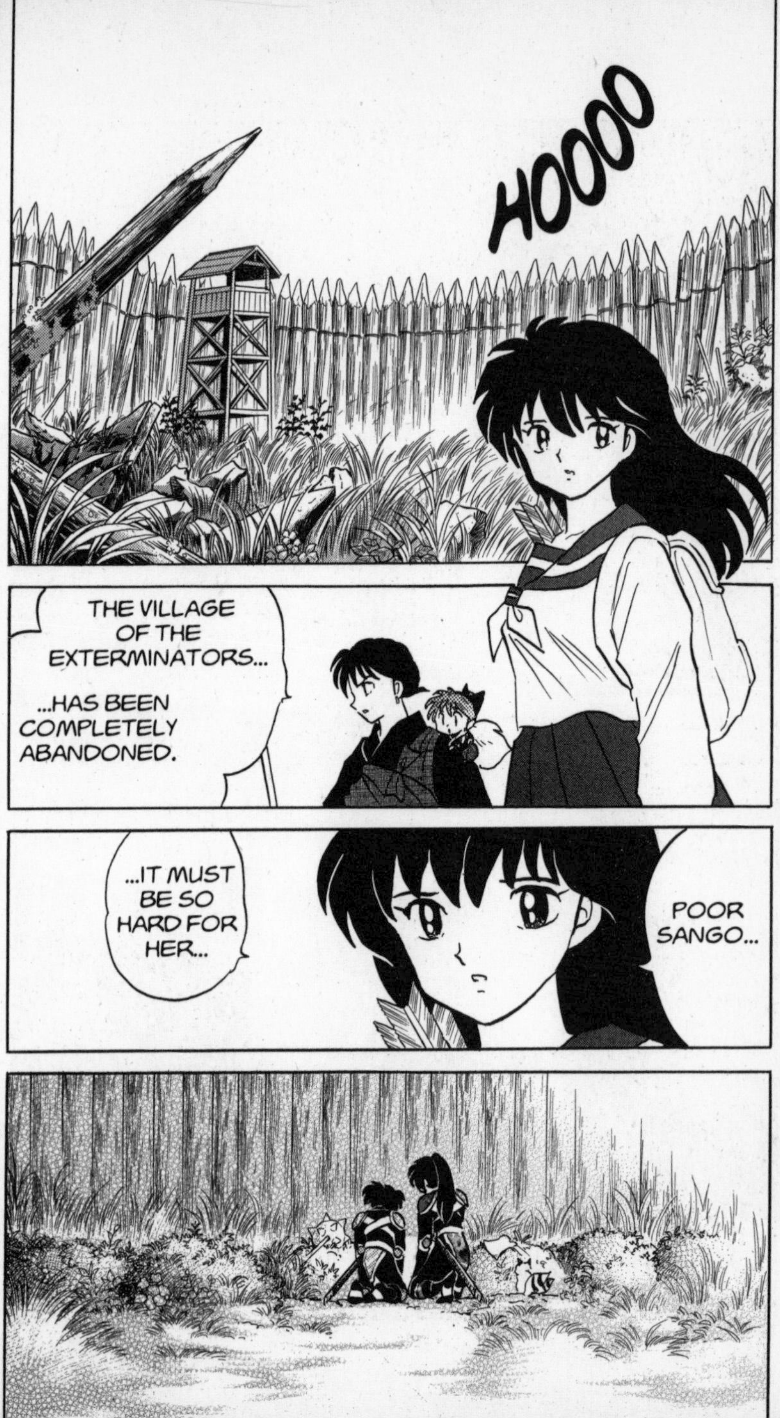
HOOOO
THE VILLAGE OF THE EXTERMINATORS...
...HAS BEEN COMPLETELY ABANDONED.
POOR SANGO...
...IT MUST BE SO HARD FOR HER...

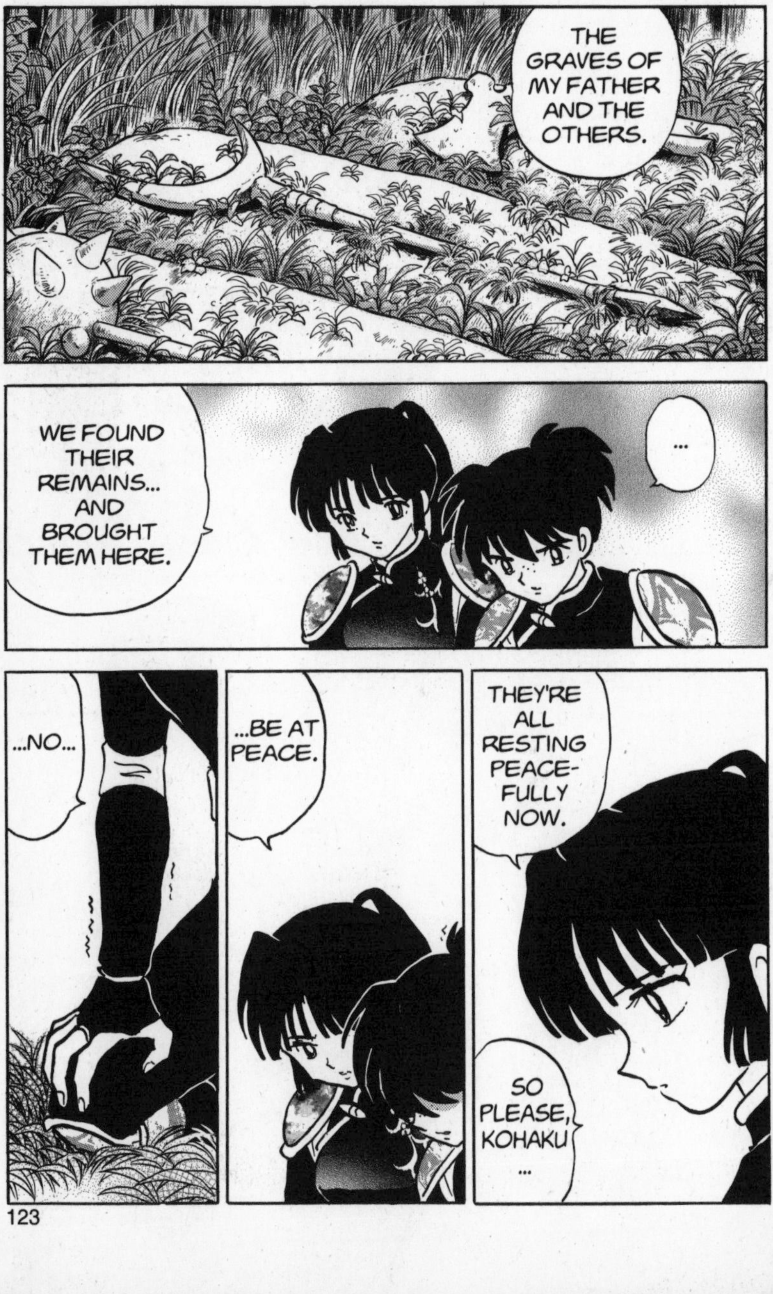
THE GRAVES OF MY FATHER AND THE OTHERS.
...
WE FOUND THEIR REMAINS... AND BROUGHT THEM HERE.
THEY'RE ALL RESTING PEACE-FULLY NOW.
SO PLEASE, KOHAKU ...
...BE AT PEACE.
...NO...

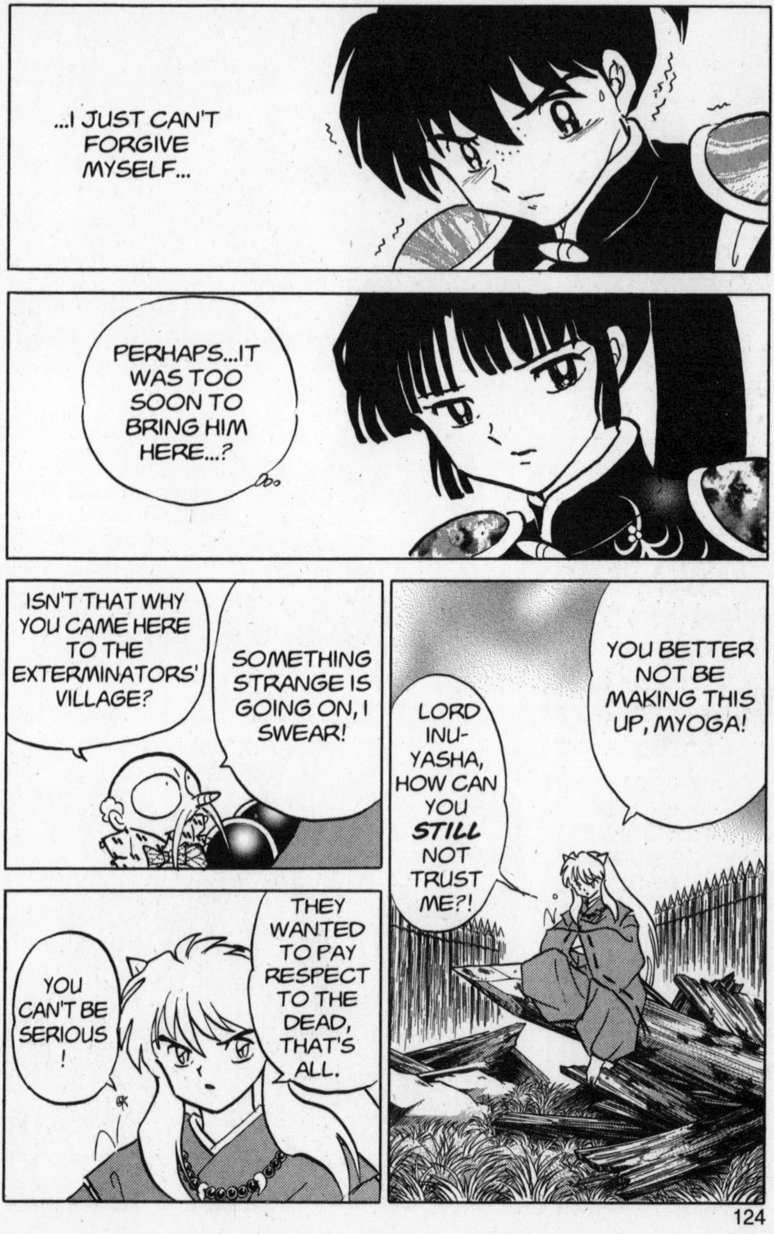
...I JUST CAN'T FORGIVE MYSELF...
PERHAPS...IT WAS TOO SOON TO BRING HIM HERE...?
YOU BETTER NOT BE MAKING THIS UP, MYOGA!
LORD INU-YASHA, HOW CAN YOU **STILL** NOT TRUST ME?!
SOMETHING STRANGE IS GOING ON, I SWEAR!
ISN'T THAT WHY YOU CAME HERE TO THE EXTERMINATORS' VILLAGE?
THEY WANTED TO PAY RESPECT TO THE DEAD, THAT'S ALL.
YOU CAN'T BE SERIOUS!

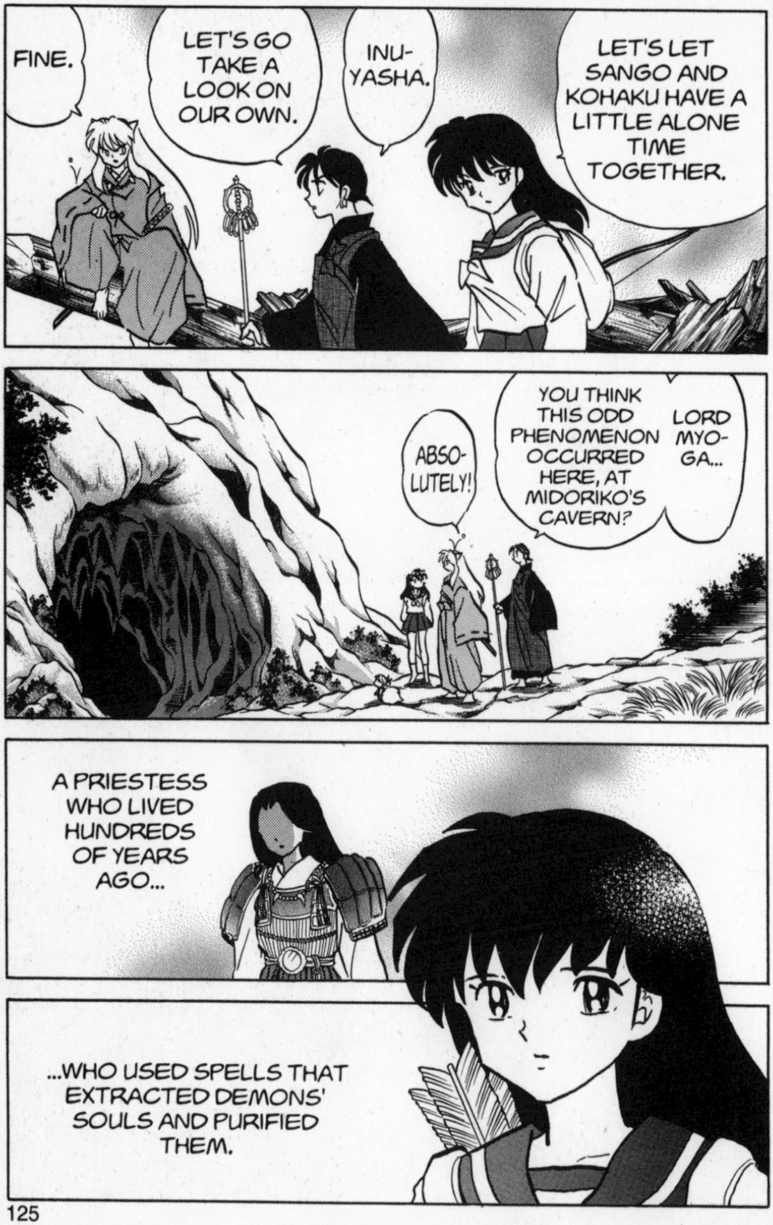
LET'S LET SANGO AND KOHAKU HAVE A LITTLE ALONE TIME TOGETHER.
INU-YASHA.
LET'S GO TAKE A LOOK ON OUR OWN.
FINE.
LORD MYO-GA...
YOU THINK THIS ODD PHENOMENON OCCURRED HERE, AT MIDORIKO'S CAVERN?
ABSO-LUTELY!
A PRIESTESS WHO LIVED HUNDREDS OF YEARS AGO...
...WHO USED SPELLS THAT EXTRACTED DEMONS' SOULS AND PURIFIED THEM.

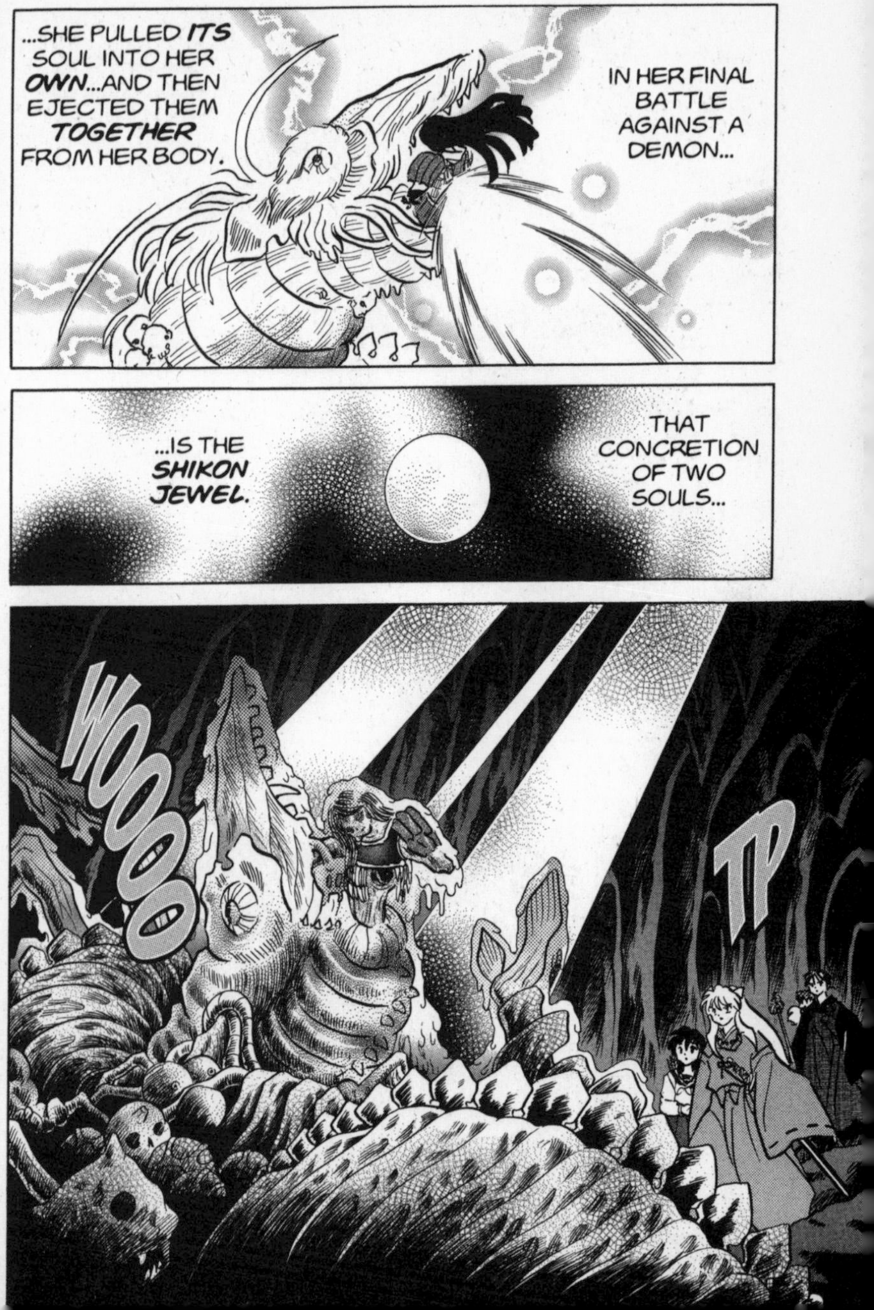
IN HER FINAL BATTLE AGAINST A DEMON...
...SHE PULLED ITS SOUL INTO HER OWN...AND THEN EJECTED THEM TOGETHER FROM HER BODY.
THAT CONCRETION OF TWO SOULS...
...IS THE SHIKON JEWEL.
TP
WOOOOO

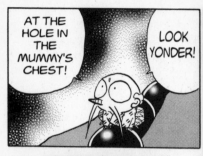

AT THE HOLE IN THE MUMMY'S CHEST!

LOOK YONDER!

IT'S GLOW- ING...?

...

GLEEM

SHHH

!

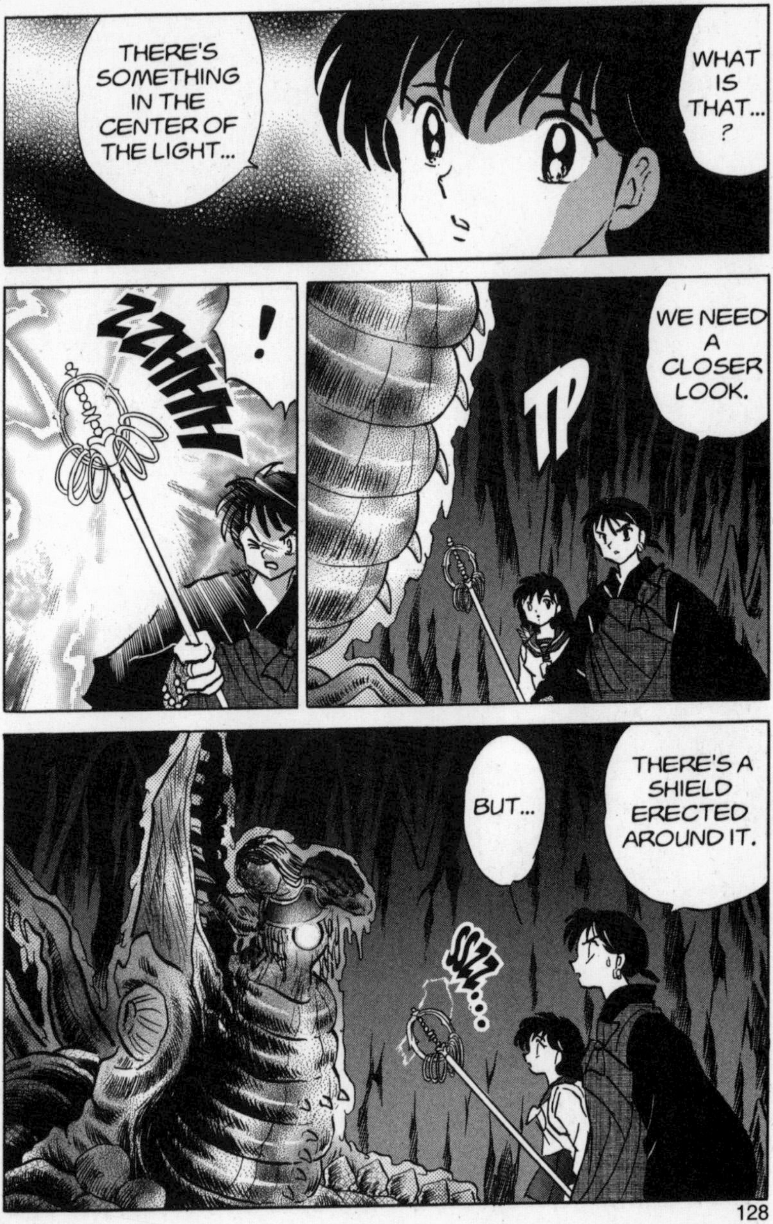
WHAT IS THAT...?
THERE'S SOMETHING IN THE CENTER OF THE LIGHT...
WE NEED A CLOSER LOOK.
TP
ZZHHHH
!
THERE'S A SHIELD ERECTED AROUND IT.
BUT...
SSZZ...

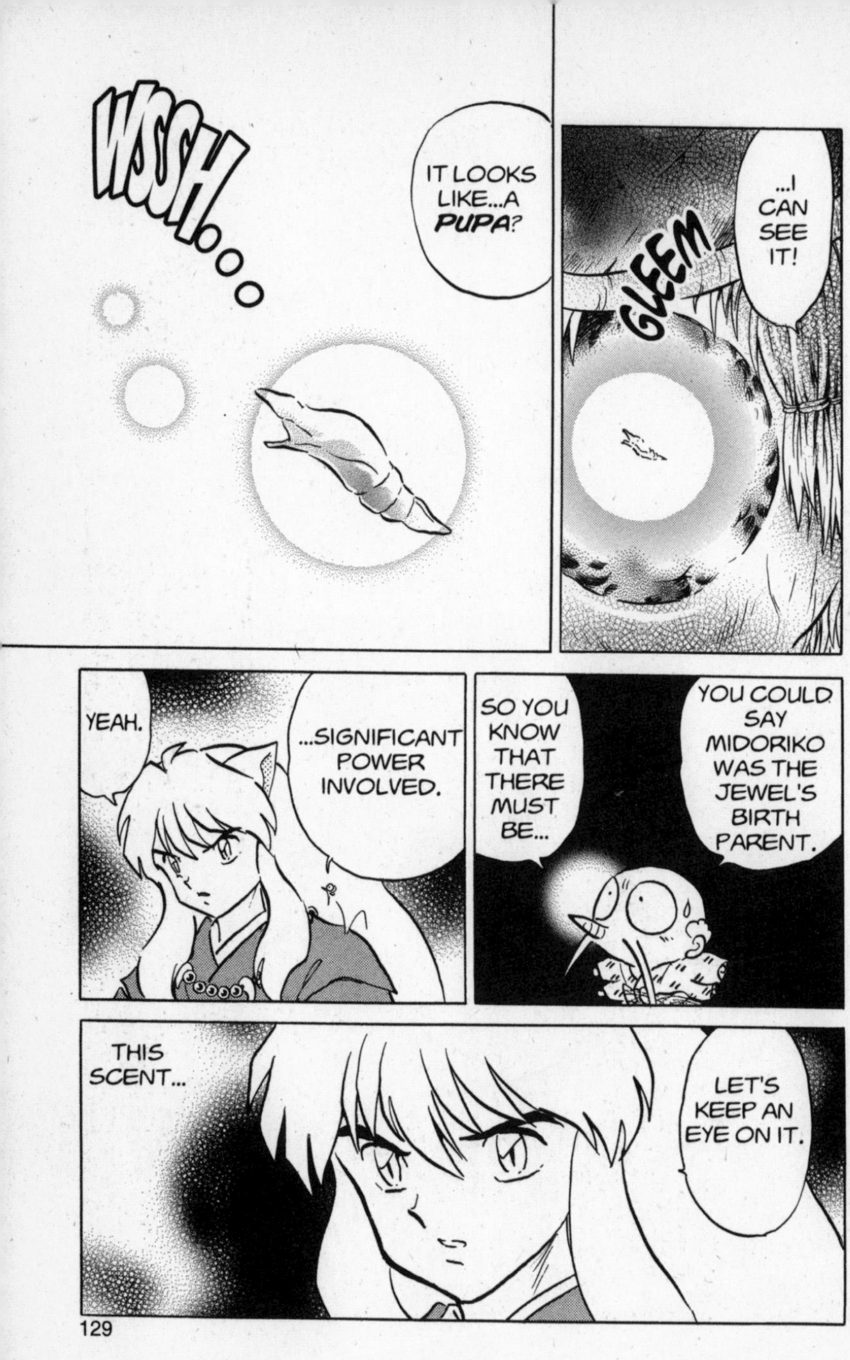
...I CAN SEE IT!
GLEEM
IT LOOKS LIKE...A *PUPA*?
WSSH
YOU COULD SAY MIDORIKO WAS THE JEWEL'S BIRTH PARENT.
SO YOU KNOW THAT THERE MUST BE...
...SIGNIFICANT POWER INVOLVED.
YEAH.
LET'S KEEP AN EYE ON IT.
THIS SCENT...

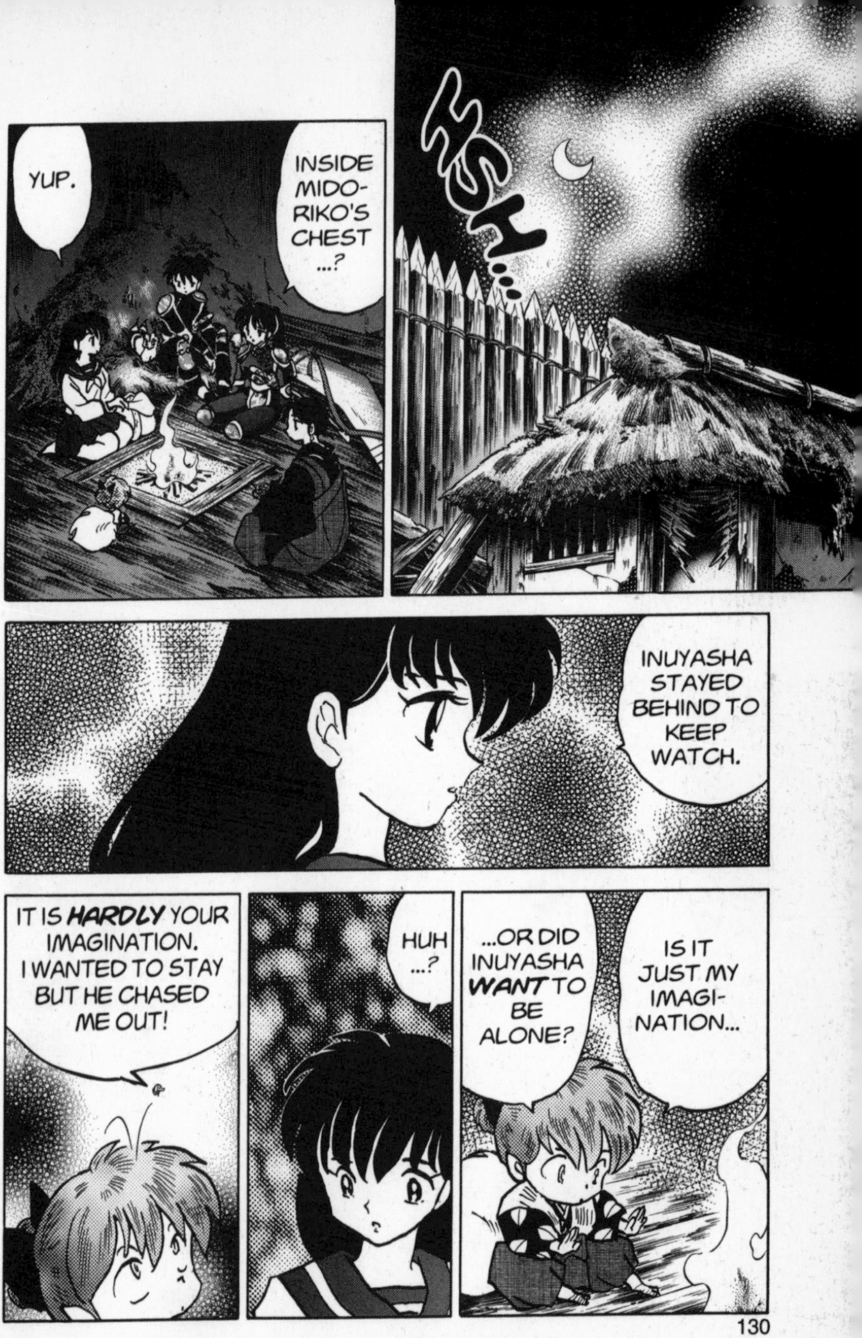
HSH...
INSIDE MIDO-RIKO'S CHEST ...?
YUP.
INUYASHA STAYED BEHIND TO KEEP WATCH.
IS IT JUST MY IMAGI-NATION...
...OR DID INUYASHA ***WANT*** TO BE ALONE?
HUH ...?
IT IS ***HARDLY*** YOUR IMAGINATION. I WANTED TO STAY BUT HE CHASED ME OUT!

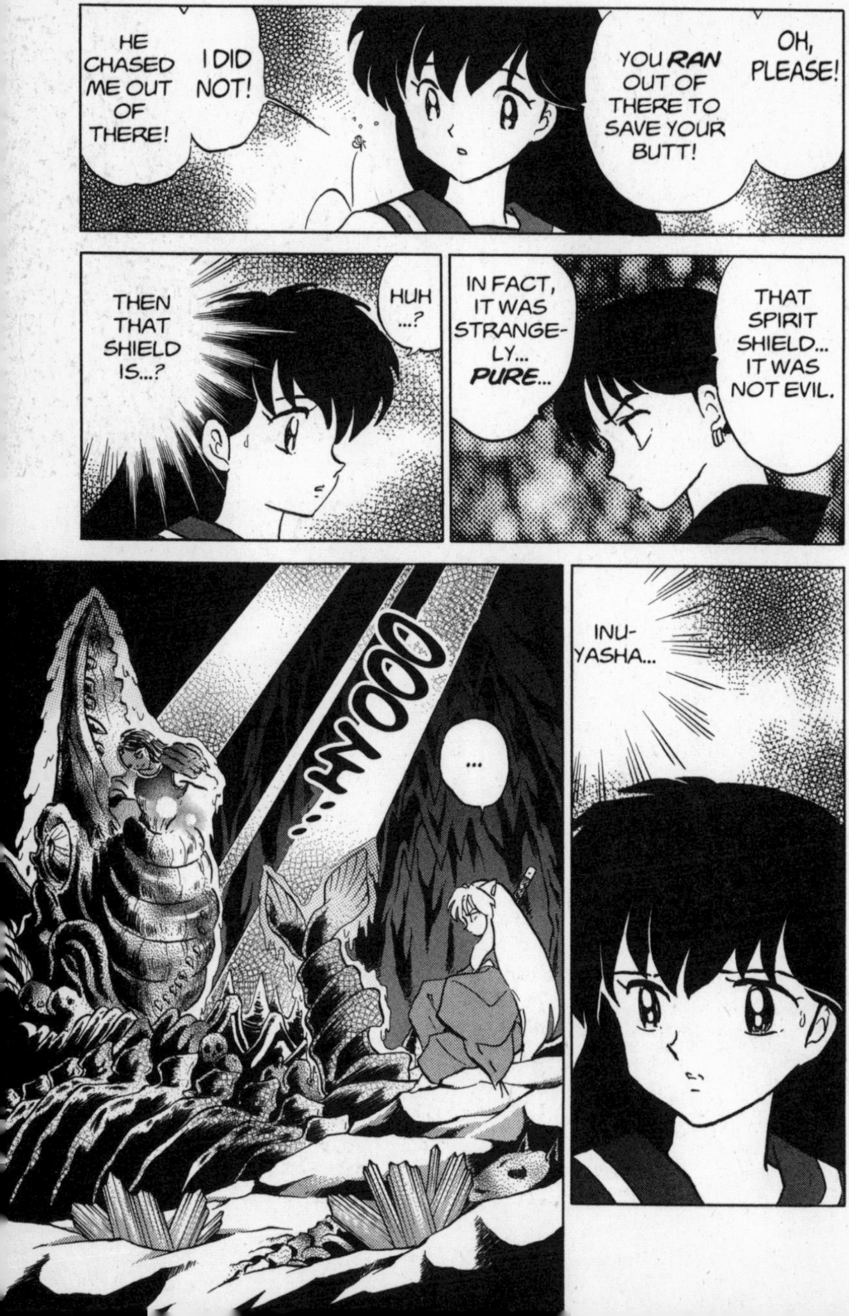
OH, PLEASE!
YOU *RAN* OUT OF THERE TO SAVE YOUR BUTT!
I DID NOT!
HE CHASED ME OUT OF THERE!
THAT SPIRIT SHIELD... IT WAS NOT EVIL.
IN FACT, IT WAS STRANGE-LY... *PURE*...
HUH ...?
THEN THAT SHIELD IS...?
INU-YASHA...
...
OOOOH...

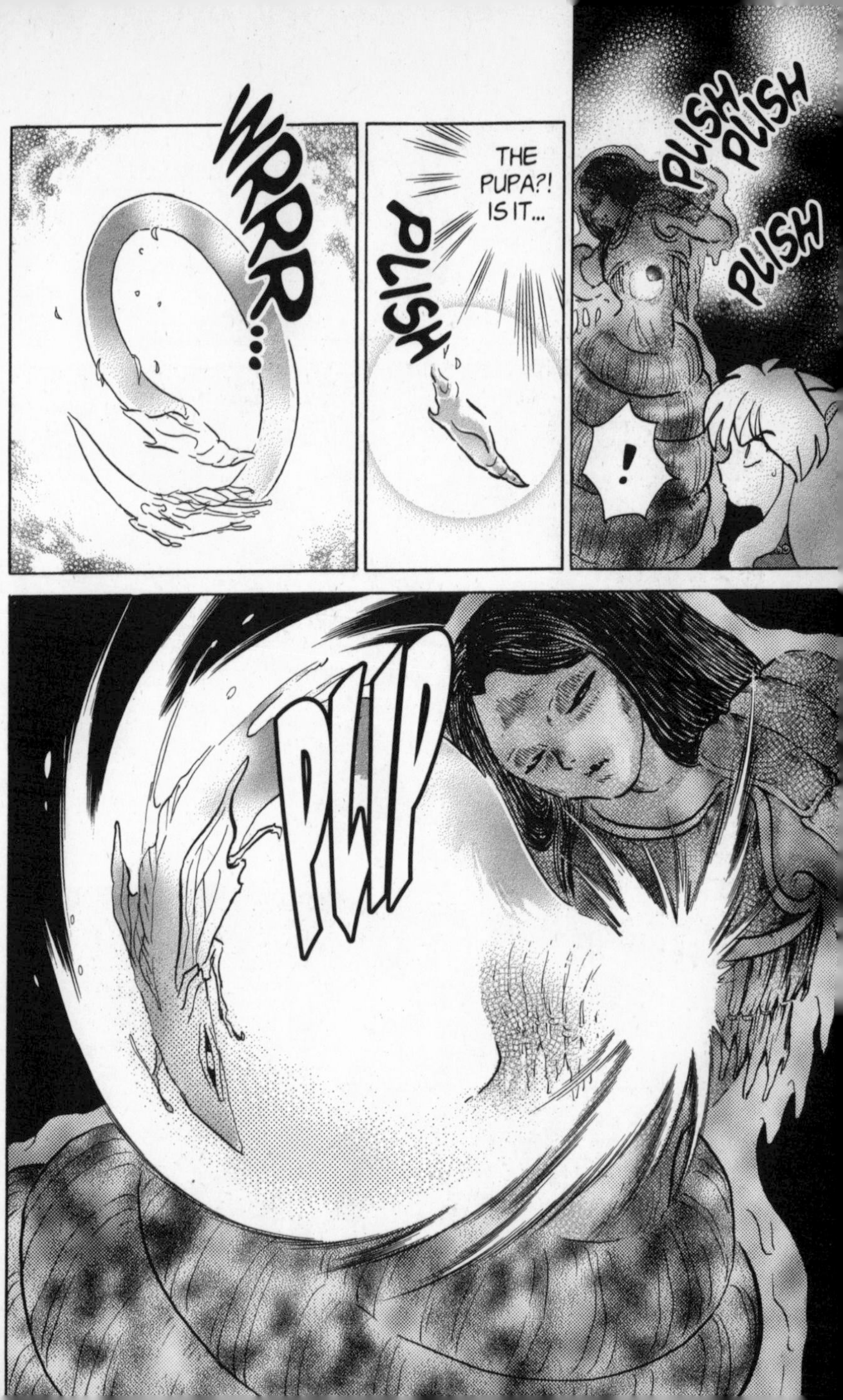
PLISH PLISH
PLISH
!
THE PUPA?! IS IT...
PLISH
WRRR...
PWIP

KIKYO'S SOUL COLLECTOR!

!

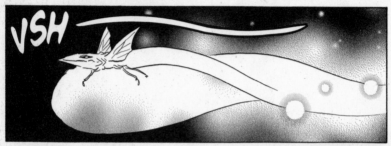

VSH

I WAS RIGHT! IT **WAS** KIKYO!

WSH

WHAT ARE YOU PLANNING?!

VZ ZZ

KIKYO--

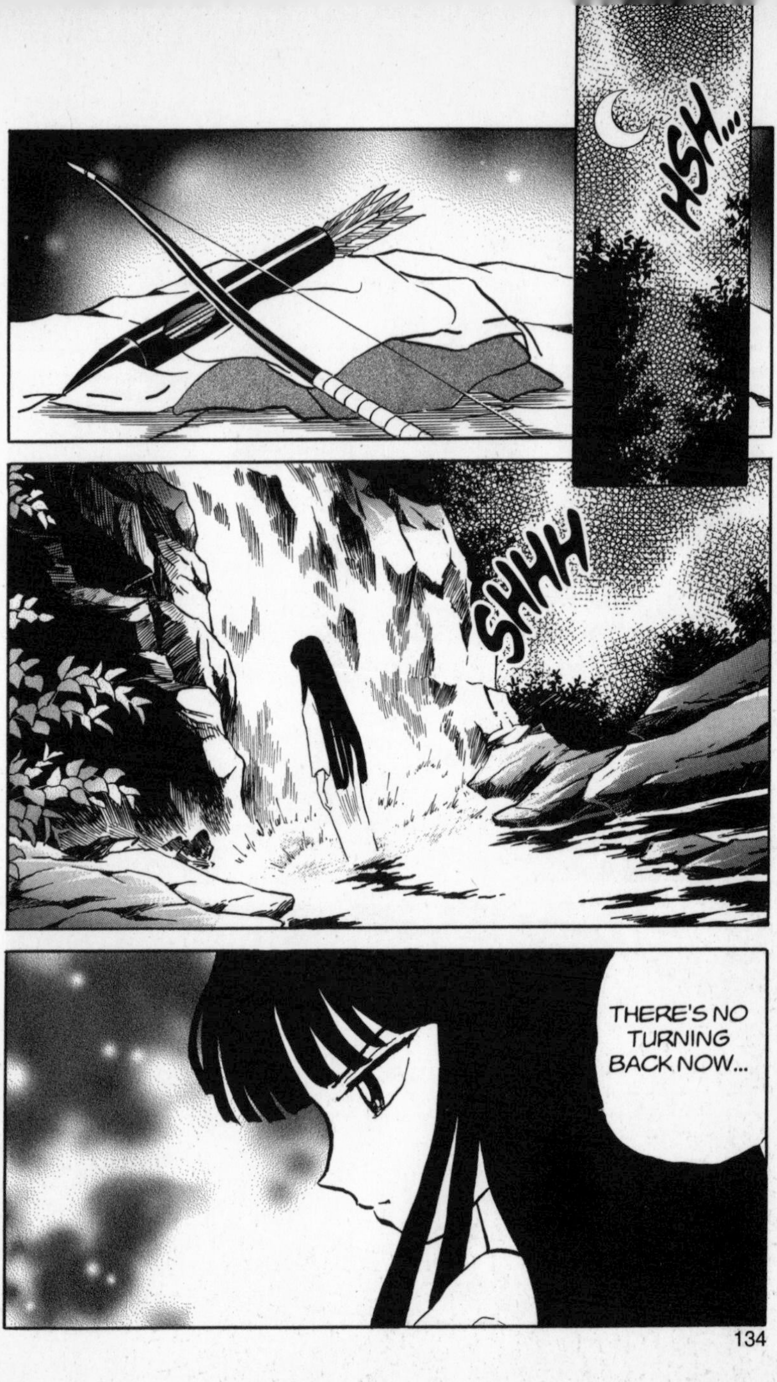
HSH...
SHHH
THERE'S NO TURNING BACK NOW...

SCROLL 8
THE SAME SOUL

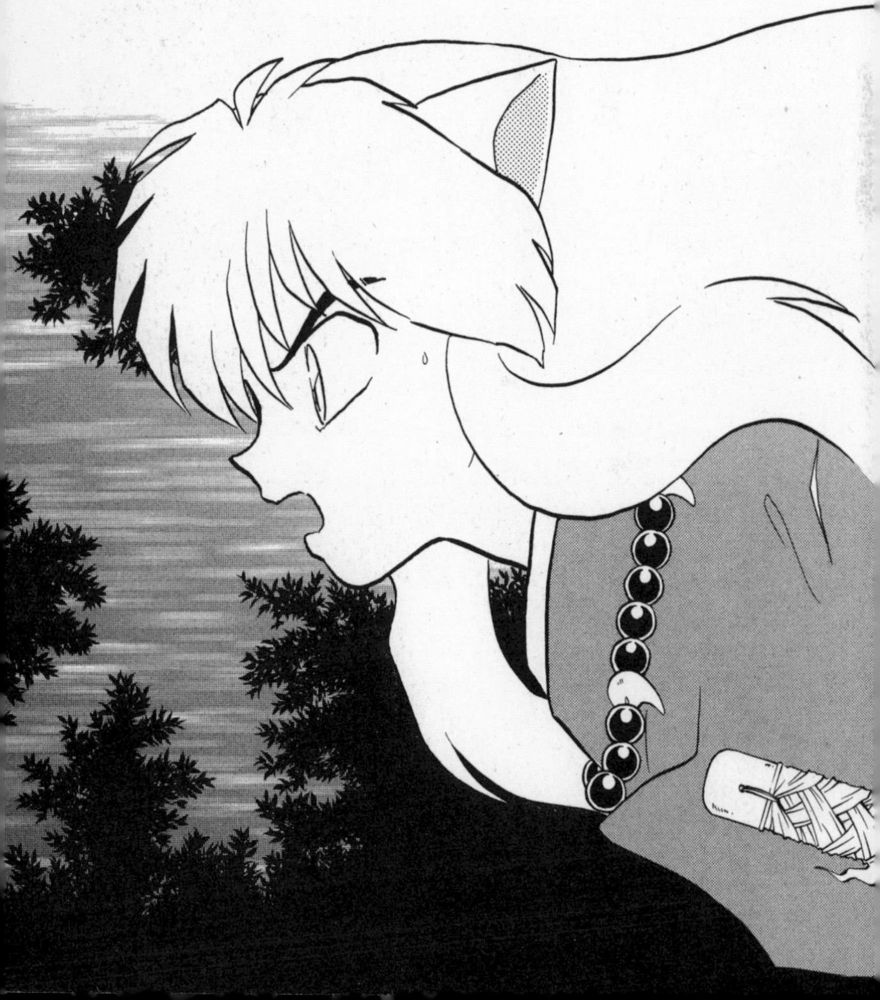

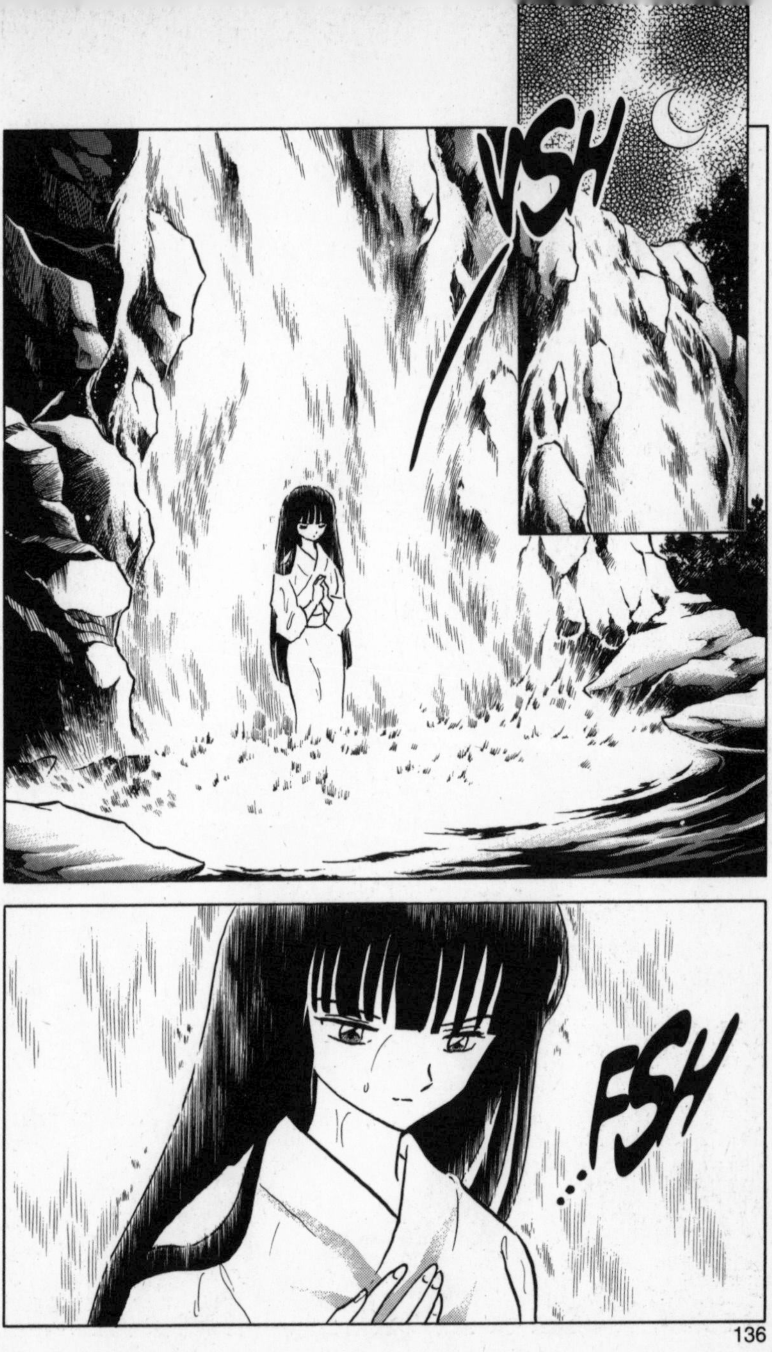
VSH
...FSH

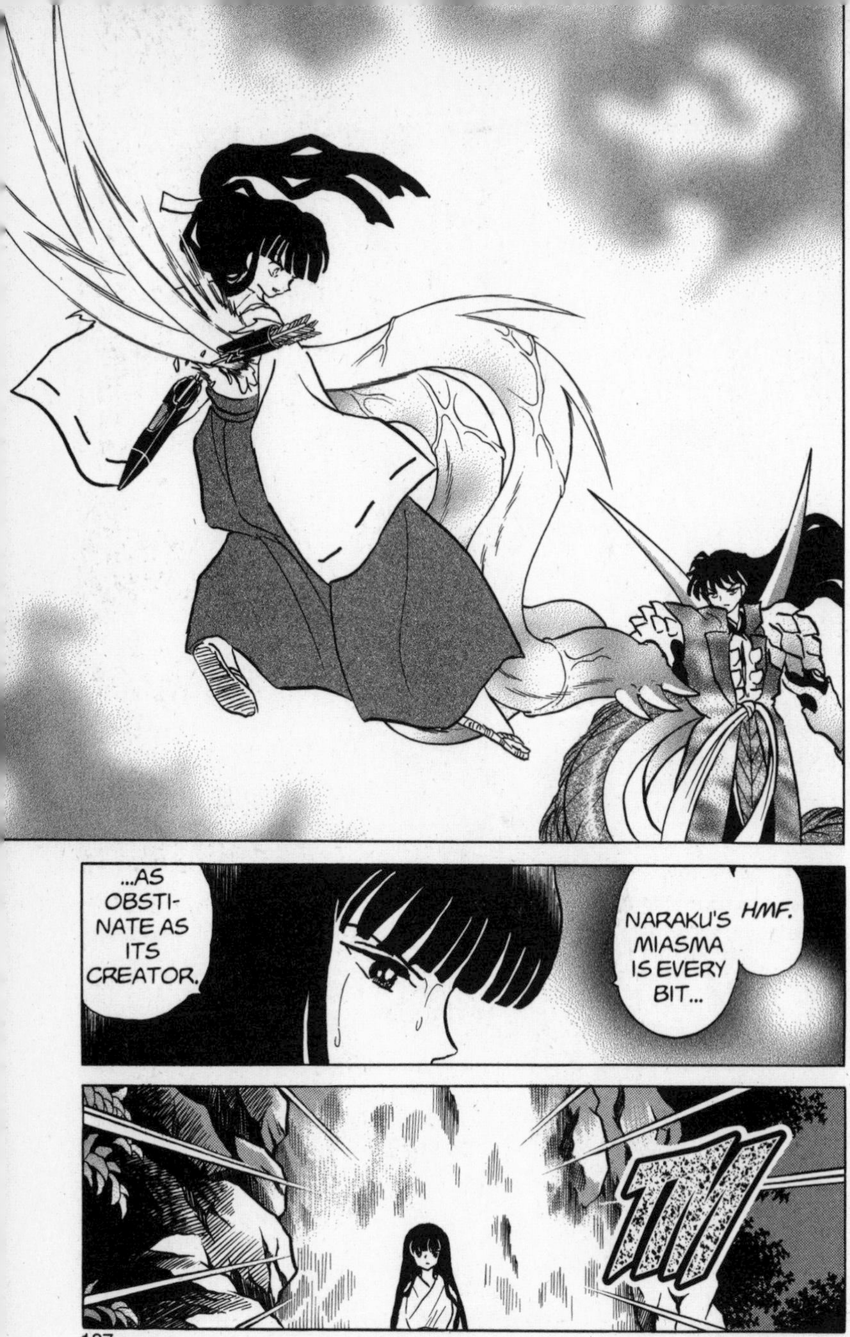
HMF.
NARAKU'S MIASMA IS EVERY BIT...
...AS OBSTINATE AS ITS CREATOR.

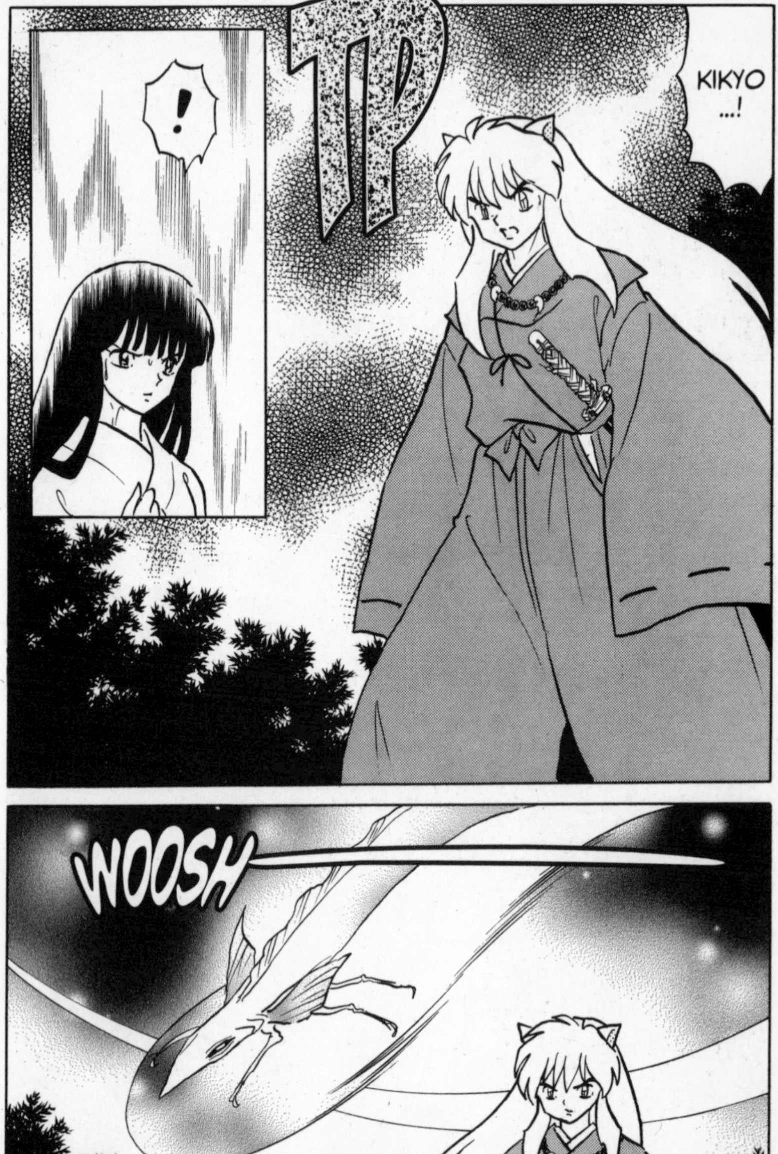
KIKYO ...!
TP
!
WOOSH

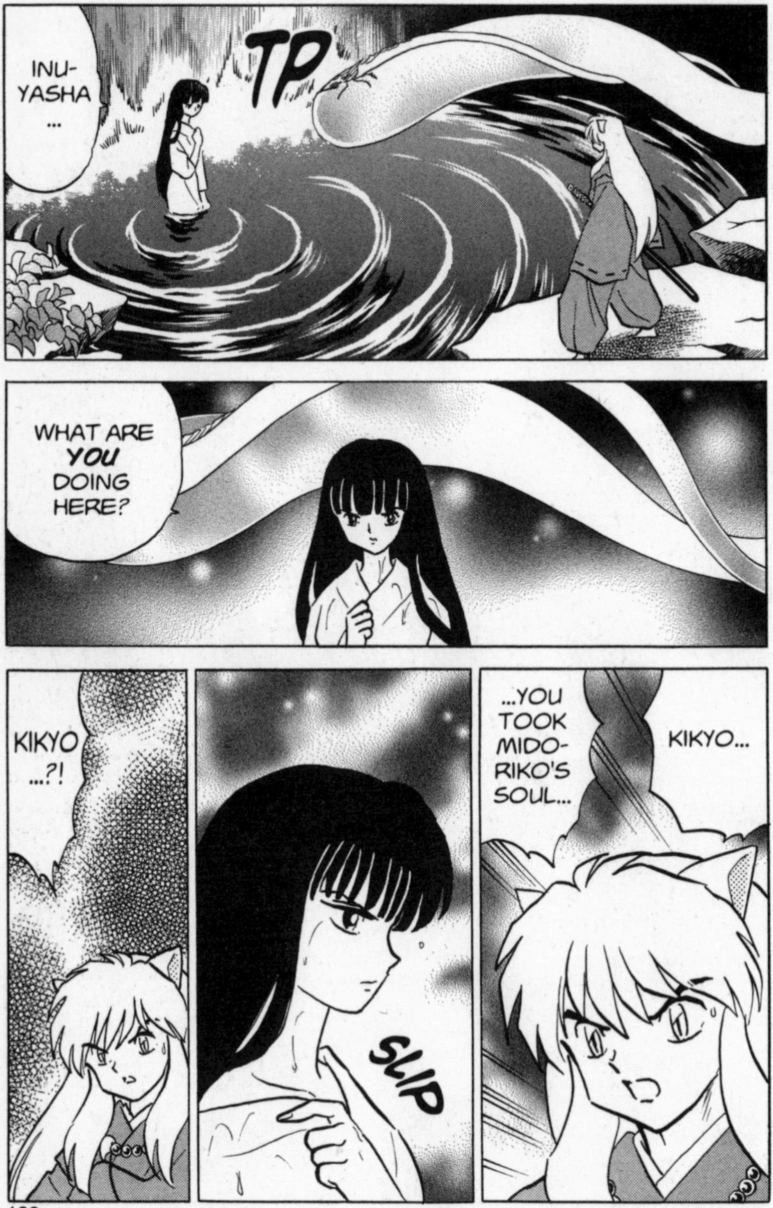
TP
INU-YASHA ...
WHAT ARE YOU DOING HERE?
KIKYO...
...YOU TOOK MIDO-RIKO'S SOUL...
SLIP
KIKYO ...?!

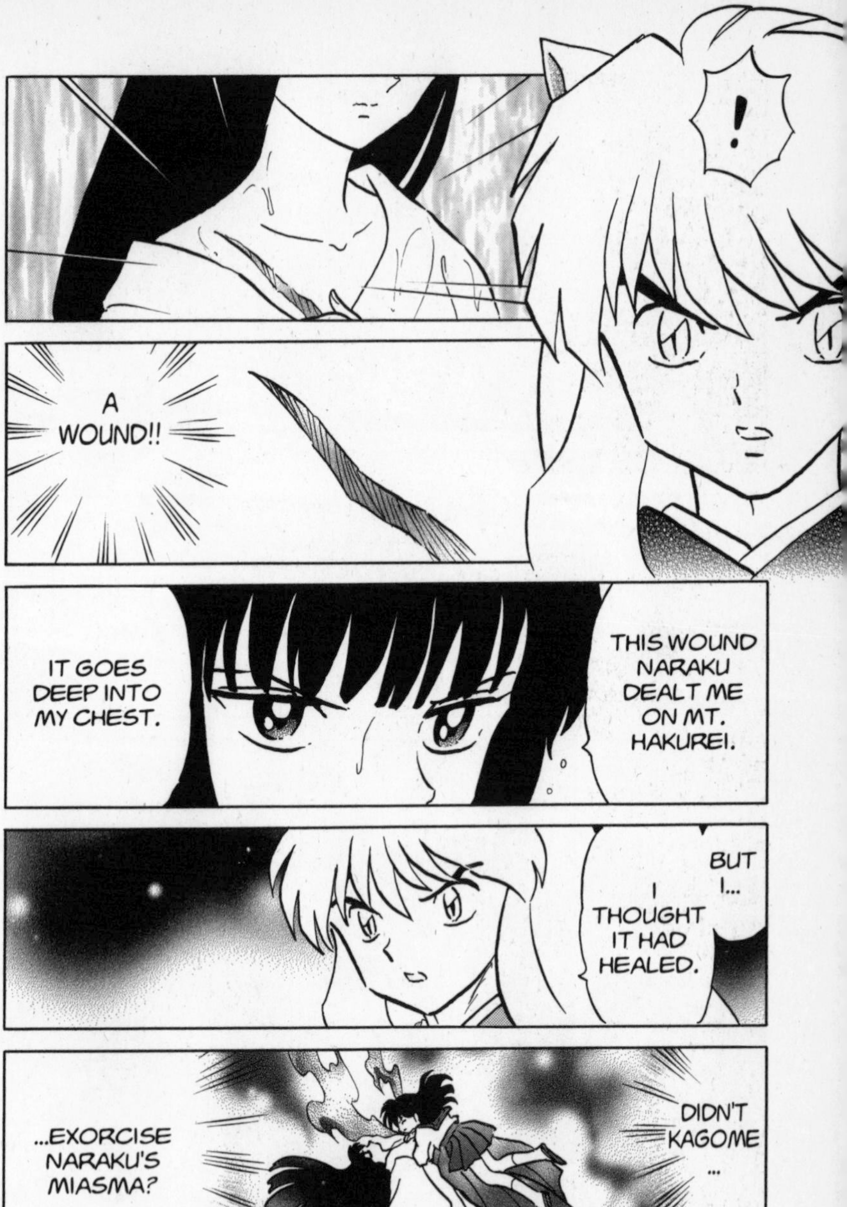
!
A WOUND!!
THIS WOUND NARAKU DEALT ME ON MT. HAKUREI.
IT GOES DEEP INTO MY CHEST.
BUT I...
I THOUGHT IT HAD HEALED.
DIDN'T KAGOME ...
...EXORCISE NARAKU'S MIASMA?

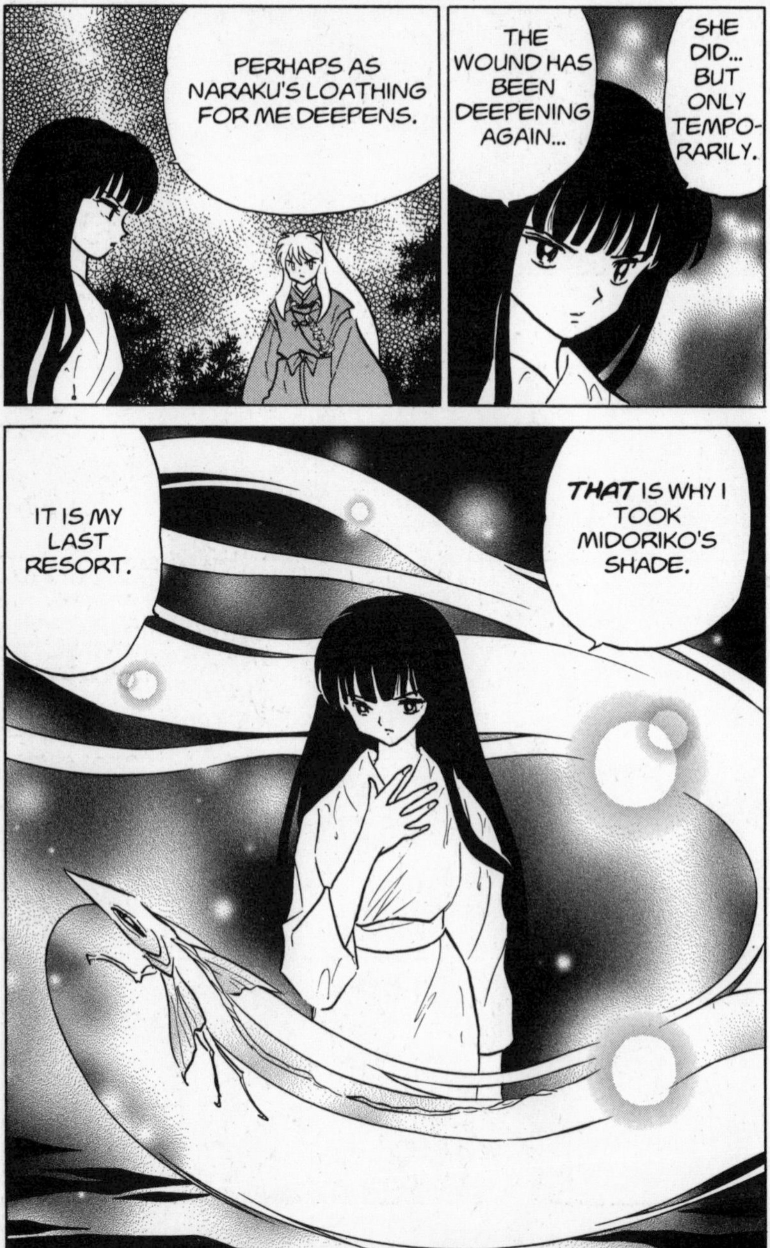
SHE DID... BUT ONLY TEMPO-RARILY.
THE WOUND HAS BEEN DEEPENING AGAIN...
PERHAPS AS NARAKU'S LOATHING FOR ME DEEPENS.
THAT IS WHY I TOOK MIDORIKO'S SHADE.
IT IS MY LAST RESORT.

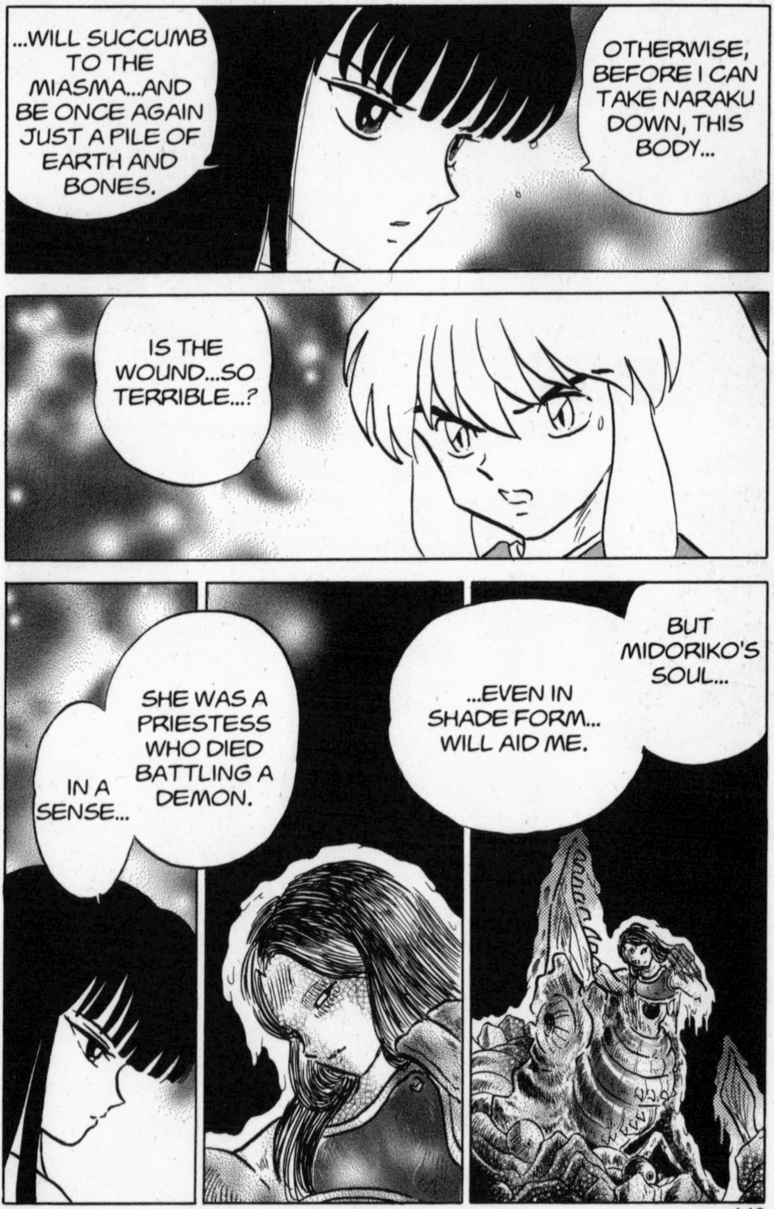
OTHERWISE, BEFORE I CAN TAKE NARAKU DOWN, THIS BODY...
...WILL SUCCUMB TO THE MIASMA...AND BE ONCE AGAIN JUST A PILE OF EARTH AND BONES.
IS THE WOUND...SO TERRIBLE...?
BUT MIDORIKO'S SOUL...
...EVEN IN SHADE FORM... WILL AID ME.
SHE WAS A PRIESTESS WHO DIED BATTLING A DEMON.
IN A SENSE...

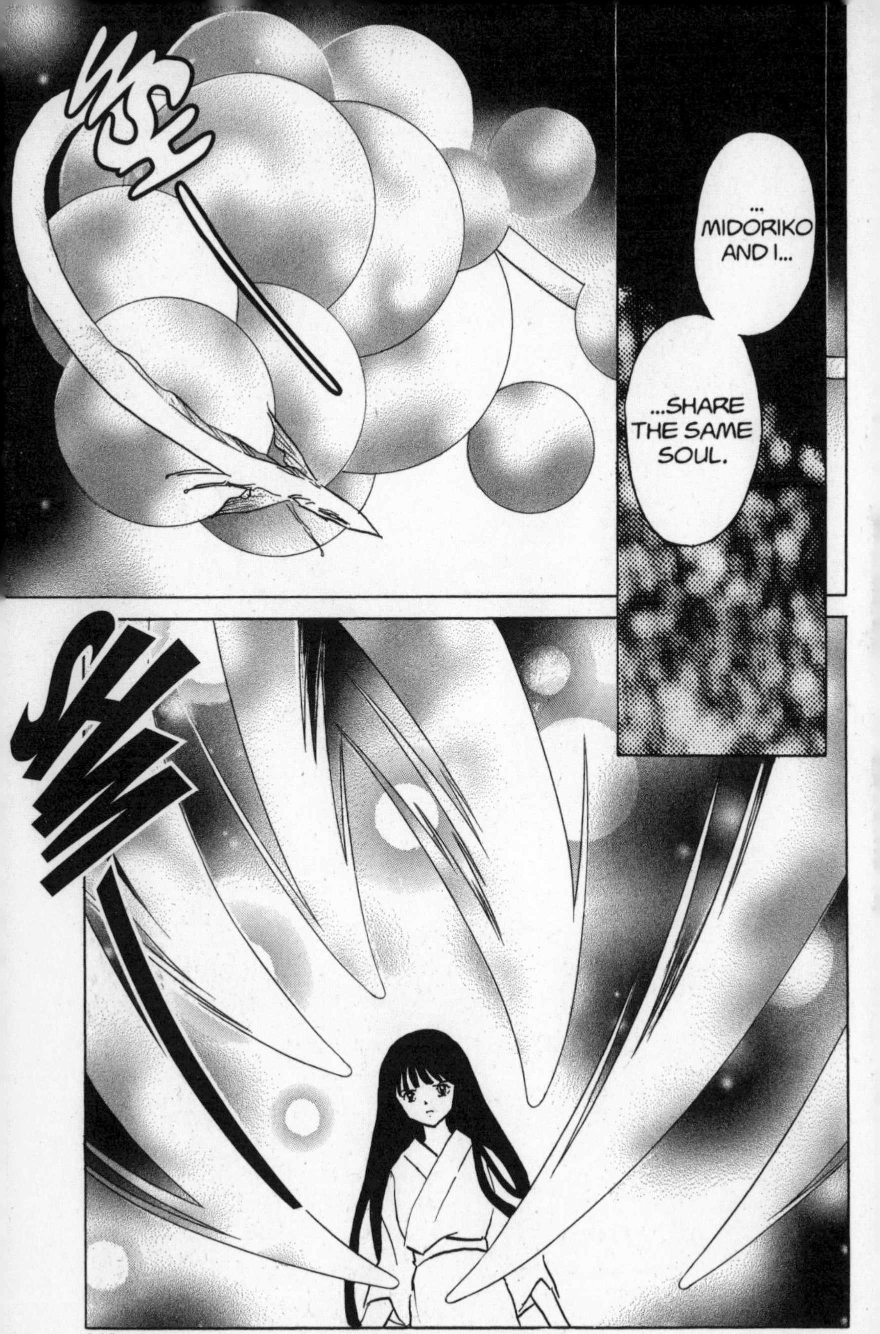
... MIDORIKO AND I...
...SHARE THE SAME SOUL.

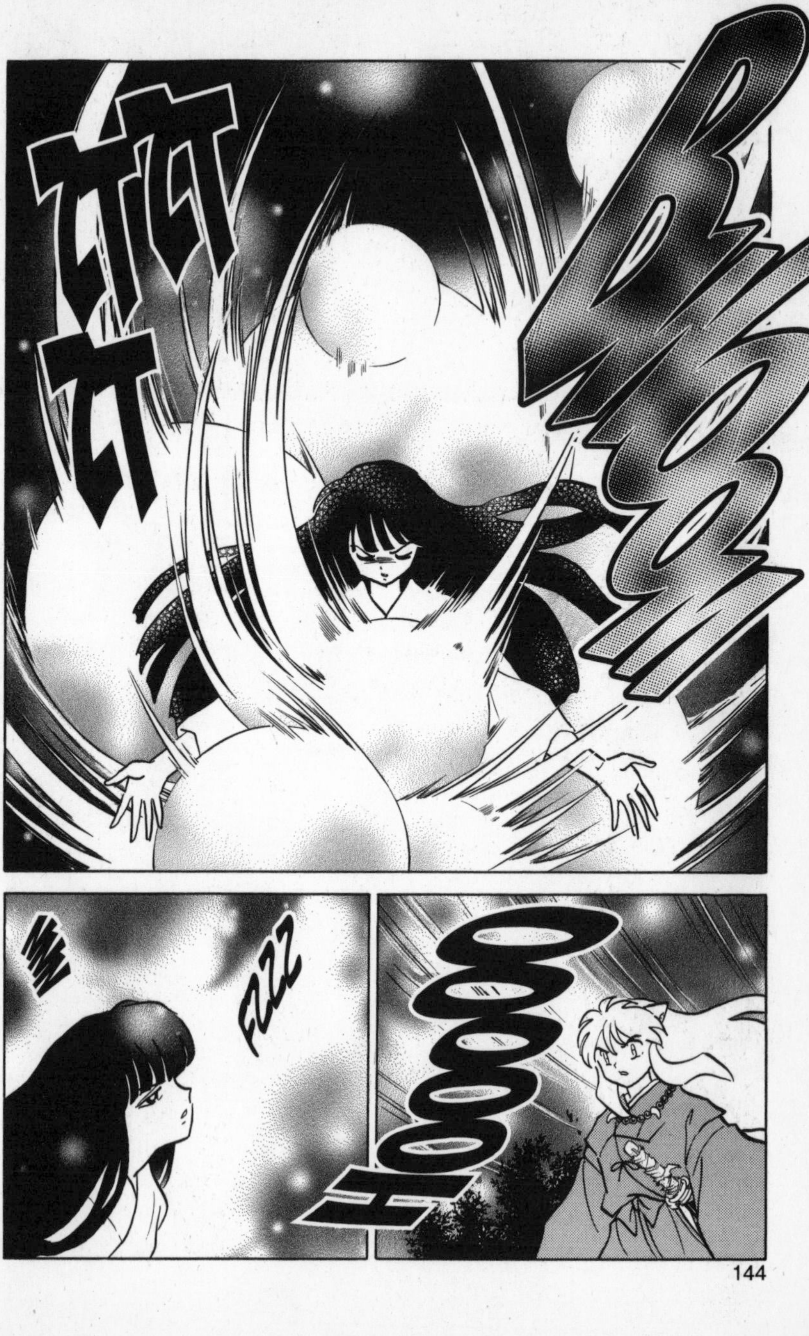
OOOOOH
FZZZ

KIKYO!

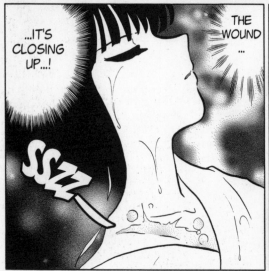

...IT'S CLOSING UP...!

THE WOUND...

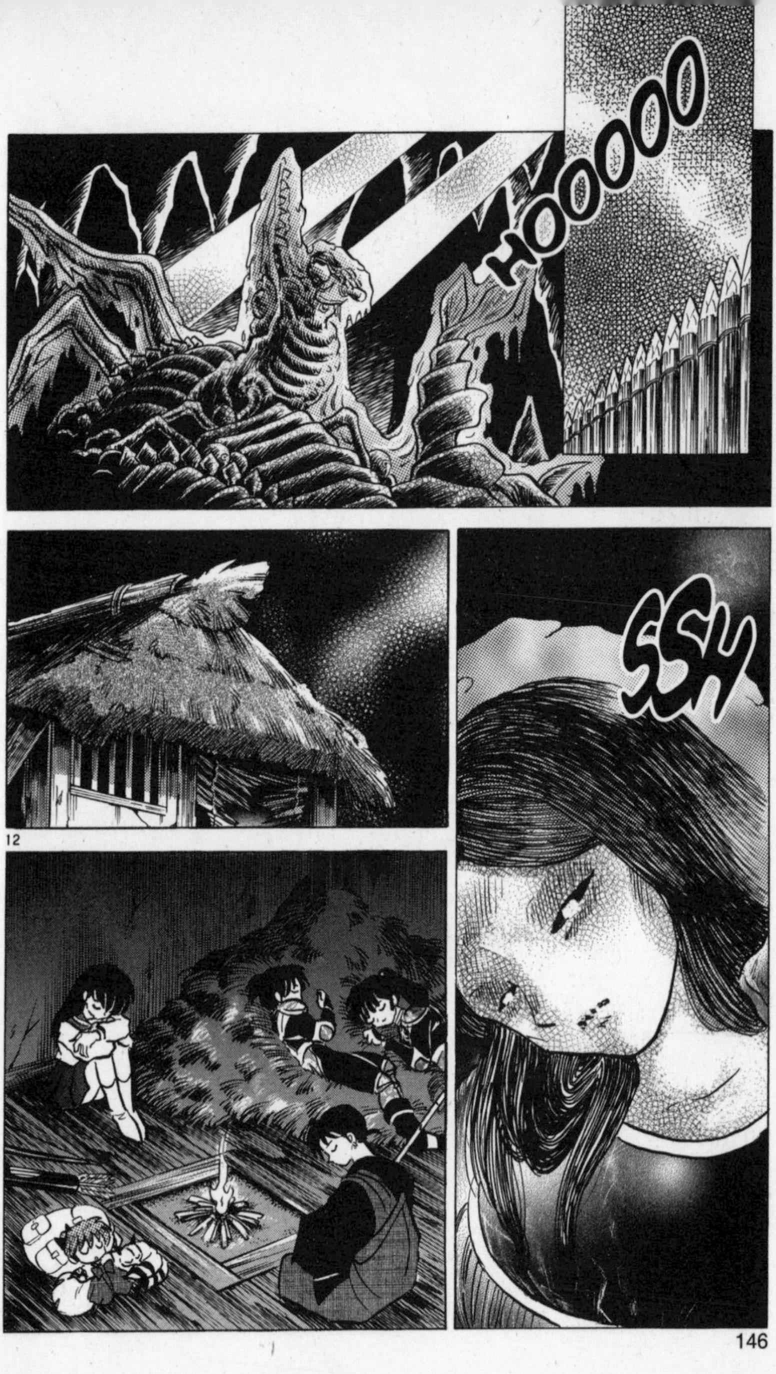
HOOOOOO
SSH

12

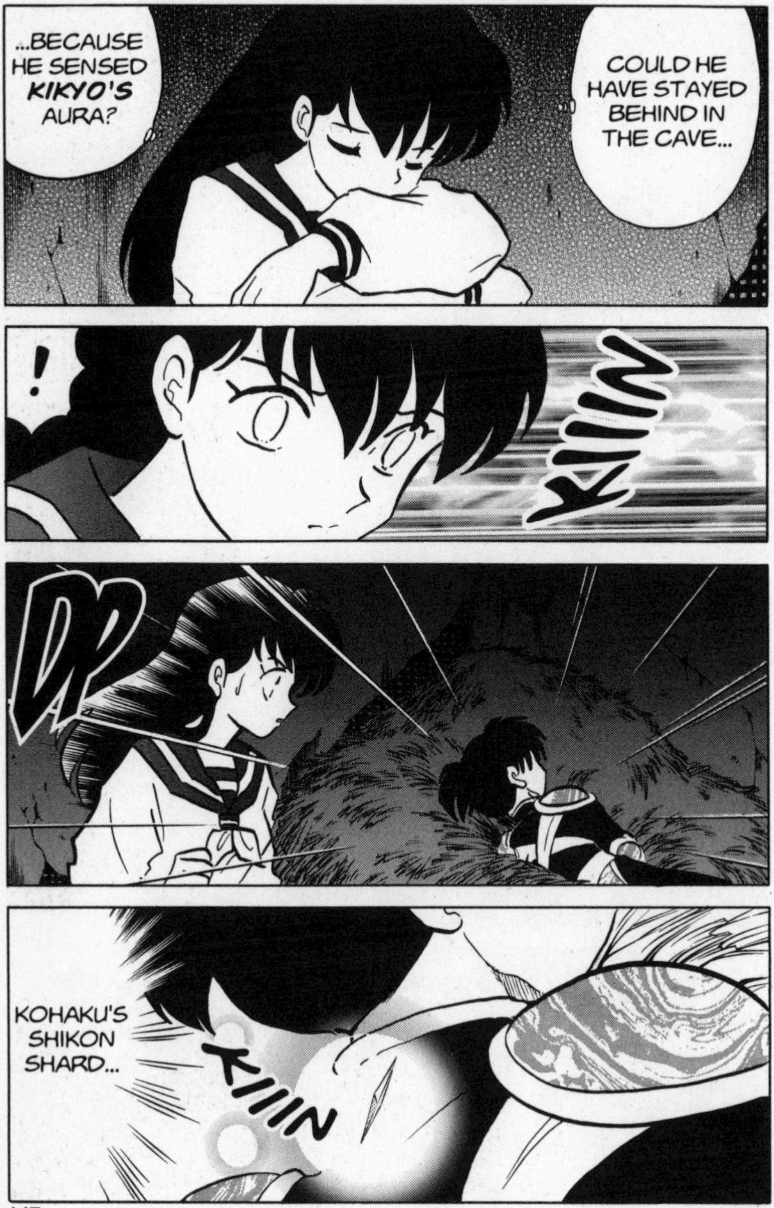
COULD HE HAVE STAYED BEHIND IN THE CAVE...
...BECAUSE HE SENSED KIKYO'S AURA?
KIIIN
!
DP
KIIIN
KOHAKU'S SHIKON SHARD...

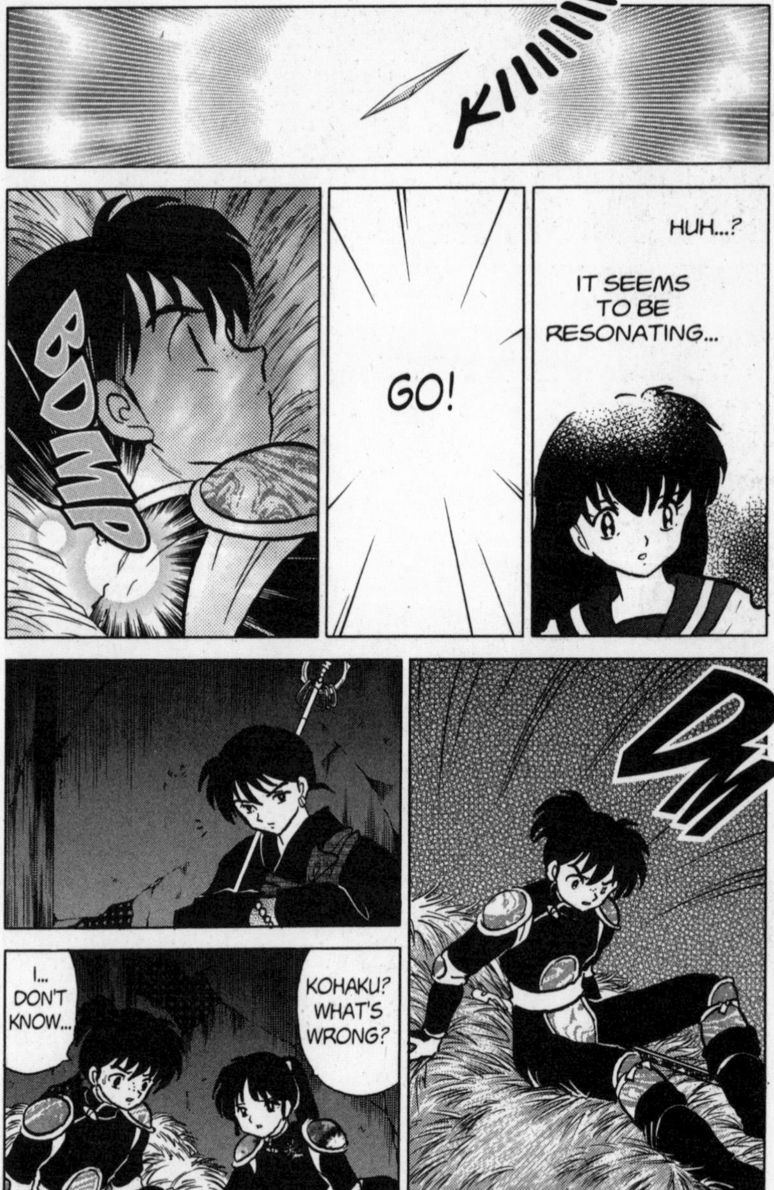
KIIIIIN
HUH...?
IT SEEMS TO BE RESONATING...
GO!
BDMP
DM
KOHAKU? WHAT'S WRONG?
I... DON'T KNOW...

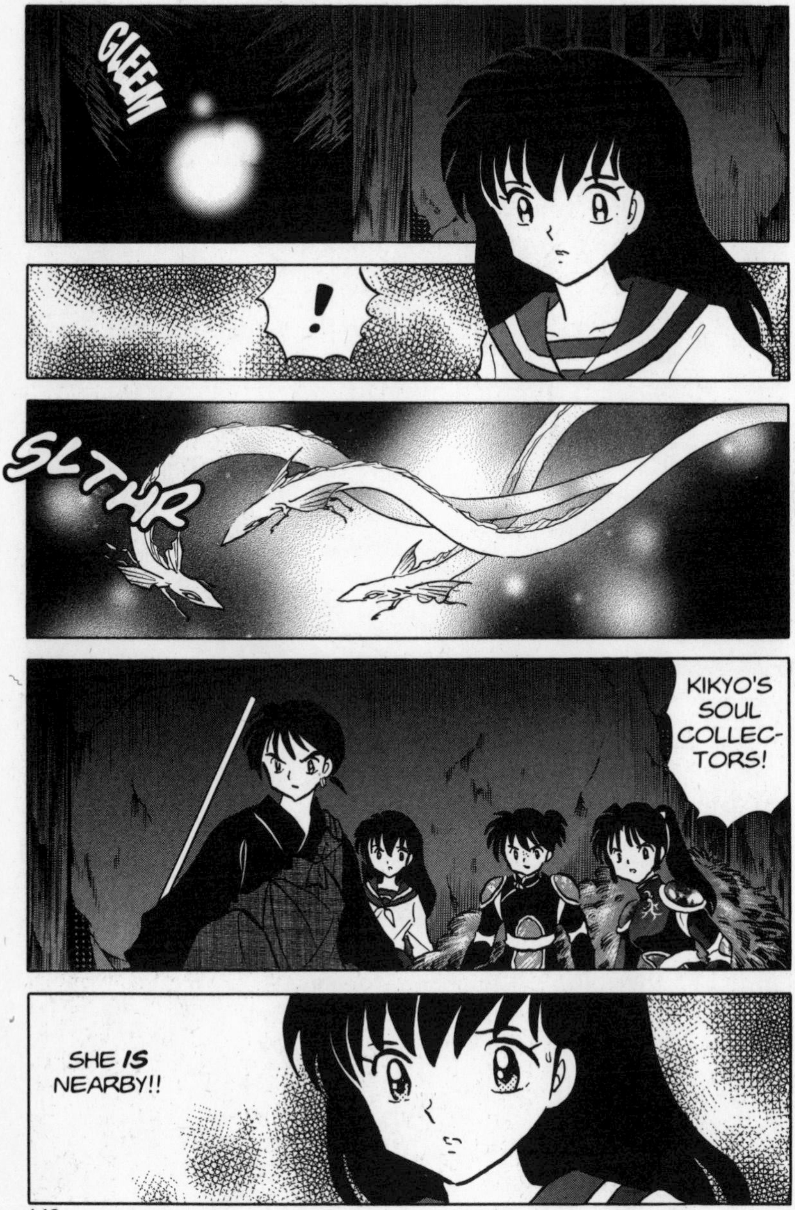
GLEEM
!
SLTHR
KIKYO'S SOUL COLLECTORS!
SHE IS NEARBY!!

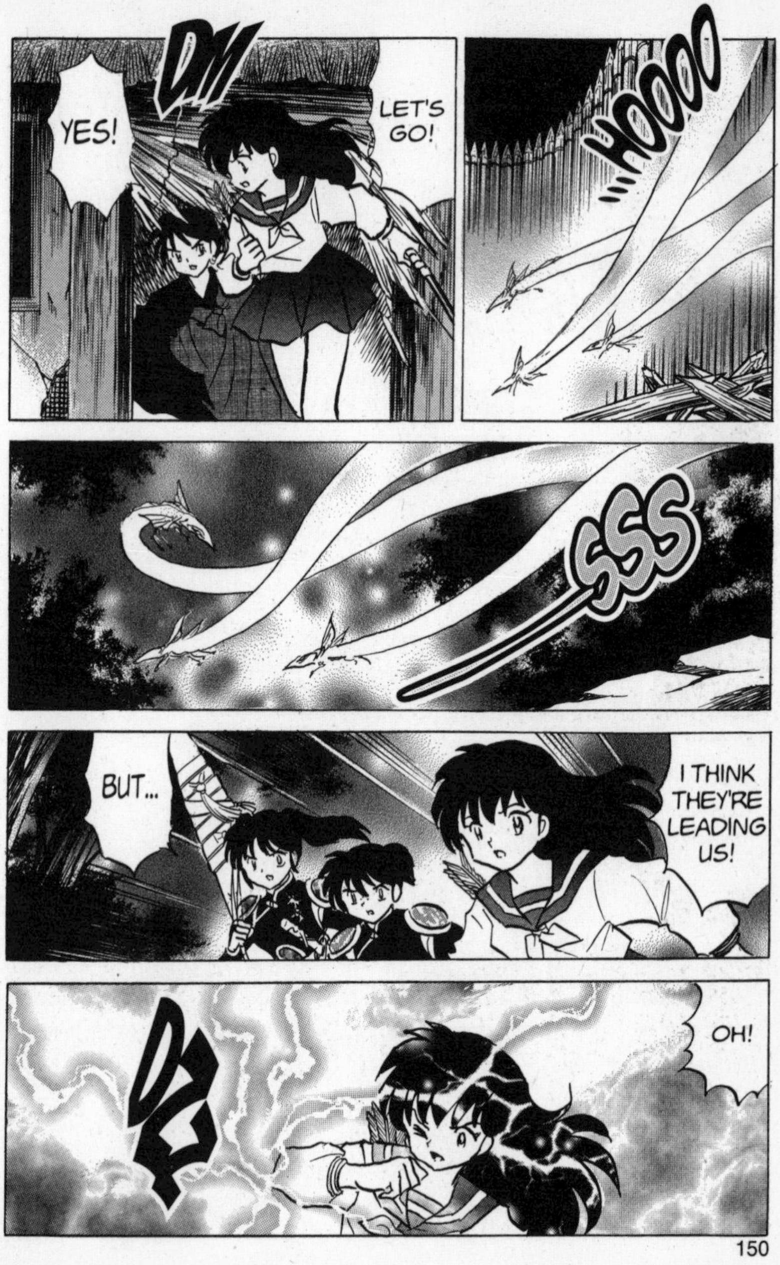
HOOOO
LET'S GO!
YES!
SSS
I THINK THEY'RE LEADING US!
BUT...
OH!

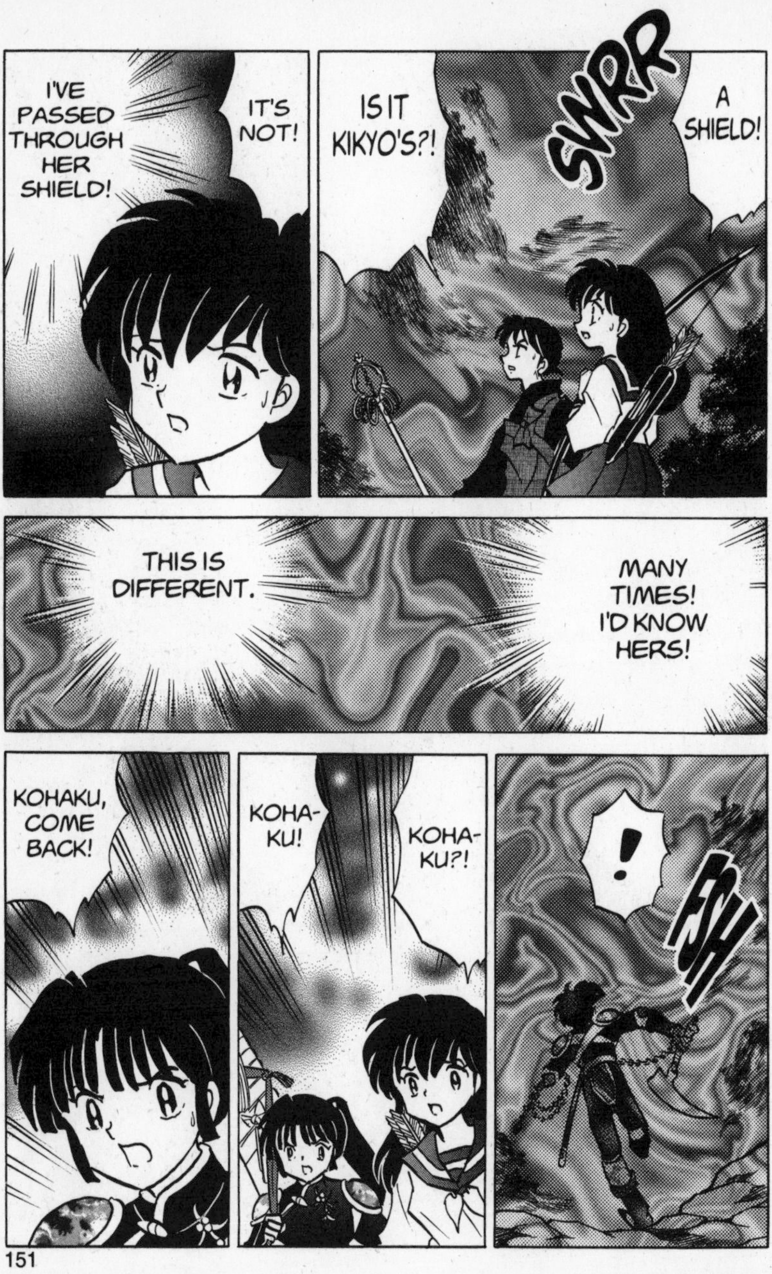
A SHIELD!
SWRR
IS IT KIKYO'S?!
IT'S NOT!
I'VE PASSED THROUGH HER SHIELD!
MANY TIMES! I'D KNOW HERS!
THIS IS DIFFERENT.
!
FSH
KOHA-KU?!
KOHA-KU!
KOHAKU, COME BACK!

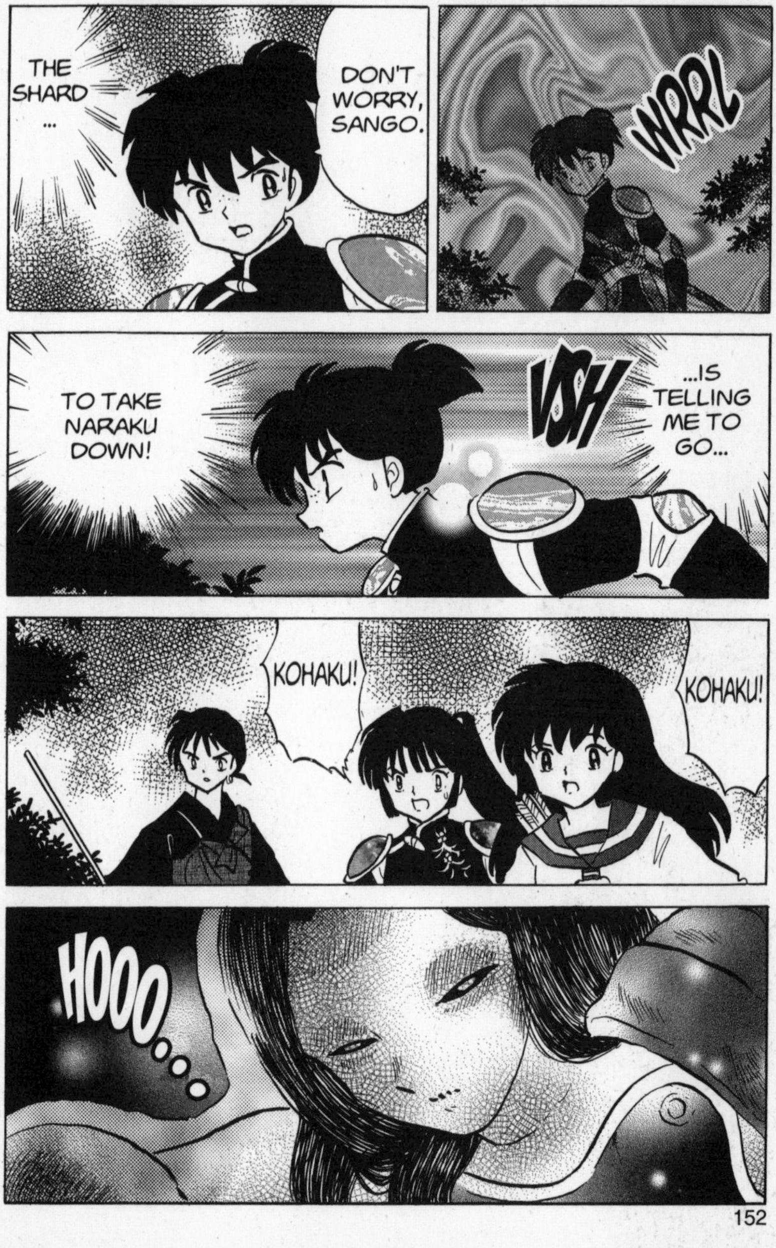
WRRL
DON'T WORRY, SANGO.
THE SHARD ...
VSH
...IS TELLING ME TO GO...
TO TAKE NARAKU DOWN!
KOHAKU!
KOHAKU!
HOOO....

SCROLL 9
DESTINIES

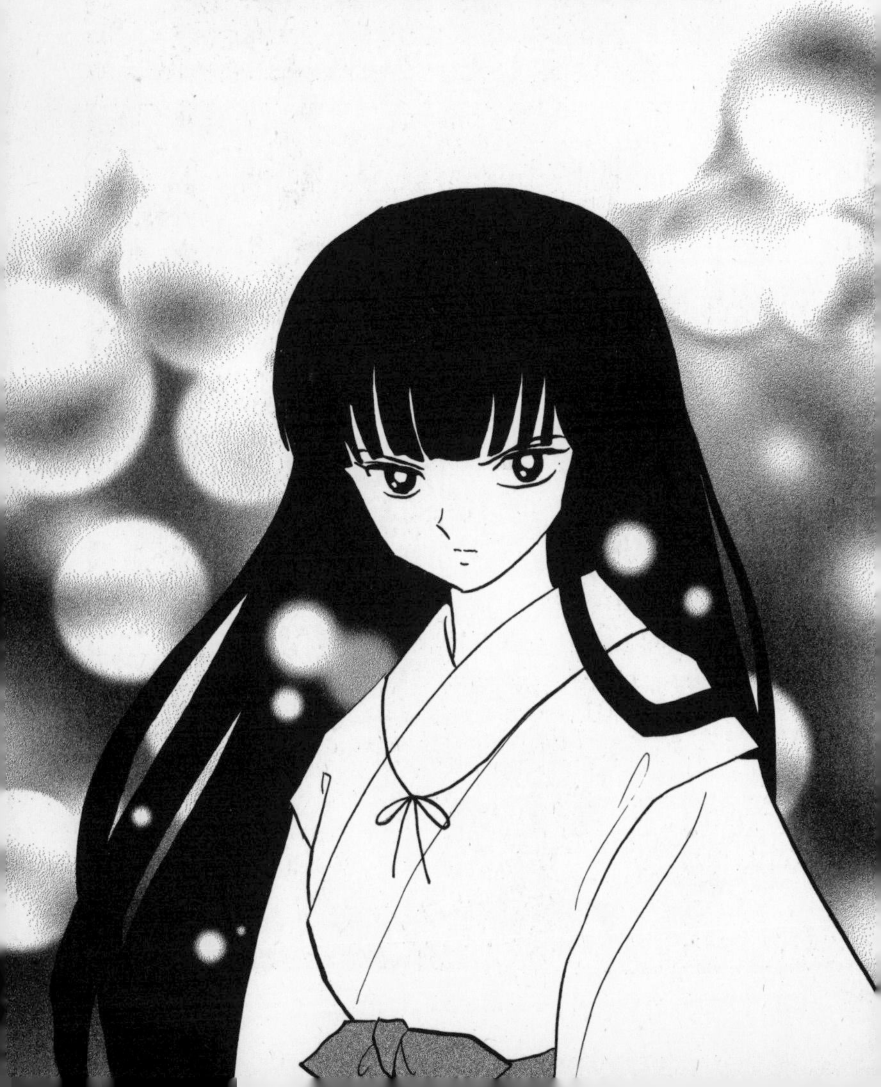

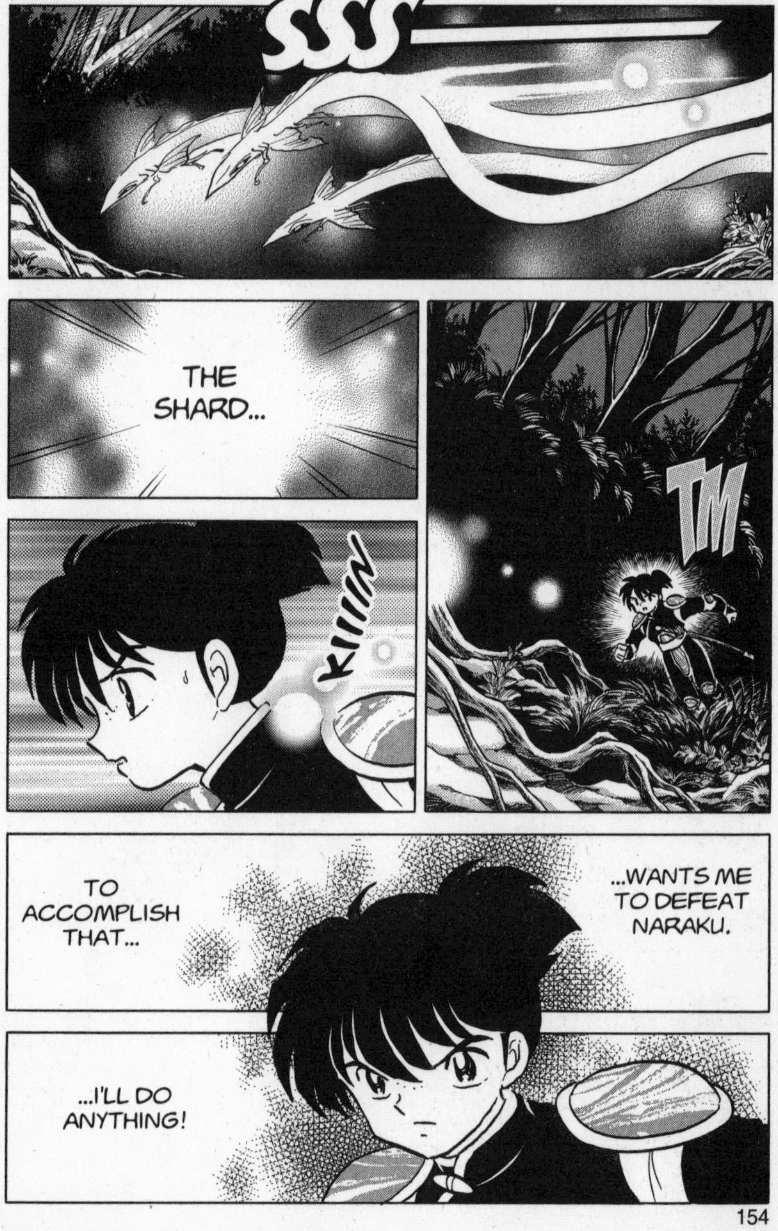
SSS
TM
THE SHARD...
KIIIIN
...WANTS ME TO DEFEAT NARAKU.
TO ACCOMPLISH THAT...
...I'LL DO ANYTHING!

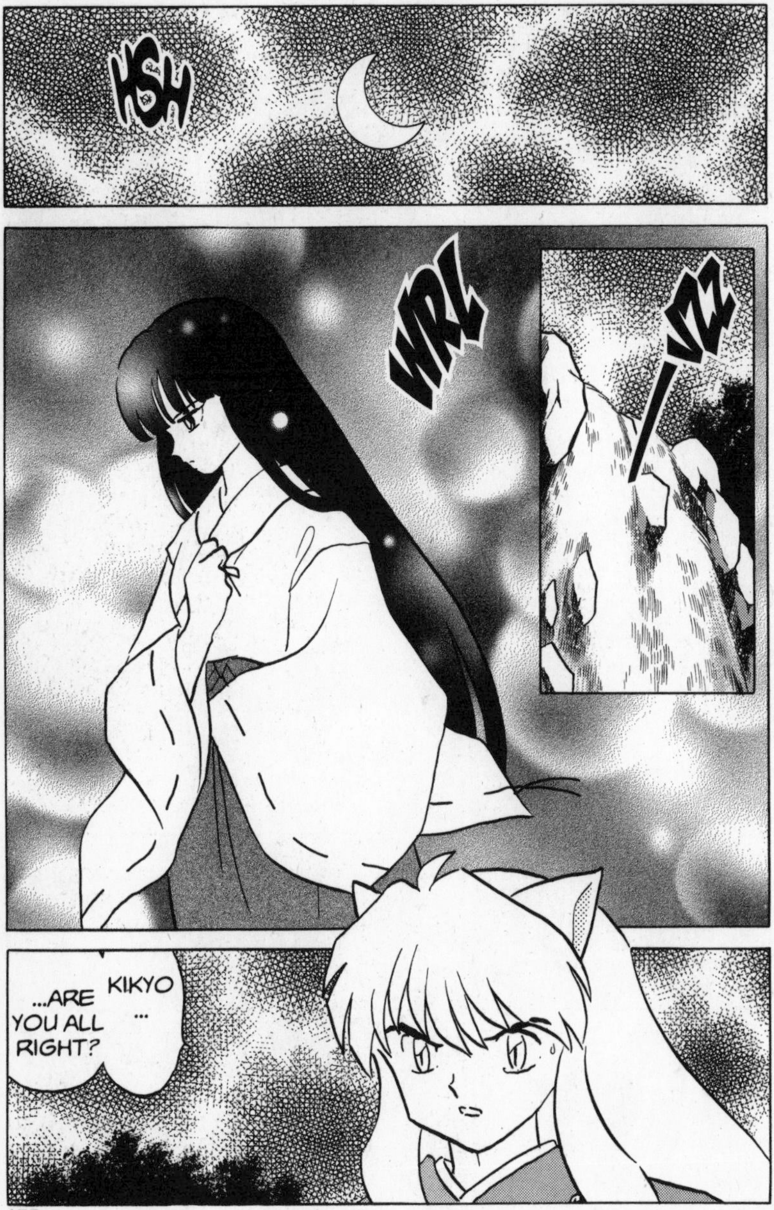
HSH
VZZ
WRL
KIKYO ...
...ARE YOU ALL RIGHT?

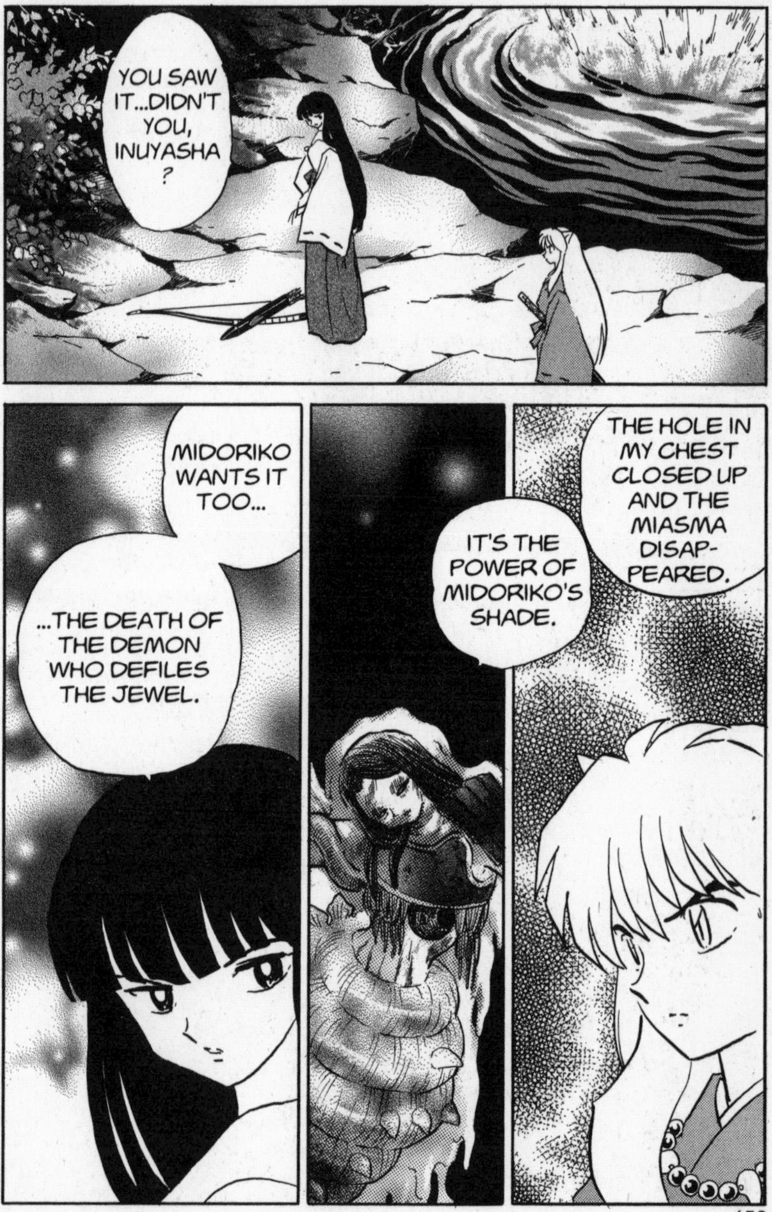
YOU SAW IT...DIDN'T YOU, INUYASHA?
THE HOLE IN MY CHEST CLOSED UP AND THE MIASMA DISAP-PEARED.
IT'S THE POWER OF MIDORIKO'S SHADE.
MIDORIKO WANTS IT TOO...
...THE DEATH OF THE DEMON WHO DEFILES THE JEWEL.

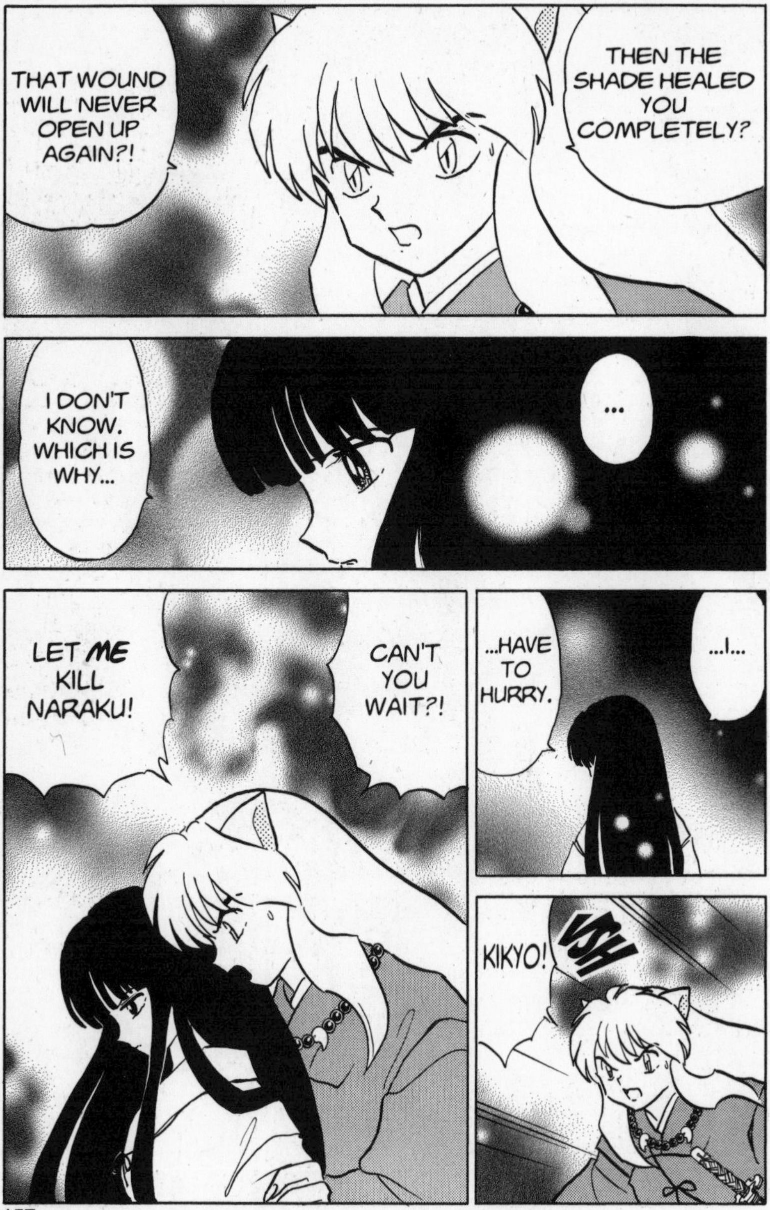
THEN THE SHADE HEALED YOU COMPLETELY?
THAT WOUND WILL NEVER OPEN UP AGAIN?!
...
I DON'T KNOW. WHICH IS WHY...
...I...
...HAVE TO HURRY.
VSH!
KIKYO!
CAN'T YOU WAIT?!
LET *ME* KILL NARAKU!

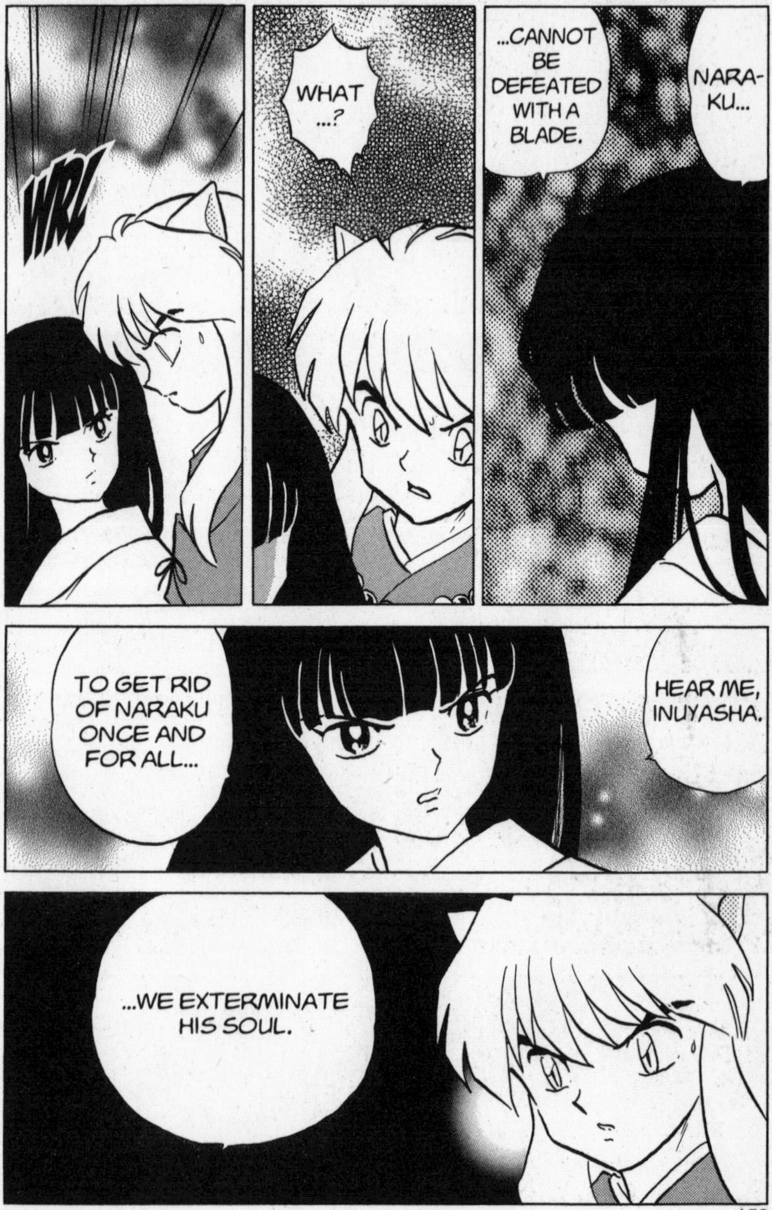
NARAKU...
...CANNOT BE DEFEATED WITH A BLADE.
WHAT ...?
WRI
HEAR ME, INUYASHA.
TO GET RID OF NARAKU ONCE AND FOR ALL...
...WE EXTERMINATE HIS SOUL.

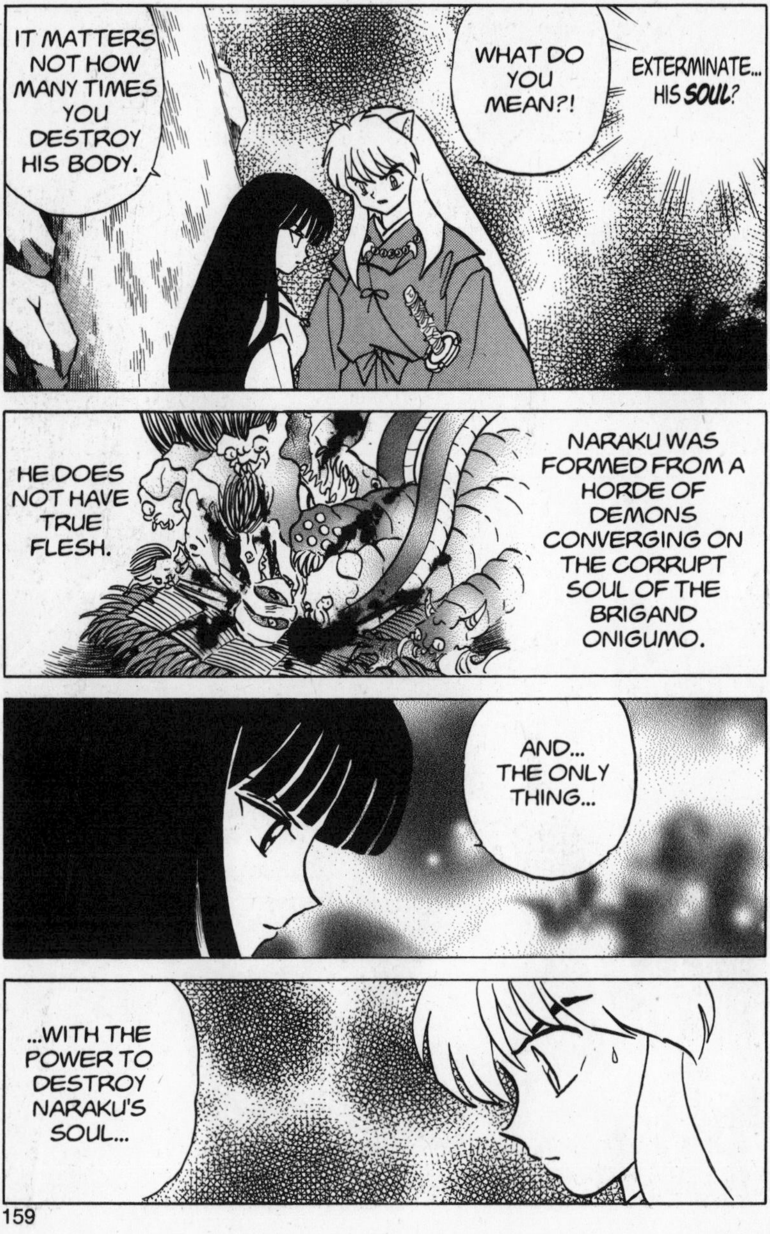
EXTERMINATE... HIS SOUL?
WHAT DO YOU MEAN?!
IT MATTERS NOT HOW MANY TIMES YOU DESTROY HIS BODY.
NARAKU WAS FORMED FROM A HORDE OF DEMONS CONVERGING ON THE CORRUPT SOUL OF THE BRIGAND ONIGUMO.
HE DOES NOT HAVE TRUE FLESH.
AND... THE ONLY THING...
...WITH THE POWER TO DESTROY NARAKU'S SOUL...

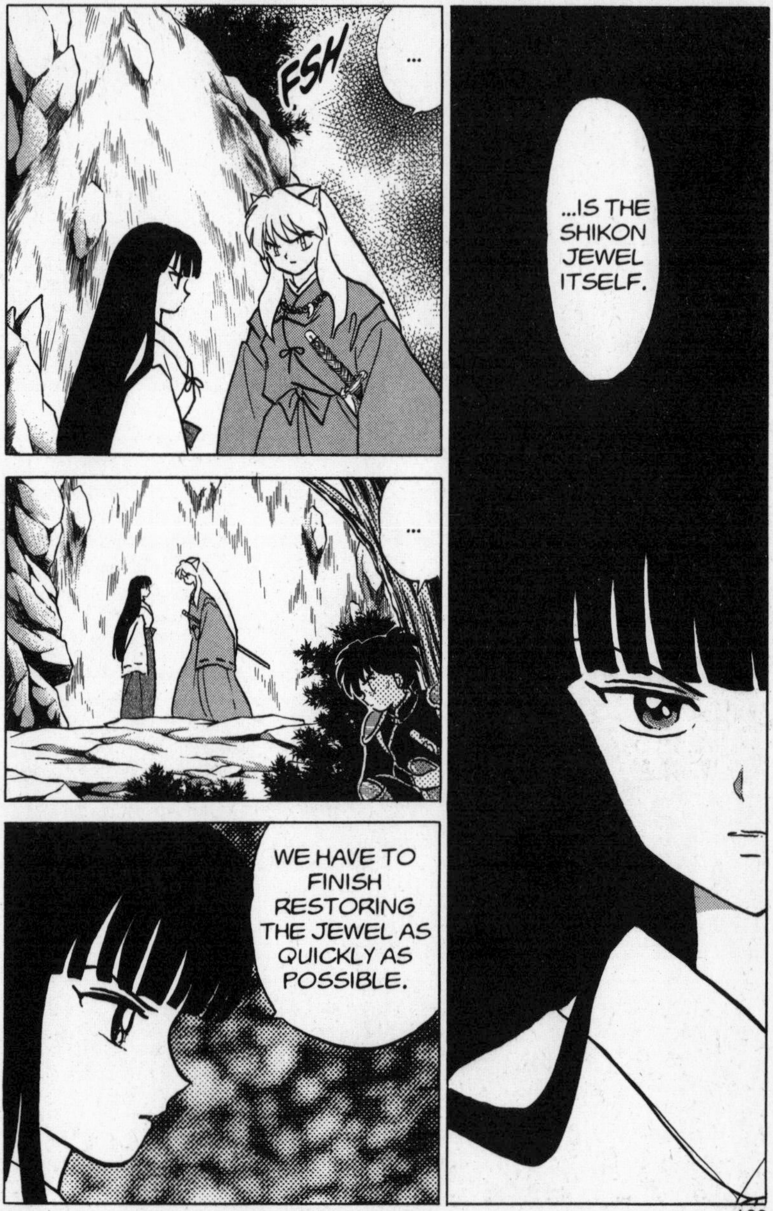
...IS THE SHIKON JEWEL ITSELF.
FSH
...
...
WE HAVE TO FINISH RESTORING THE JEWEL AS QUICKLY AS POSSIBLE.

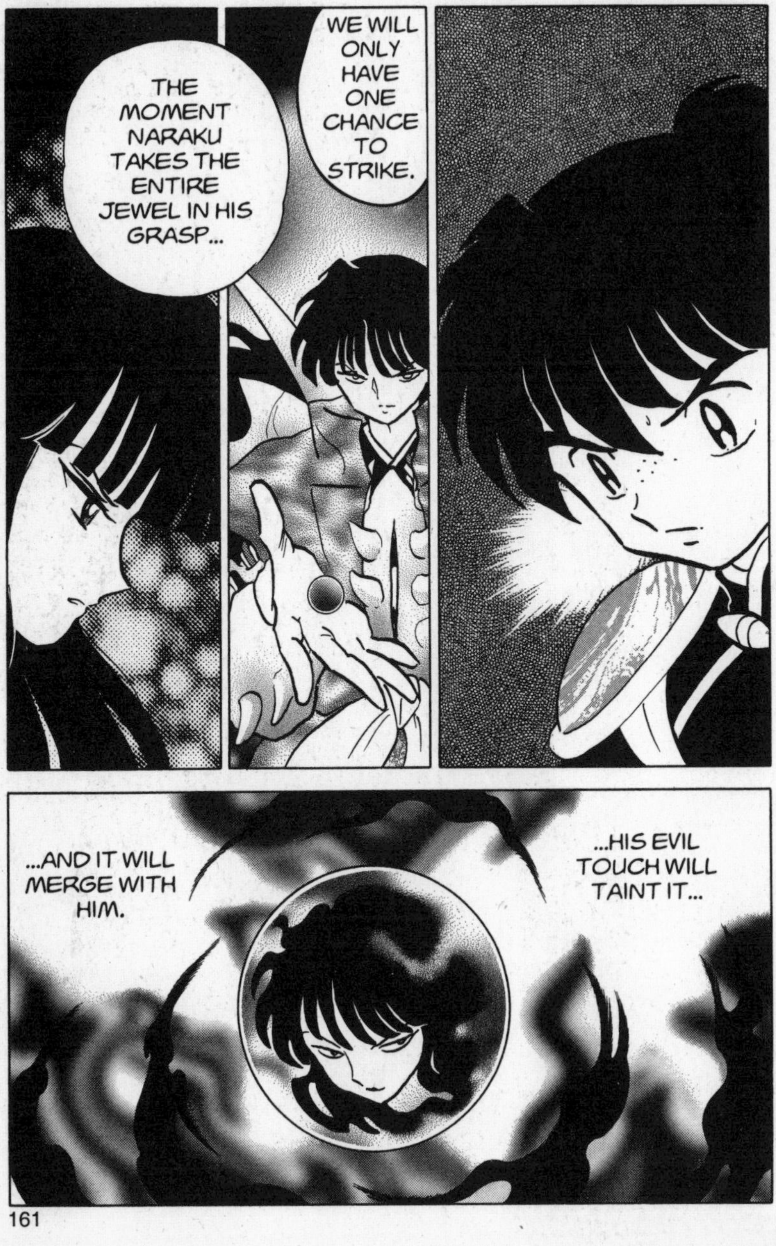
WE WILL ONLY HAVE ONE CHANCE TO STRIKE.
THE MOMENT NARAKU TAKES THE ENTIRE JEWEL IN HIS GRASP...
...HIS EVIL TOUCH WILL TAINT IT...
...AND IT WILL MERGE WITH HIM.

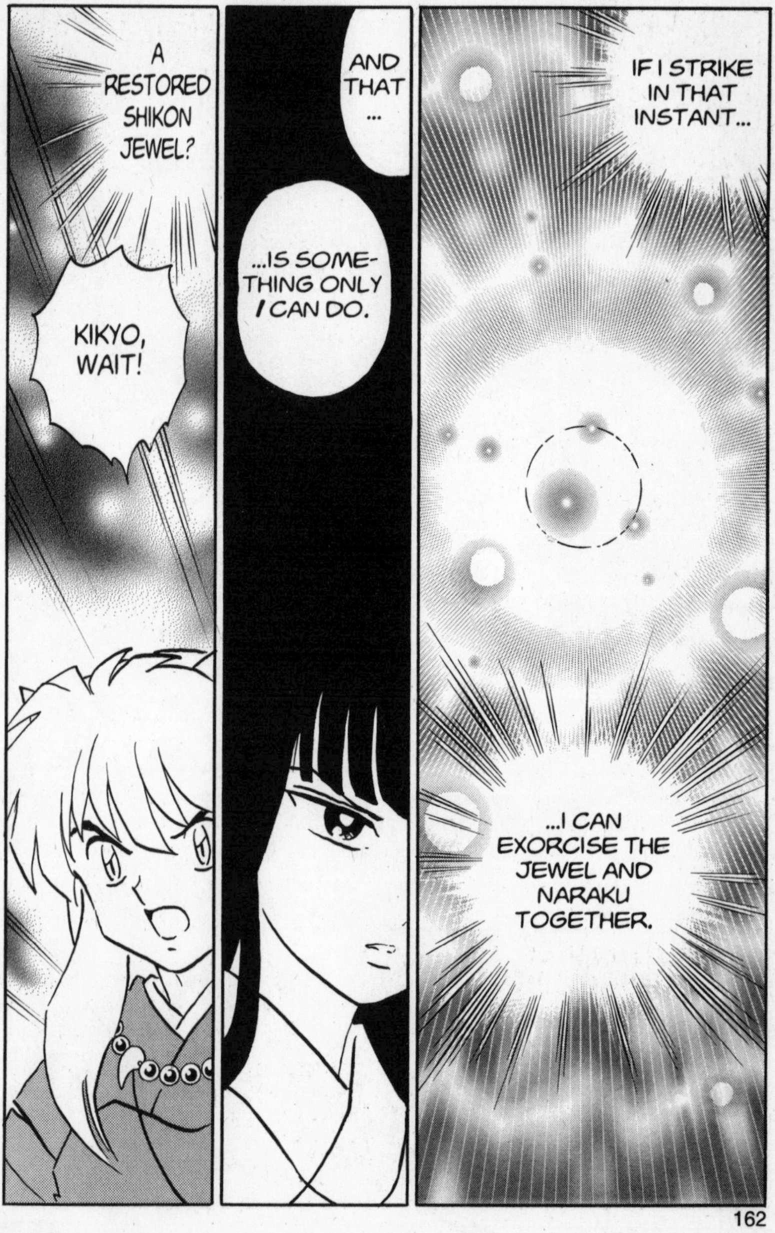
IF I STRIKE IN THAT INSTANT...
...I CAN EXORCISE THE JEWEL AND NARAKU TOGETHER.
AND THAT ...
...IS SOMETHING ONLY I CAN DO.
A RESTORED SHIKON JEWEL?
KIKYO, WAIT!

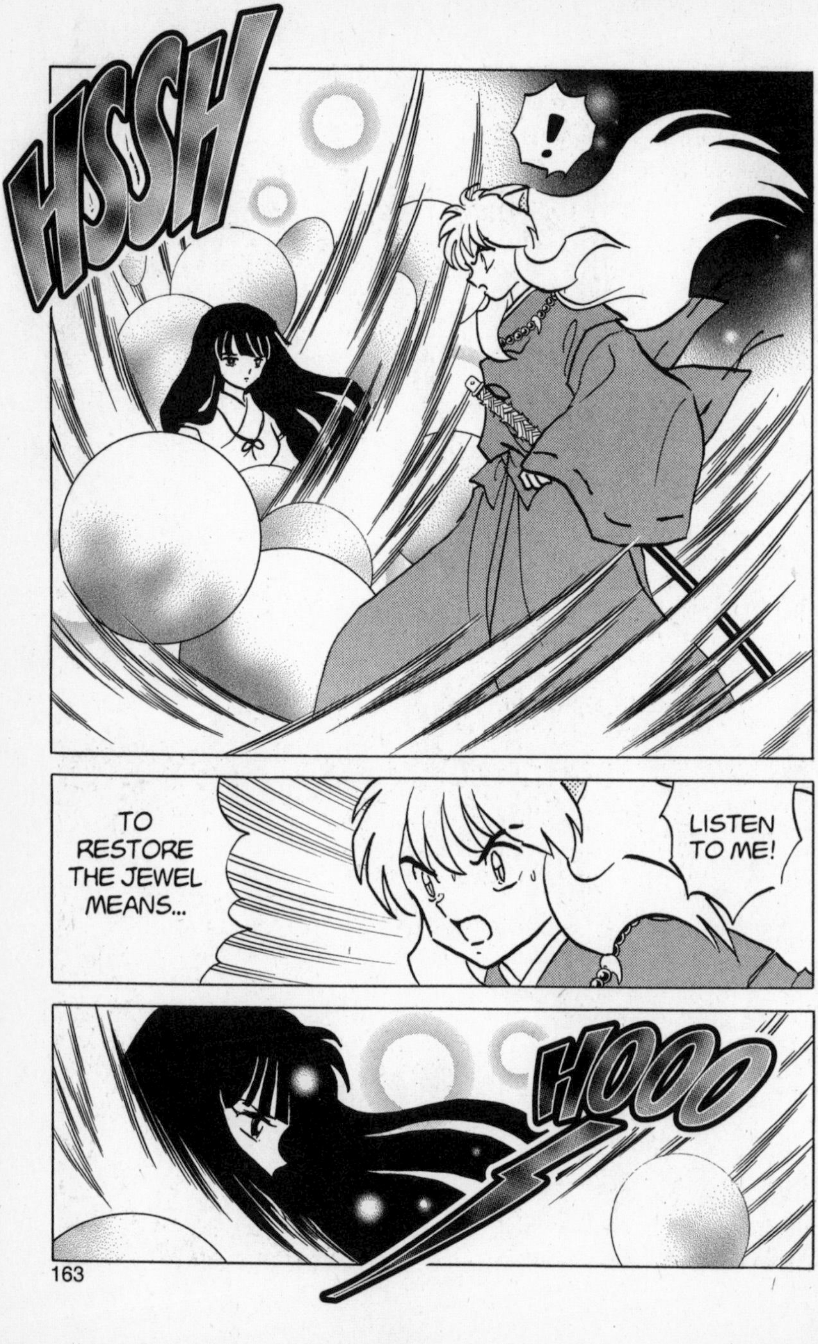
HSSH
!
LISTEN TO ME!
TO RESTORE THE JEWEL MEANS...
HOOO

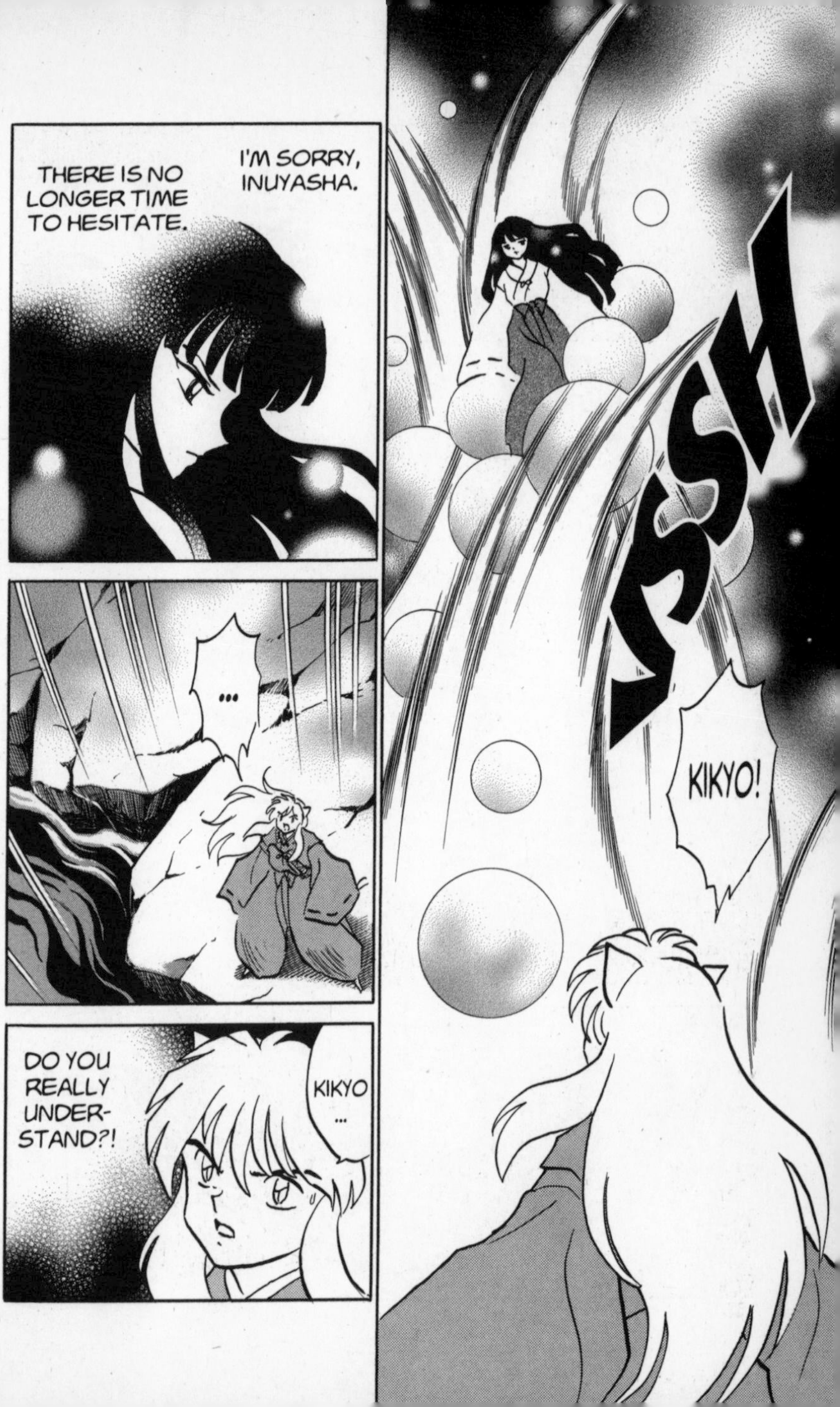
VSSH!
KIKYO!
I'M SORRY, INUYASHA.
THERE IS NO LONGER TIME TO HESITATE.
...
KIKYO ...
DO YOU REALLY UNDER-STAND?!

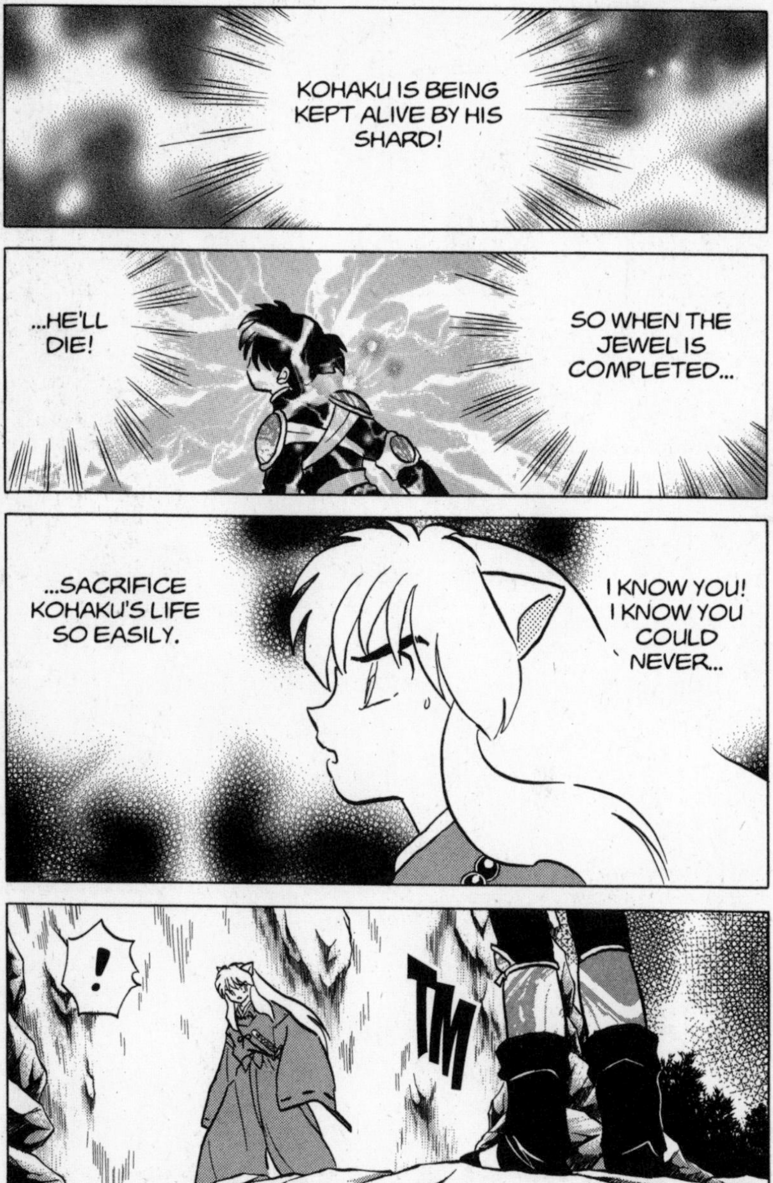
KOHAKU IS BEING KEPT ALIVE BY HIS SHARD!
SO WHEN THE JEWEL IS COMPLETED...
...HE'LL DIE!
I KNOW YOU! I KNOW YOU COULD NEVER...
...SACRIFICE KOHAKU'S LIFE SO EASILY.
TM
!

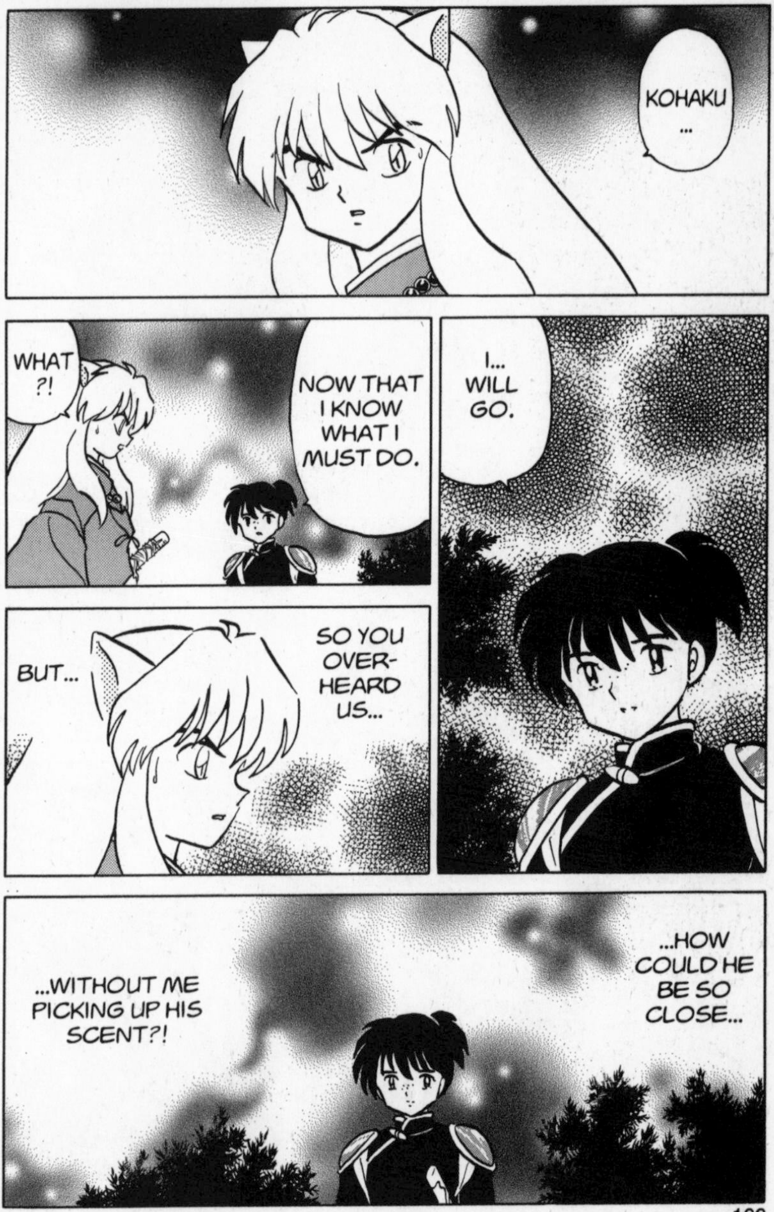
KOHAKU ...
I... WILL GO.
NOW THAT I KNOW WHAT I MUST DO.
WHAT?!
SO YOU OVER-HEARD US...
BUT...
...HOW COULD HE BE SO CLOSE...
...WITHOUT ME PICKING UP HIS SCENT?!

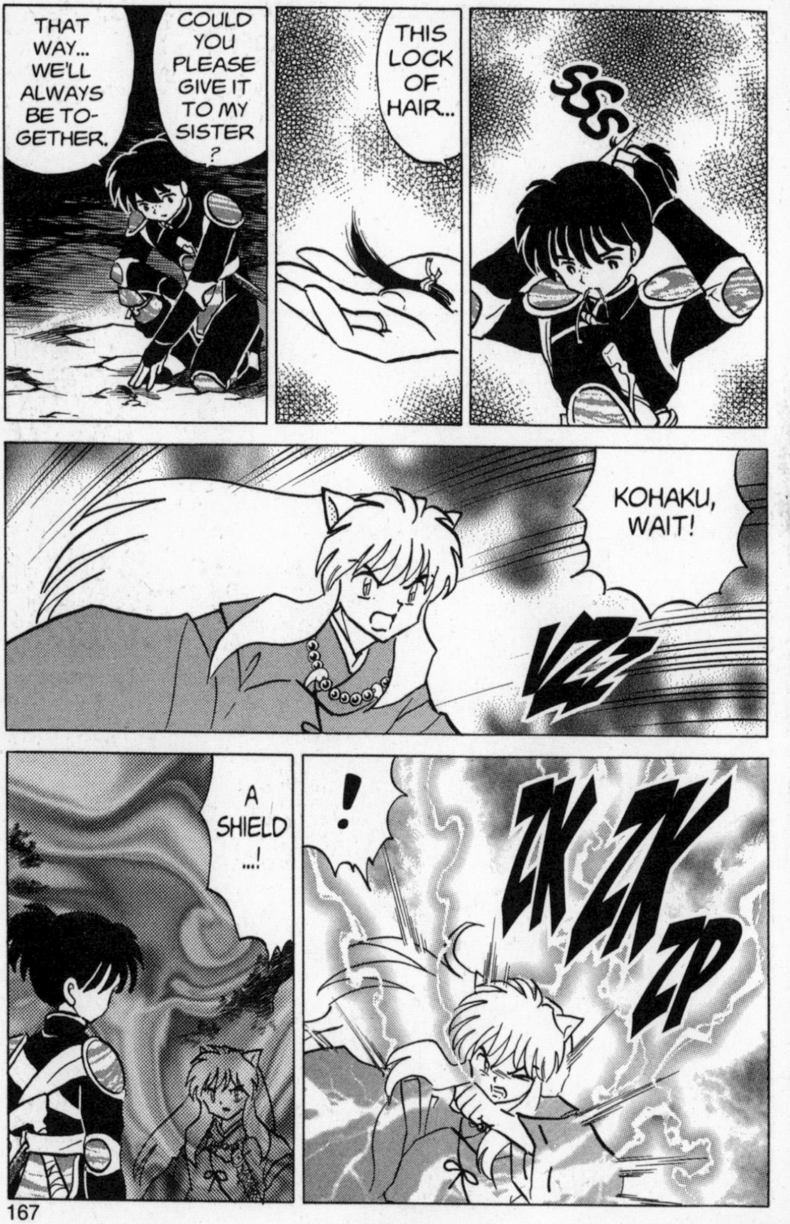
SSS
THIS LOCK OF HAIR...
COULD YOU PLEASE GIVE IT TO MY SISTER?
THAT WAY... WE'LL ALWAYS BE TOGETHER.
KOHAKU, WAIT!
!
A SHIELD ...!

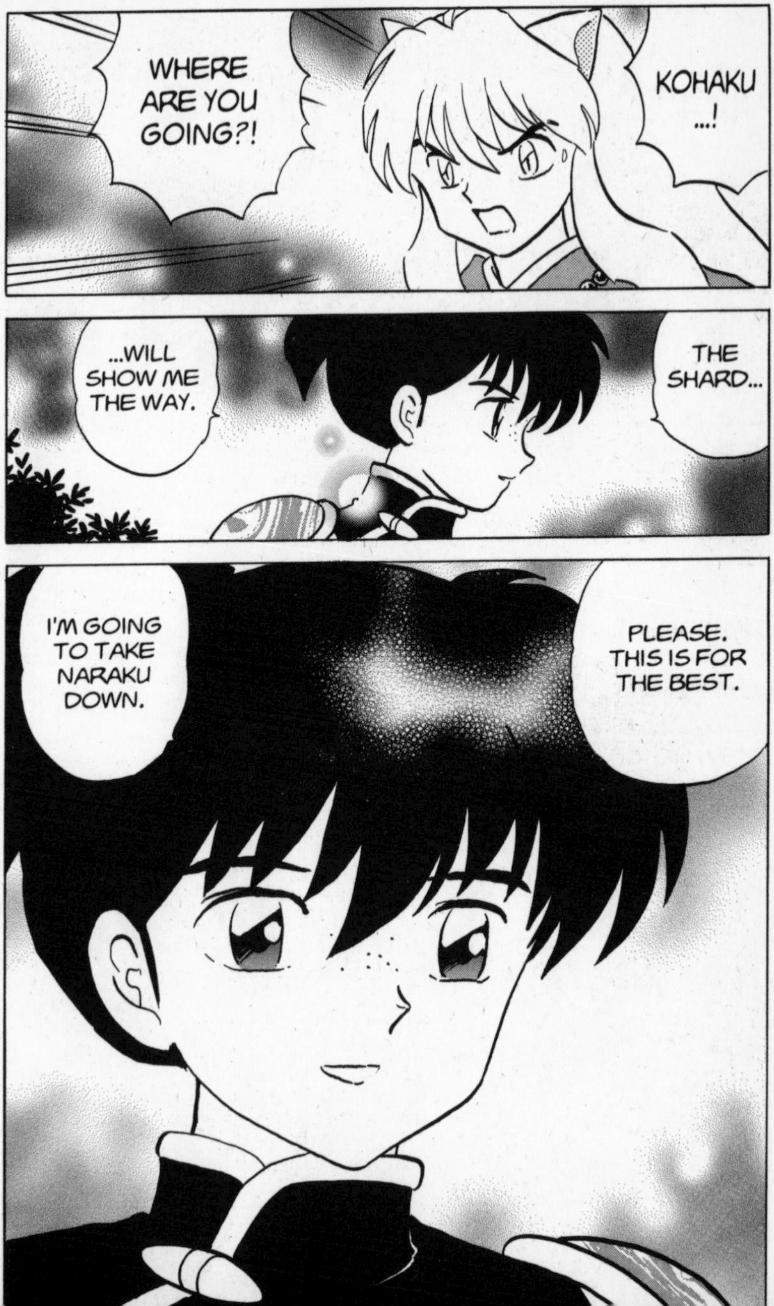
KOHAKU ...!
WHERE ARE YOU GOING?!
THE SHARD...
...WILL SHOW ME THE WAY.
PLEASE. THIS IS FOR THE BEST.
I'M GOING TO TAKE NARAKU DOWN.

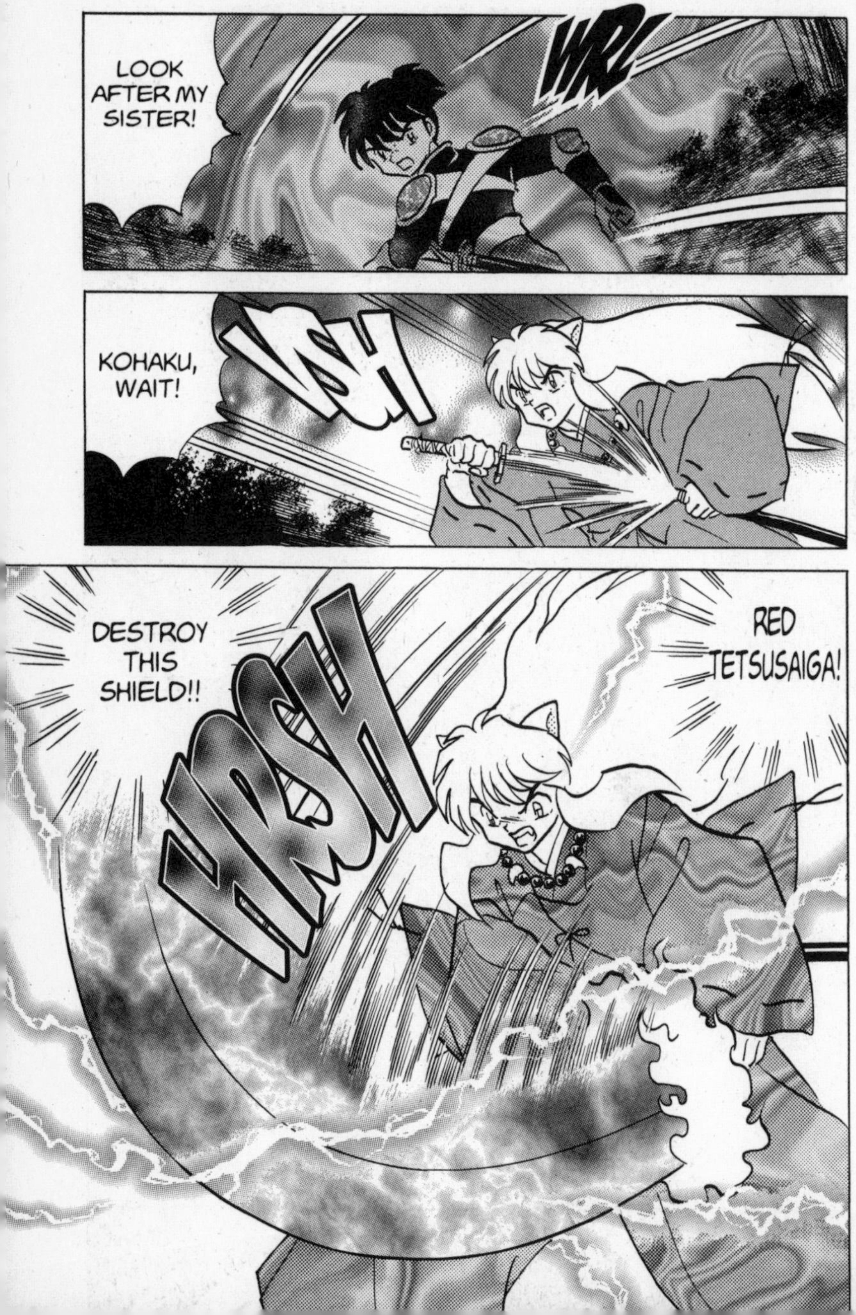
LOOK AFTER MY SISTER!
KOHAKU, WAIT!
RED TETSUSAIGA!
DESTROY THIS SHIELD!!

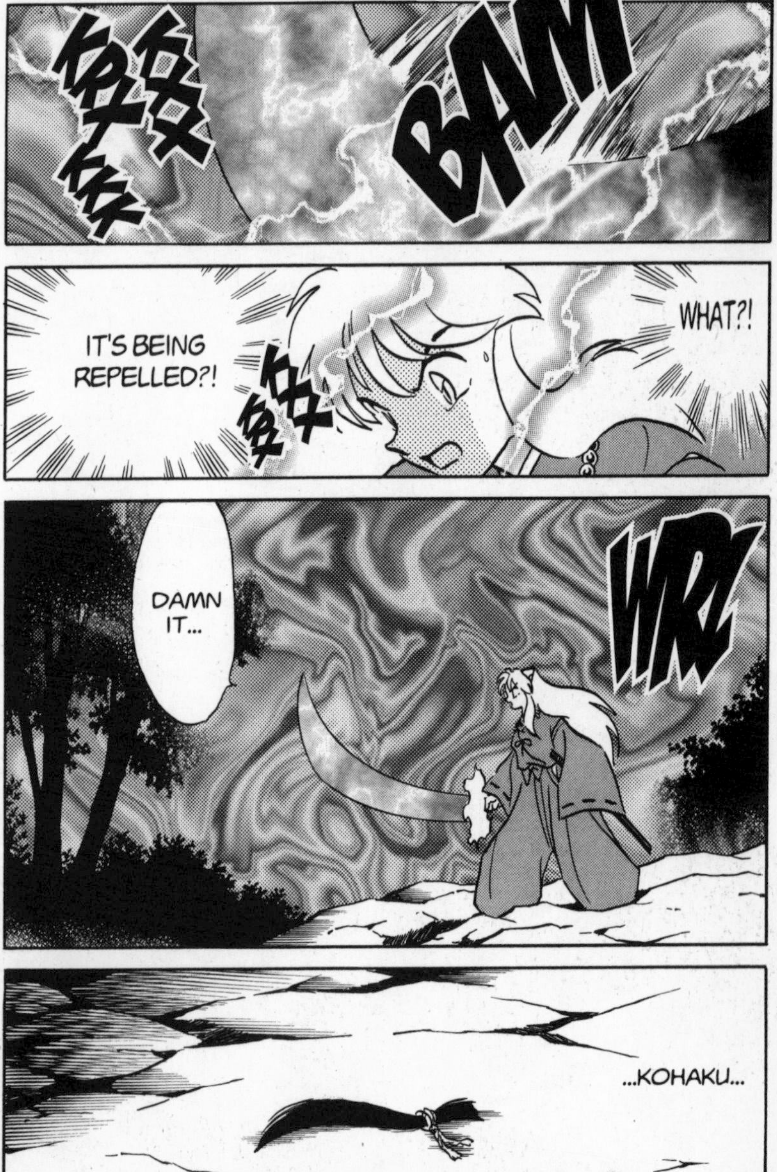
BAM
KRAKKK KRAKKK
WHAT?!
IT'S BEING REPELLED?!
KRAKKK
WRRR
DAMN IT...
...KOHAKU...

SCROLL 10

THE SNAKES' LAIR

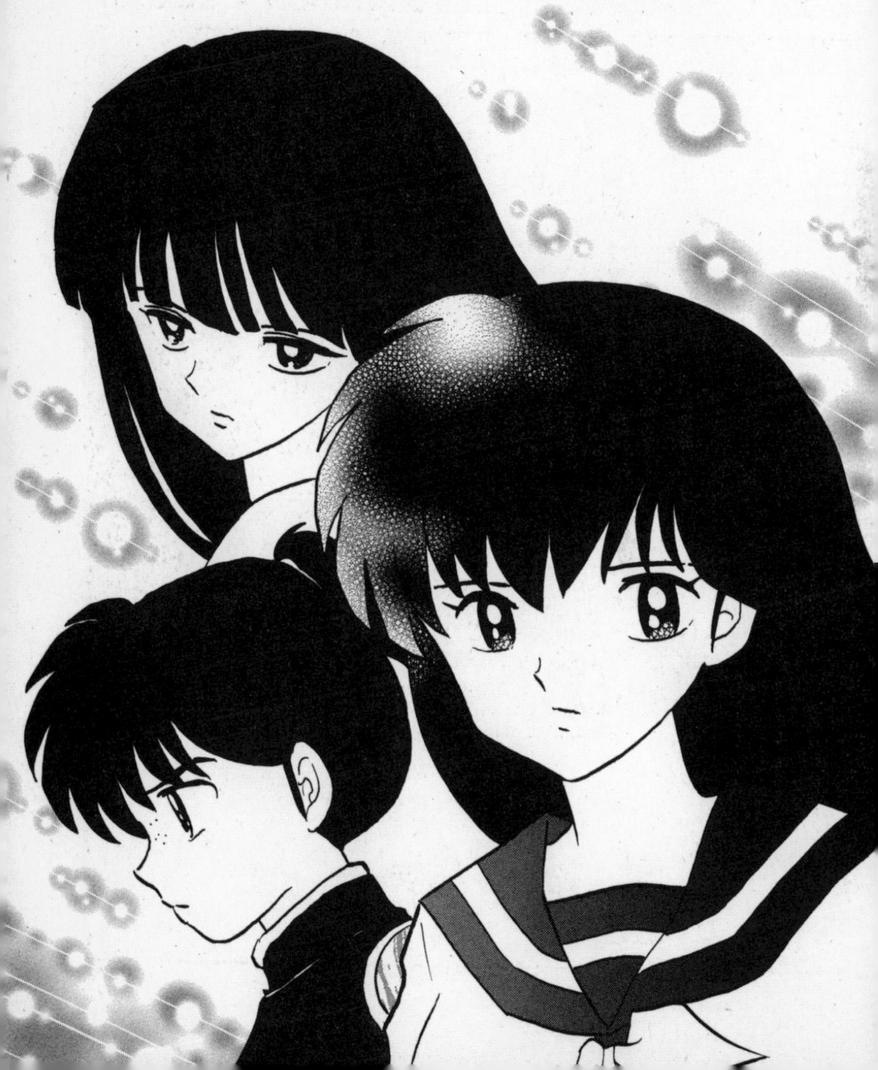

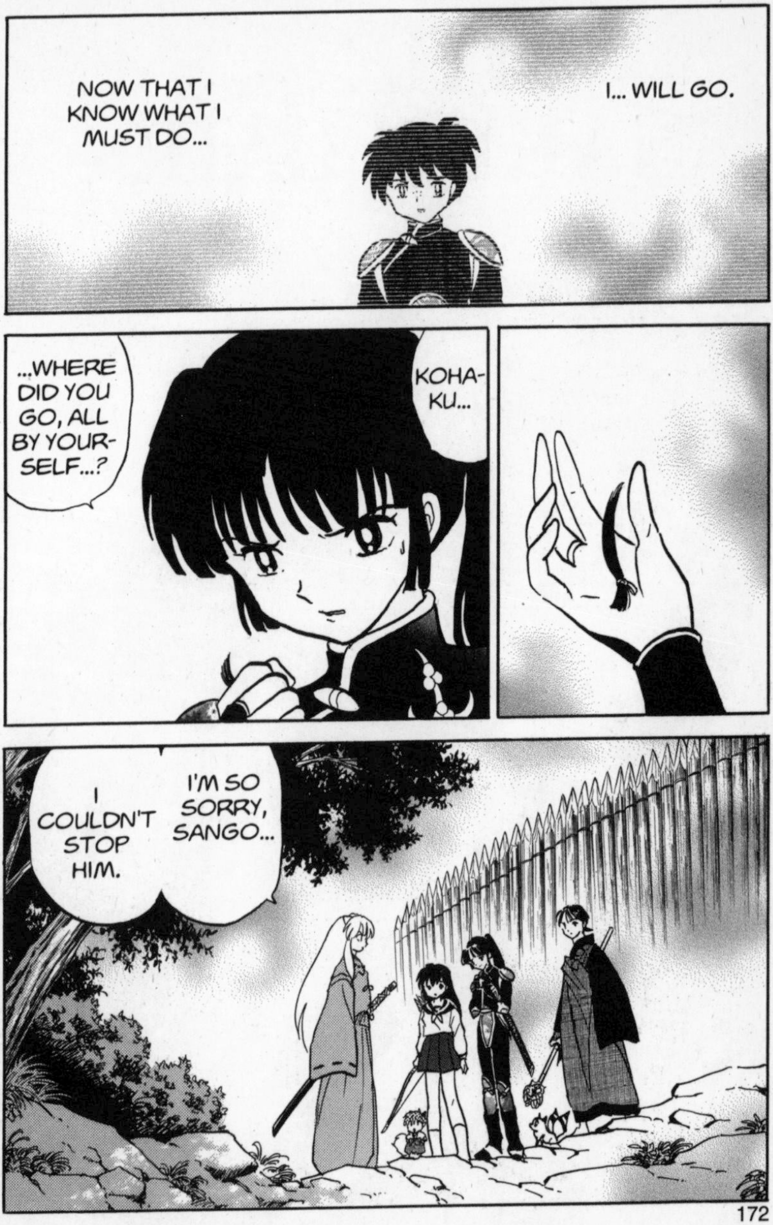
I... WILL GO.
NOW THAT I KNOW WHAT I MUST DO...
KOHA-KU...
...WHERE DID YOU GO, ALL BY YOUR-SELF...?
I'M SO SORRY, SANGO...
I COULDN'T STOP HIM.

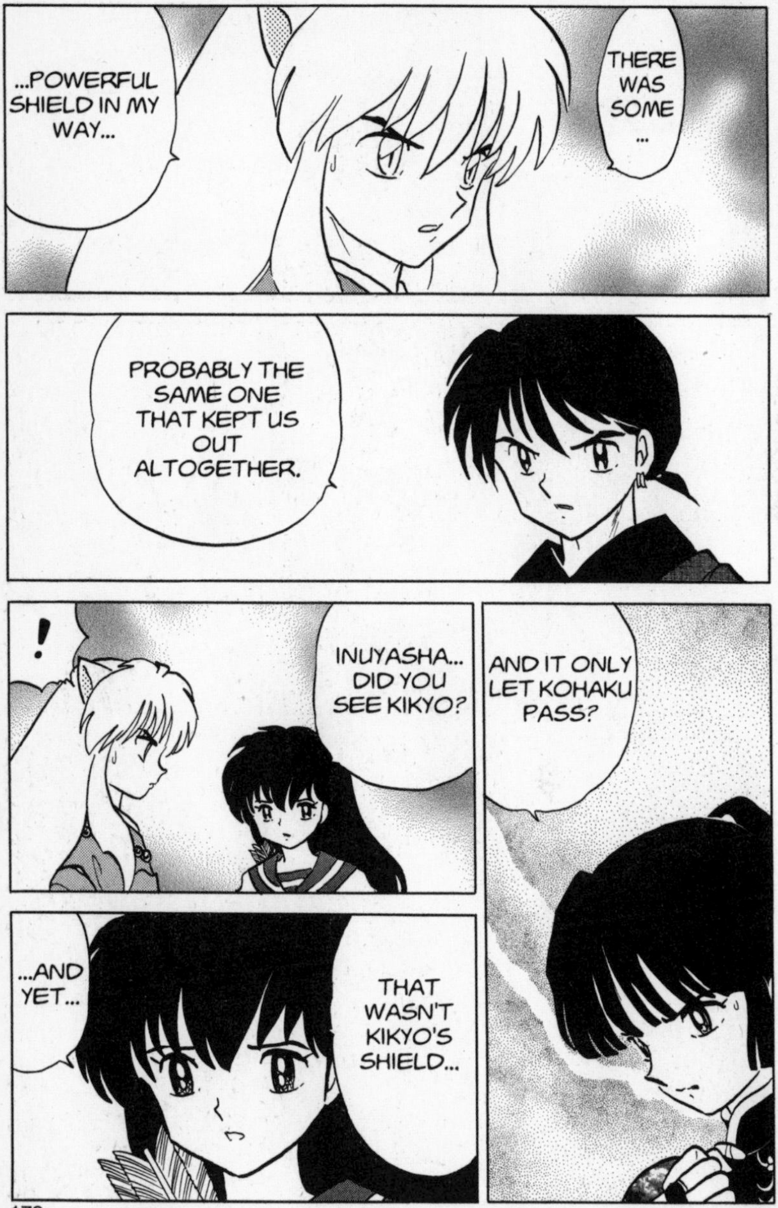
THERE WAS SOME ...
...POWERFUL SHIELD IN MY WAY...
PROBABLY THE SAME ONE THAT KEPT US OUT ALTOGETHER.
AND IT ONLY LET KOHAKU PASS?
INUYASHA... DID YOU SEE KIKYO?
!
THAT WASN'T KIKYO'S SHIELD...
...AND YET...

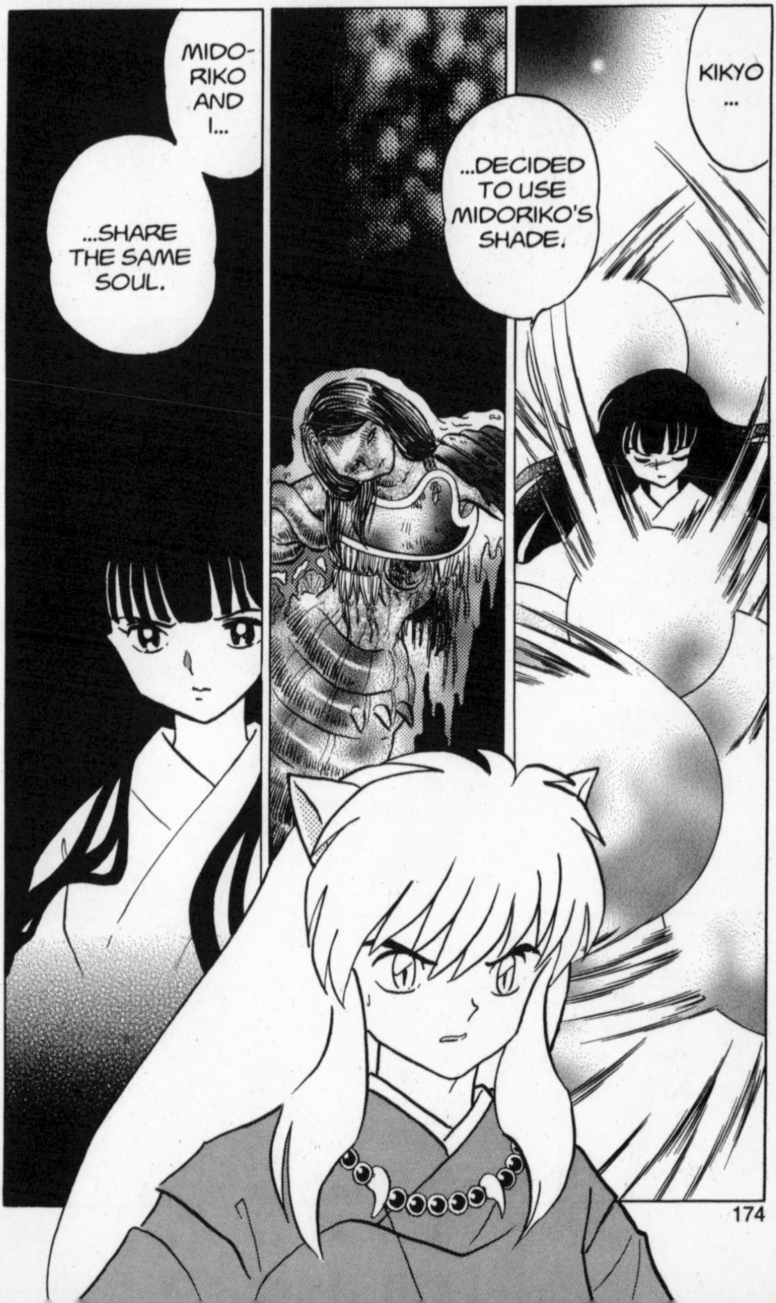
KIKYO ...
...DECIDED TO USE MIDORIKO'S SHADE.
MIDO-RIKO AND I...
...SHARE THE SAME SOUL.

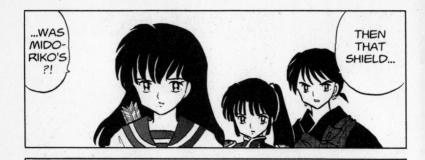

THEN THAT SHIELD...
...WAS MIDORIKO'S ?!
HOOO...
HF HF HF HF
ZEE ZEE ZEE
WELL...
I KNOW I'VE SAID THIS BEFORE, BUT...
WAIT UP, KOGA!

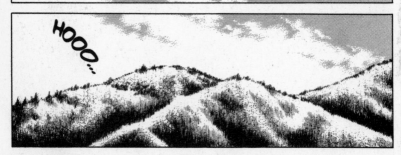

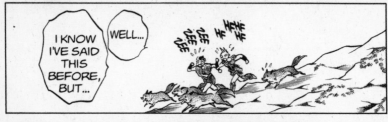

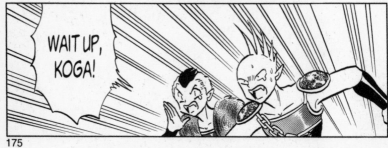

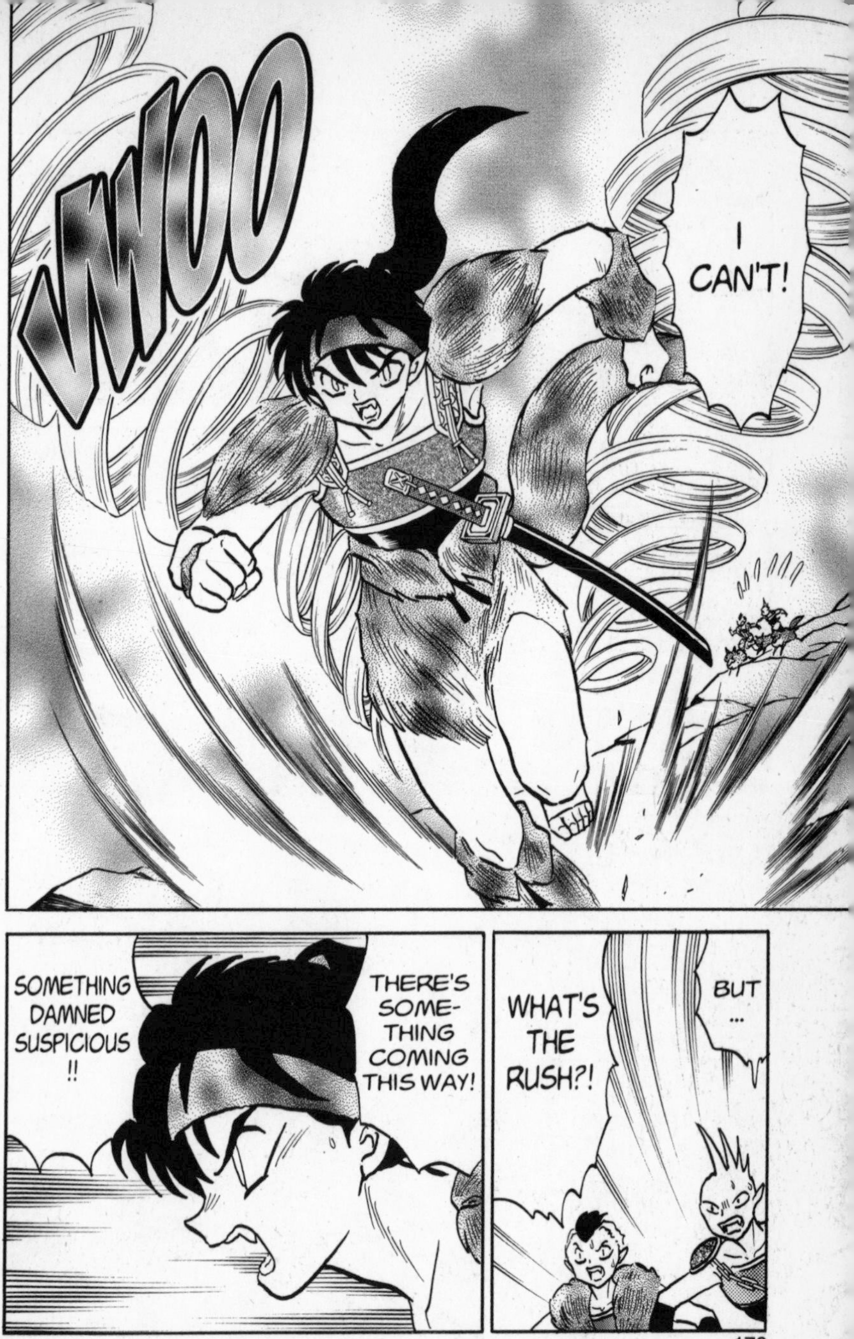
I CAN'T!
VWOO
BUT ...
WHAT'S THE RUSH?!
THERE'S SOMETHING COMING THIS WAY!
SOMETHING DAMNED SUSPICIOUS !!

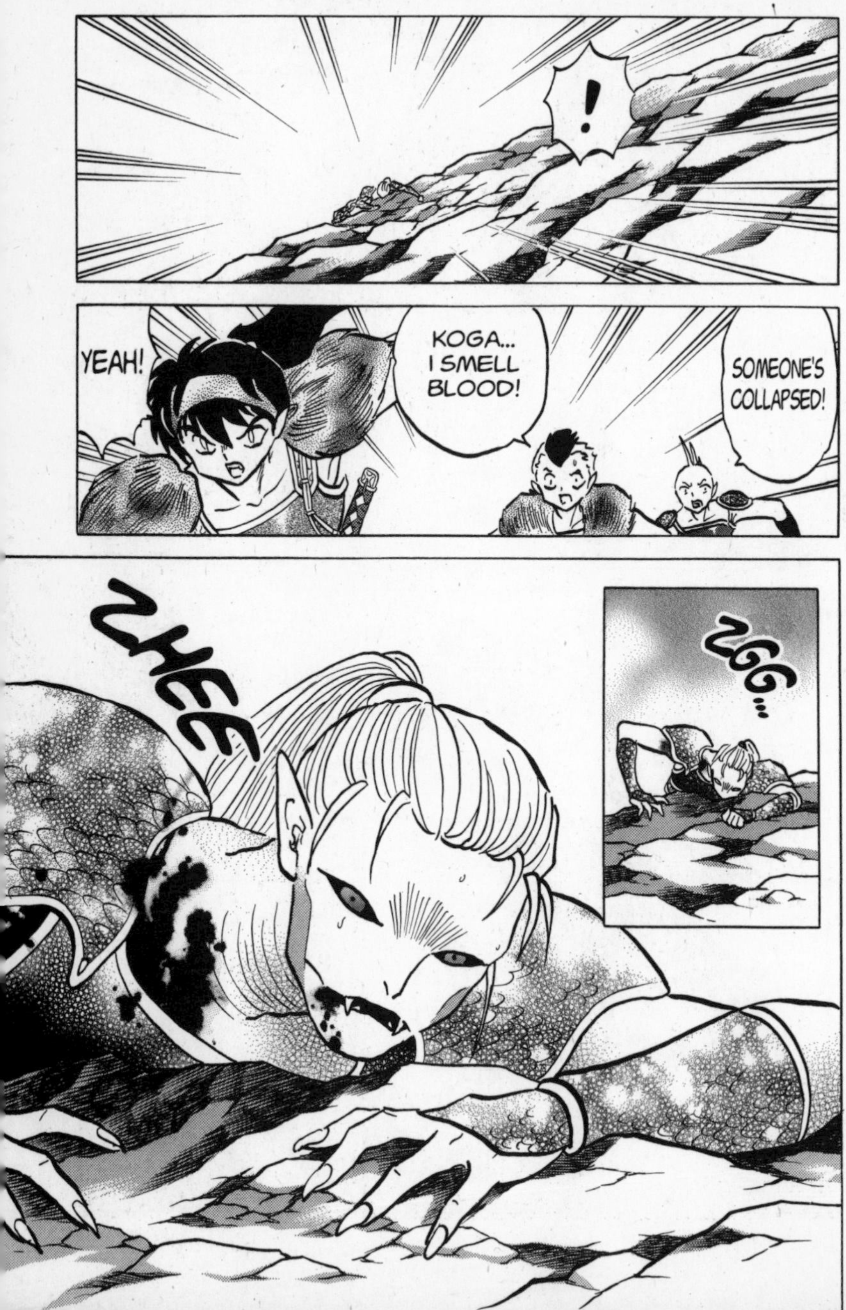
!
SOMEONE'S COLLAPSED!
KOGA... I SMELL BLOOD!
YEAH!
ZGG...
ZHEE

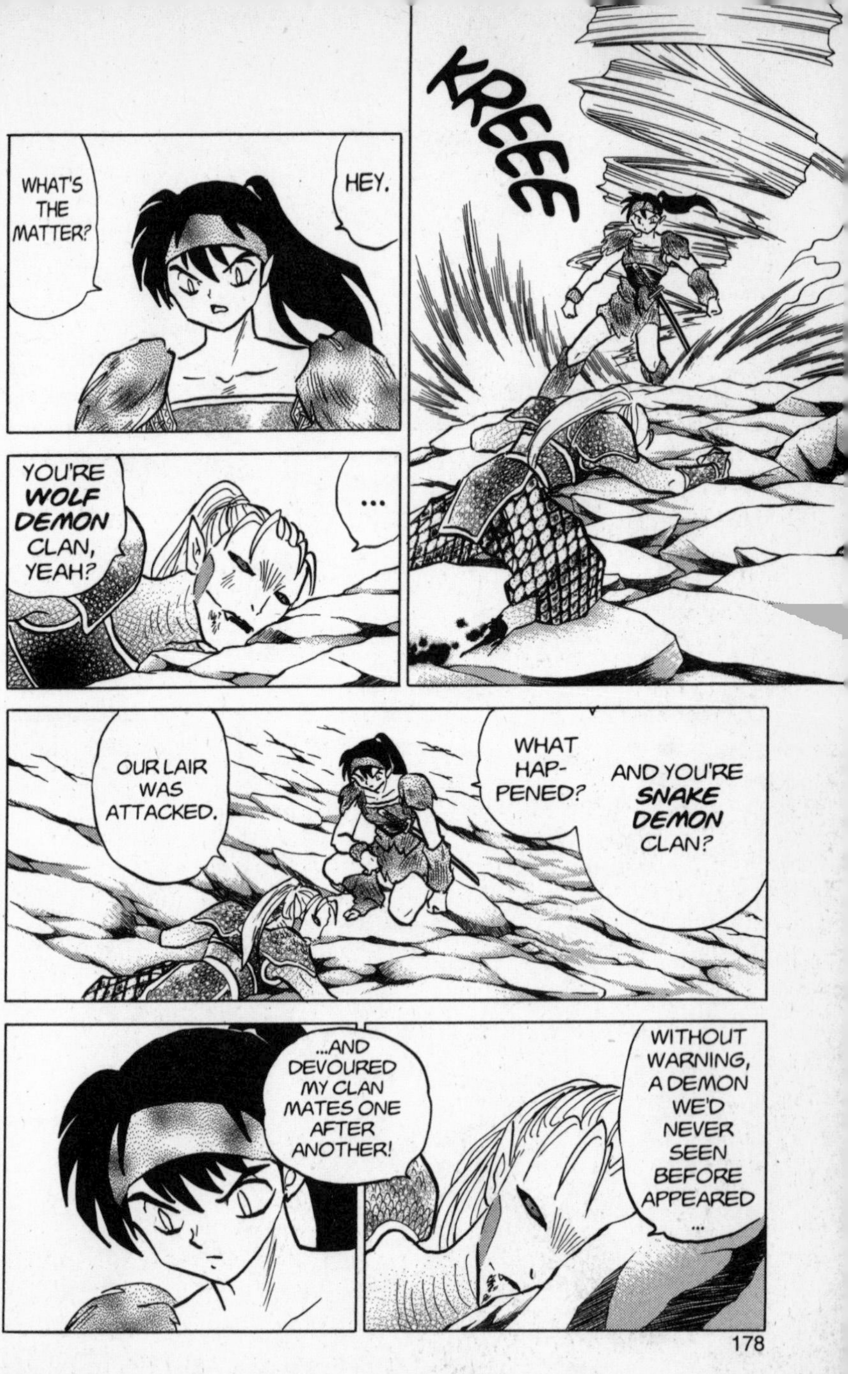
KREEE
HEY.
WHAT'S THE MATTER?
...
YOU'RE WOLF DEMON CLAN, YEAH?
AND YOU'RE SNAKE DEMON CLAN?
WHAT HAP-PENED?
OUR LAIR WAS ATTACKED.
WITHOUT WARNING, A DEMON WE'D NEVER SEEN BEFORE APPEARED ...
...AND DEVOURED MY CLAN MATES ONE AFTER ANOTHER!

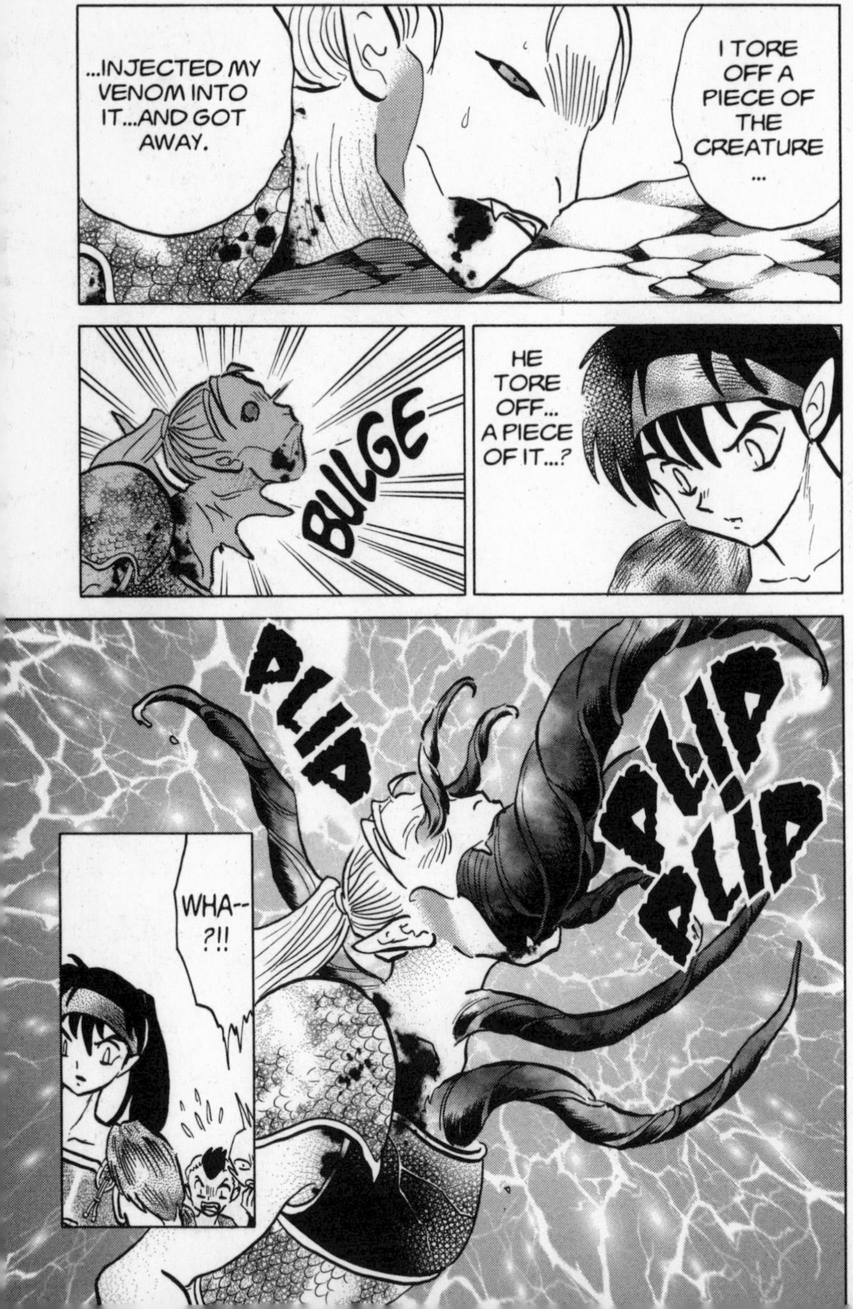
I TORE OFF A PIECE OF THE CREATURE ...
...INJECTED MY VENOM INTO IT...AND GOT AWAY.
HE TORE OFF... A PIECE OF IT...?
BULGE
PLIP PLIP
PLIP
WHA-- ?!!

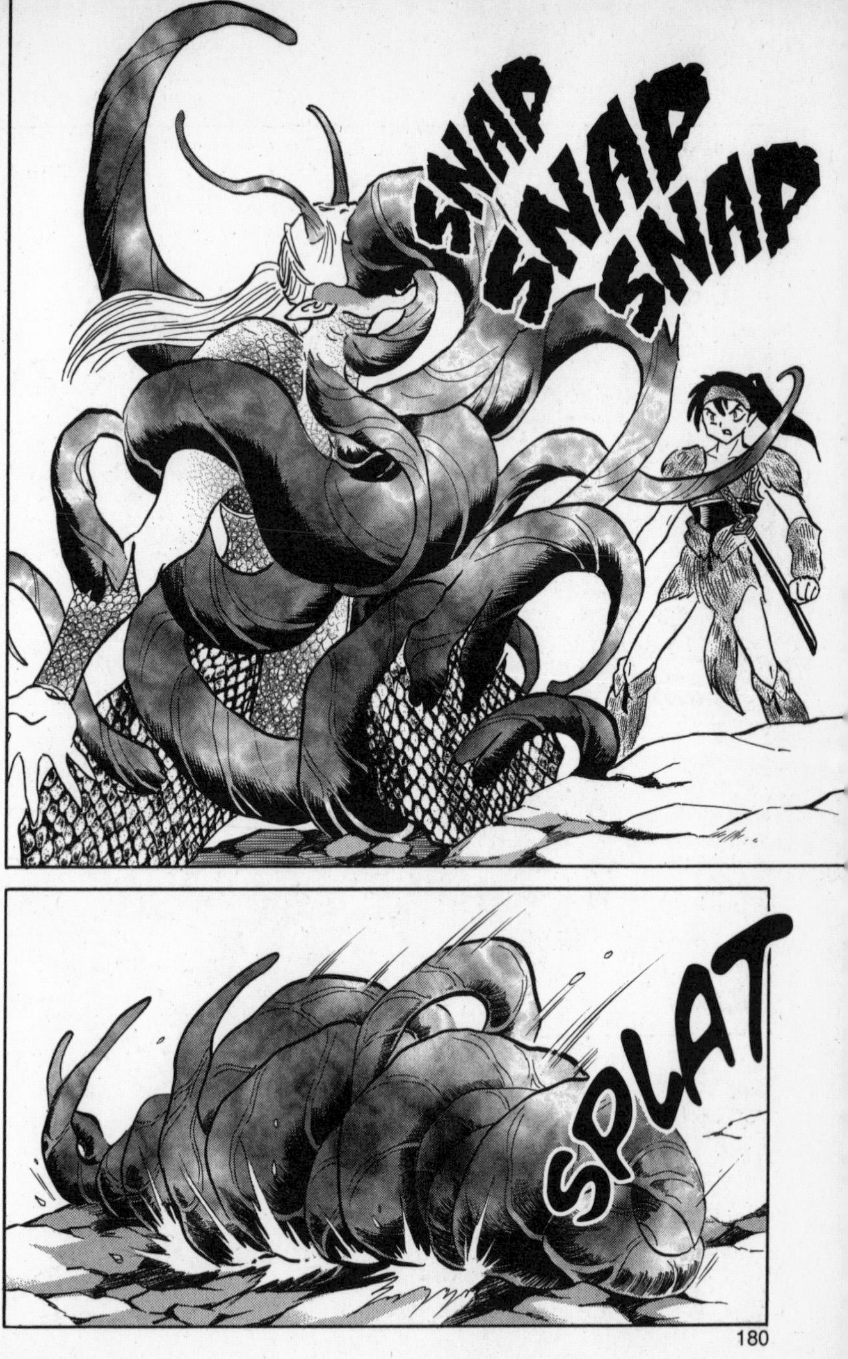
SNAP SNAP SNAP
SPLAT

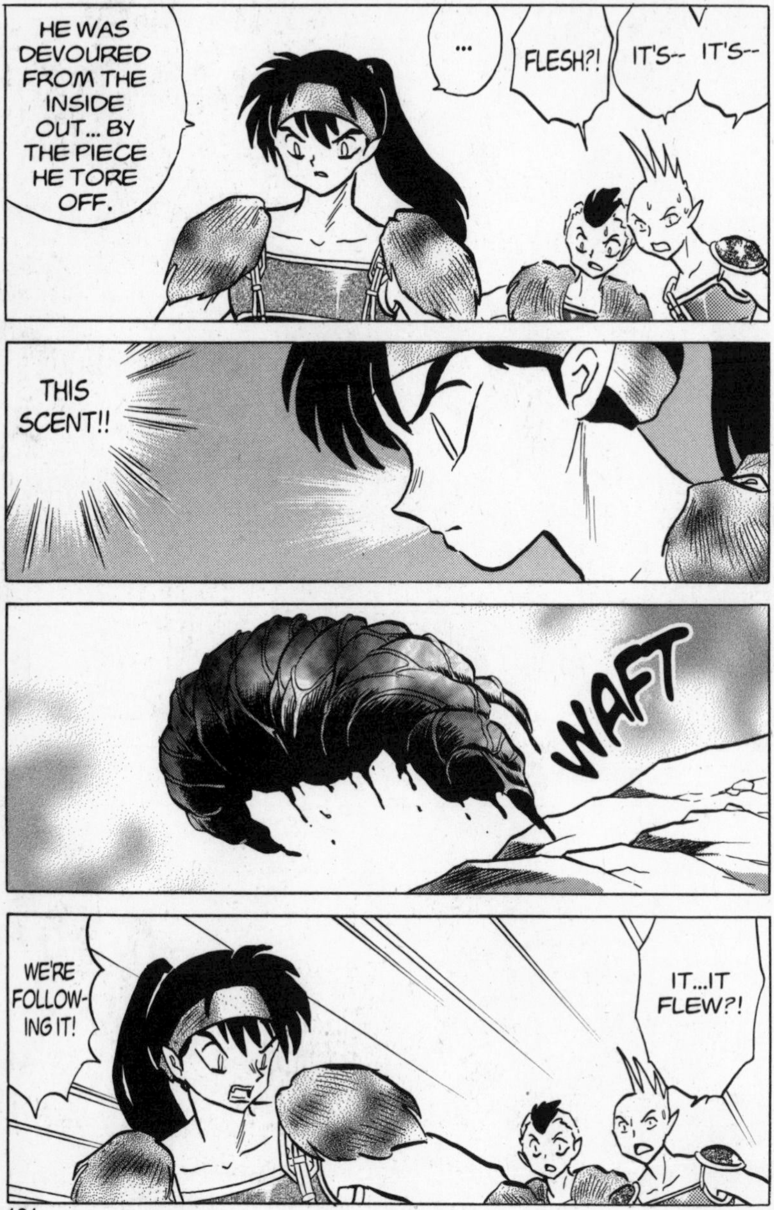
IT'S-- IT'S--
FLESH?!
...
HE WAS DEVOURED FROM THE INSIDE OUT... BY THE PIECE HE TORE OFF.
THIS SCENT!!
WAFT
IT...IT FLEW?!
WE'RE FOLLOW-ING IT!

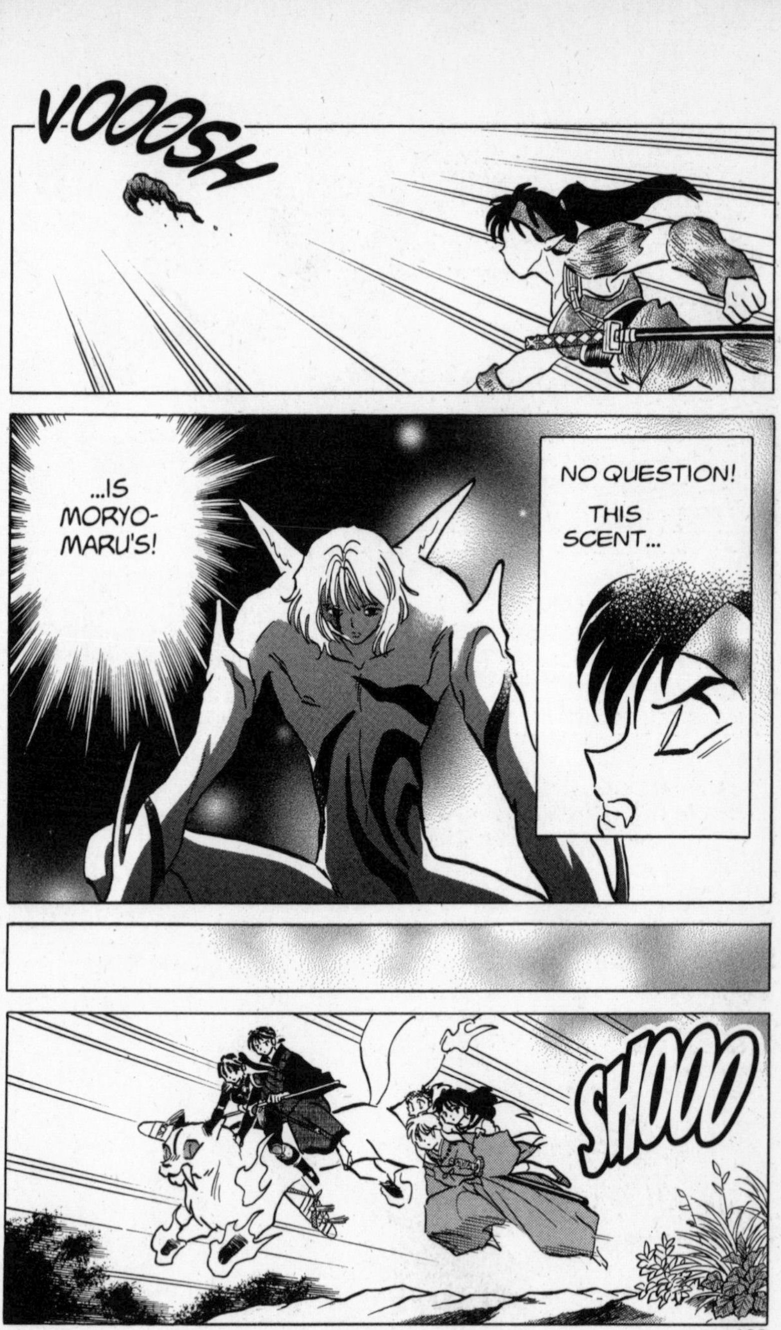
VOOSH
NO QUESTION!
THIS SCENT...
...IS MORYO-MARU'S!
SHOOO

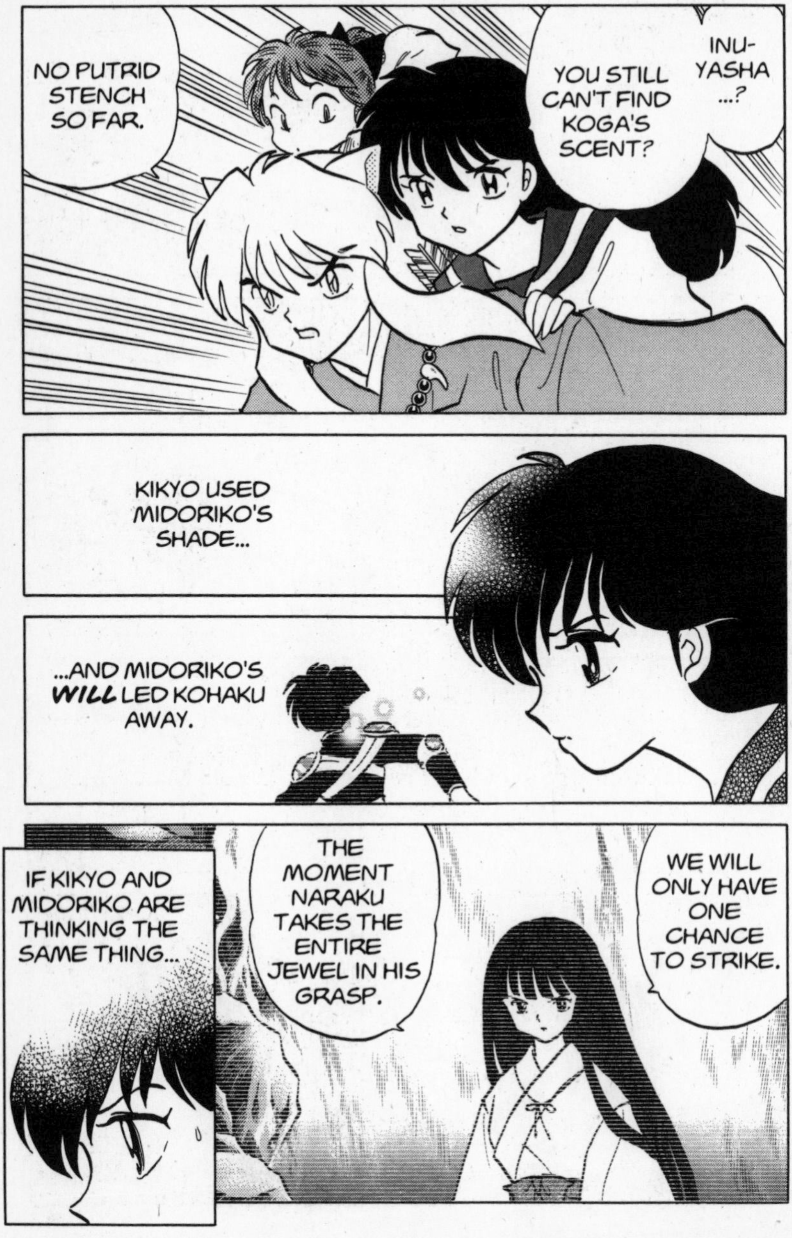
INU-YASHA ...?
YOU STILL CAN'T FIND KOGA'S SCENT?
NO PUTRID STENCH SO FAR.
KIKYO USED MIDORIKO'S SHADE...
...AND MIDORIKO'S WILL LED KOHAKU AWAY.
WE WILL ONLY HAVE ONE CHANCE TO STRIKE.
THE MOMENT NARAKU TAKES THE ENTIRE JEWEL IN HIS GRASP.
IF KIKYO AND MIDORIKO ARE THINKING THE SAME THING...

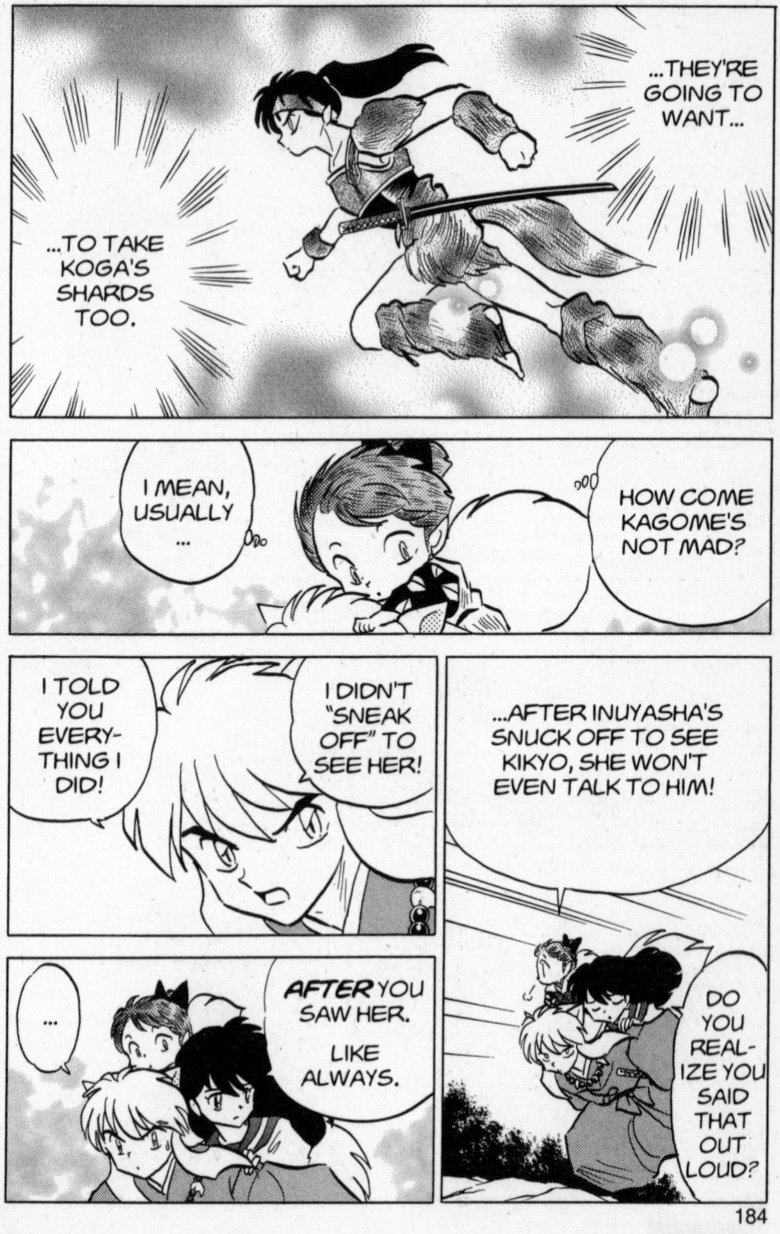
...THEY'RE GOING TO WANT...
...TO TAKE KOGA'S SHARDS TOO.
HOW COME KAGOME'S NOT MAD?
I MEAN, USUALLY ...
...AFTER INUYASHA'S SNUCK OFF TO SEE KIKYO, SHE WON'T EVEN TALK TO HIM!
DO YOU REAL-IZE YOU SAID THAT OUT LOUD?
I DIDN'T "SNEAK OFF" TO SEE HER!
I TOLD YOU EVERY-THING I DID!
AFTER YOU SAW HER.
LIKE ALWAYS.
...

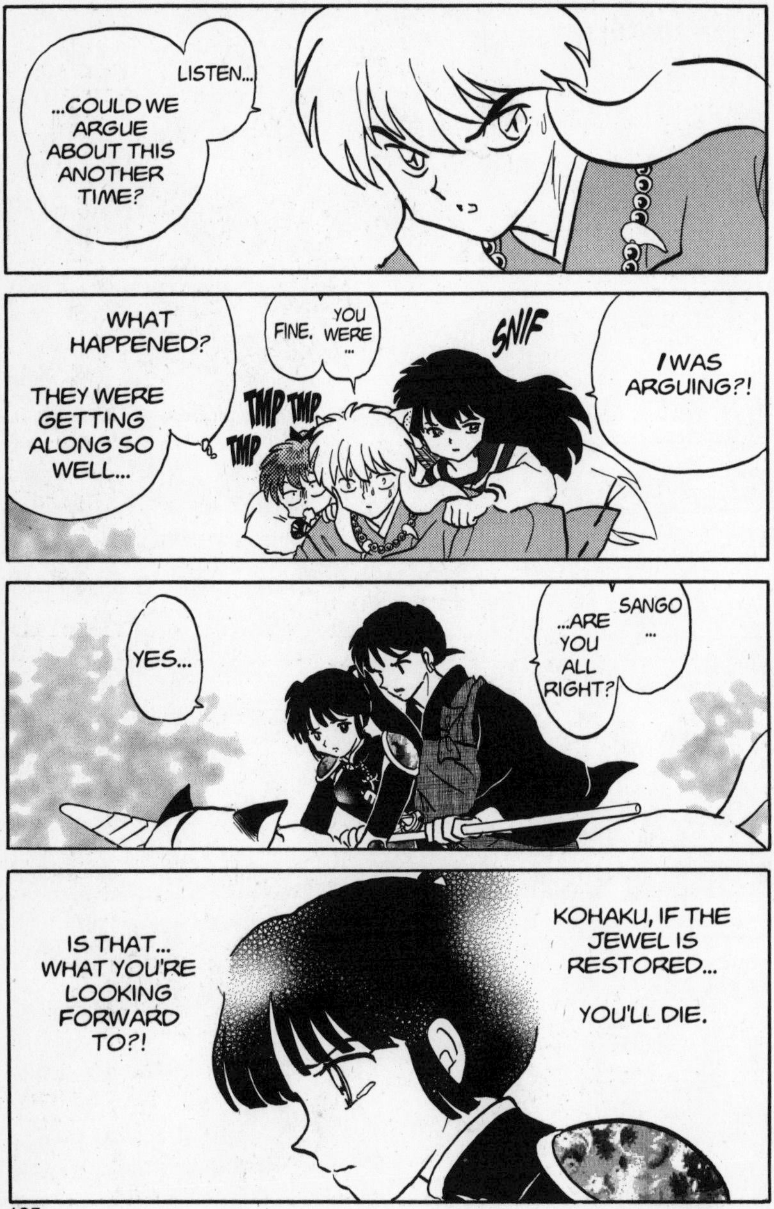
LISTEN...
...COULD WE ARGUE ABOUT THIS ANOTHER TIME?
I WAS ARGUING?!
SNIF
YOU WERE...
FINE.
TMP TMP
TMP
WHAT HAPPENED?
THEY WERE GETTING ALONG SO WELL...
SANGO...
...ARE YOU ALL RIGHT?
YES...
KOHAKU, IF THE JEWEL IS RESTORED...
YOU'LL DIE.
IS THAT... WHAT YOU'RE LOOKING FORWARD TO?!

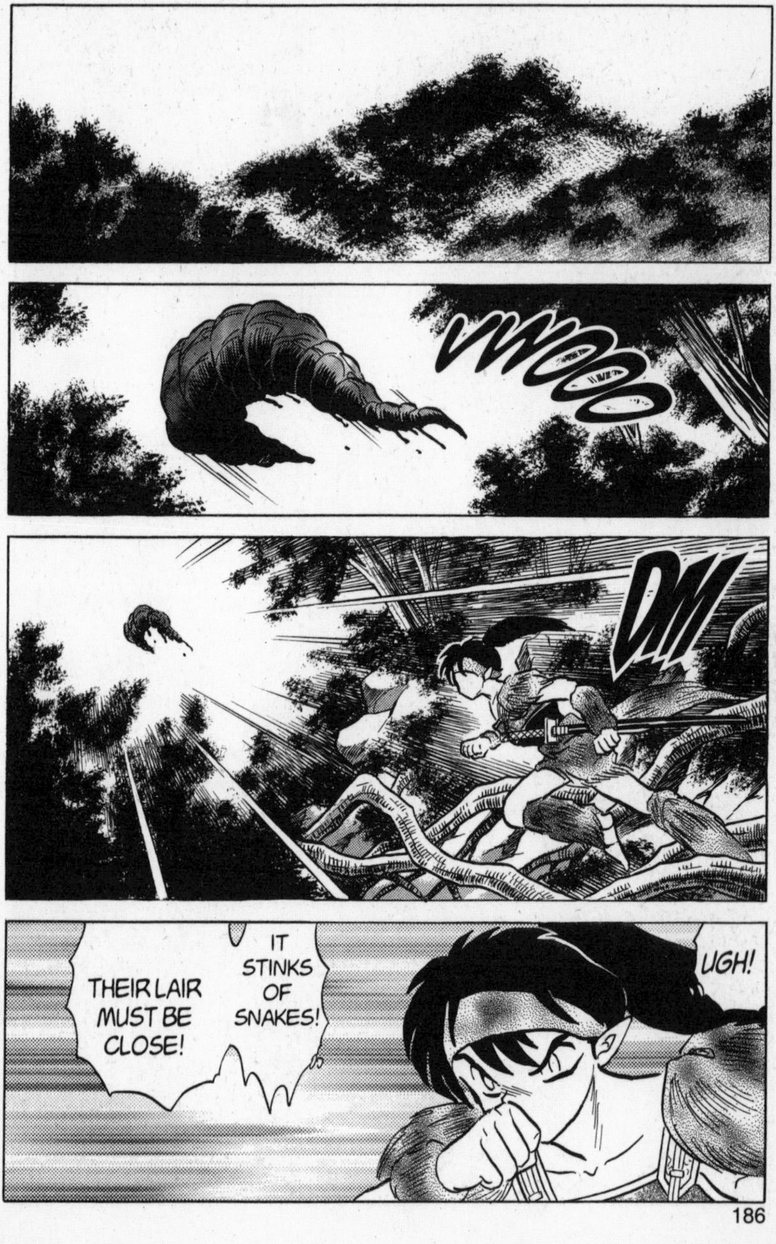
VWOOO
DM
UGH!
IT STINKS OF SNAKES!
THEIR LAIR MUST BE CLOSE!

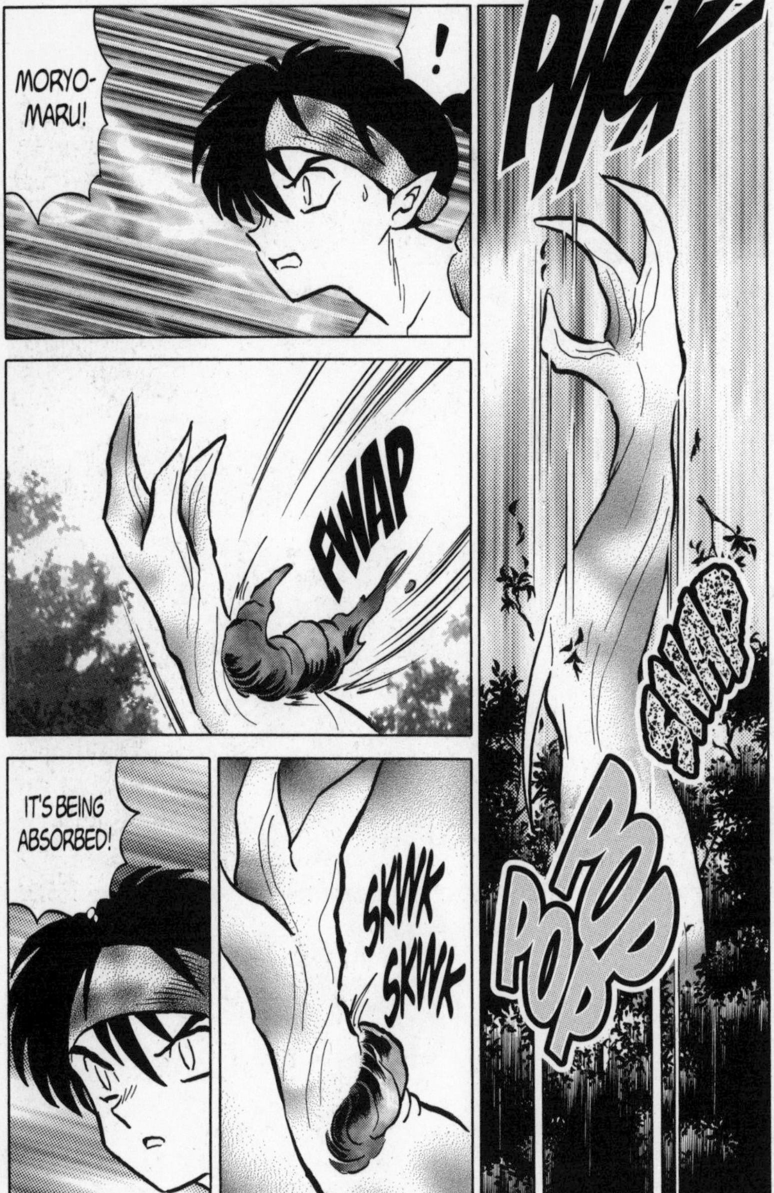

PWK
SNAP
POP POP
!
MORYO-MARU!
FWAP
SKWK SKWK
IT'S BEING ABSORBED!

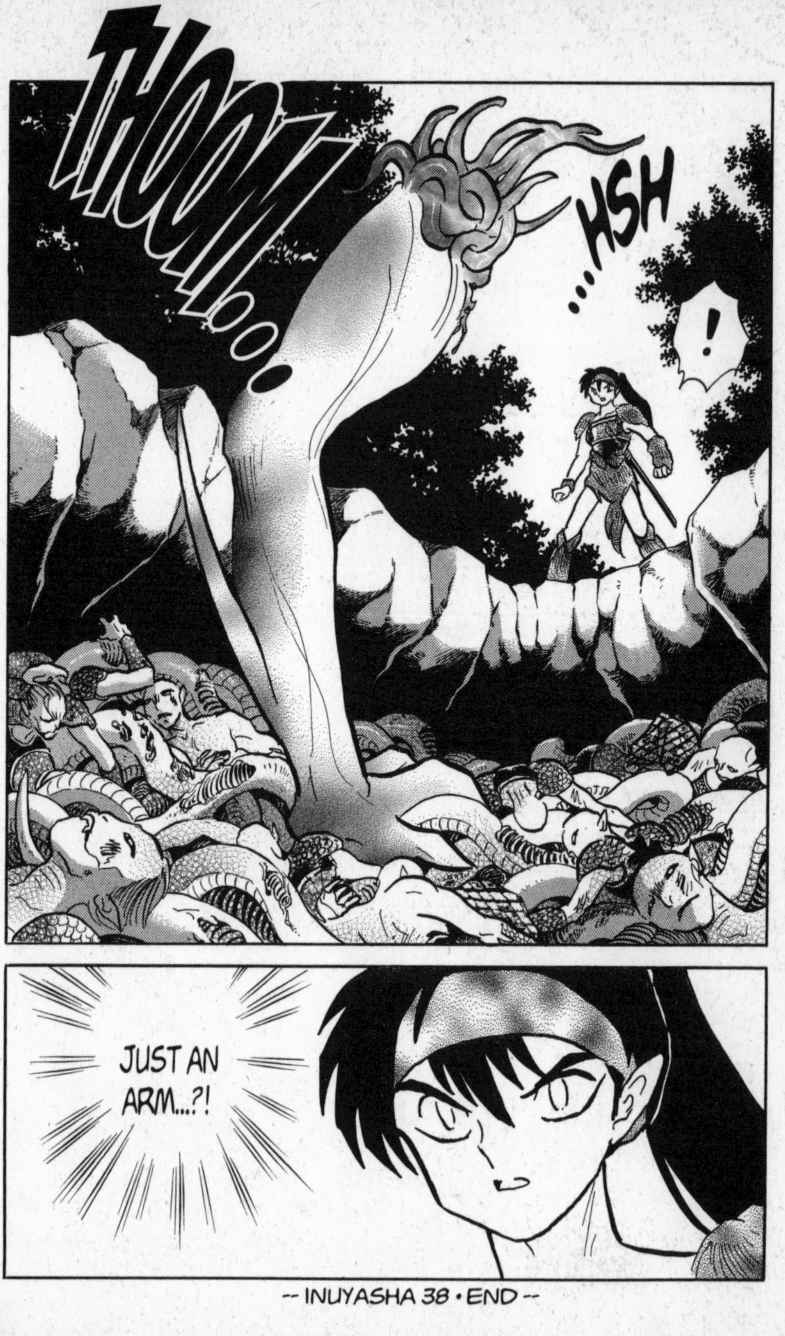
THOOM...
...HSH
!
JUST AN ARM...?!

Half Human, Half

When Kagome discovers a well that transports her to feudal era Japan, she unwittingly frees a half-demon, Inuyasha, and shatters the sacred Jewel of Four Souls. Now they must work together to restore the jewel before it falls into the wrong hands...

INUYASHA

The manga that inspired a phenomenon!

Only $9.95!

FULL COLOR adaptation of the TV series!

Only $11.95!